KU-349-203

ST. MARK IN TRADITION
From an eighth-century Gospel-Book in Vienna

THE CLARENDON BIBLE

The Gospel according to
SAINT MARK

IN THE REVISED VERSION

With introduction and commentary
by the late

A. W. F. BLUNT, D.D.
FORMERLY BISHOP OF BRADFORD

OXFORD
AT THE CLARENDON PRESS

Oxford University Press, Amen House, London E.C.4

GLASGOW NEW YORK TORONTO MELBOURNE WELLINGTON
BOMBAY CALCUTTA MADRAS KARACHI LAHORE DACCA
CAPE TOWN SALISBURY NAIROBI IBADAN ACCRA
KUALA LUMPUR HONG KONG

FIRST PUBLISHED 1929
REPRINTED 1935, 1939 (WITH CORRECTIONS)
1943, 1947, 1949, 1953, 1957, 1963

PRINTED IN GREAT BRITAIN

PREFACE

THE problem of the teaching of Holy Scripture at the present time presents many difficulties. There is a large and growing class of persons who feel bound to recognize that the progress of archaeological and critical studies has made it impossible for them to read, and still more to teach, it precisely in the old way. However strongly they may believe in inspiration, they cannot any longer set before their pupils, or take as the basis of their interpretation, the doctrine of the verbal inspiration of the Holy Scripture. It is with the object of meeting the requirements not only of the elder pupils in public schools, their teachers, students in training colleges, and others engaged in education, but also of the clergy, and the growing class of the general public which we believe takes an interest in Biblical studies, that the present series is projected.

The writers will be responsible each for his own contribution only, and their interpretation is based upon the belief that the books of the Bible require to be placed in their historical context, so that, as far as possible, we may recover the sense which they bore when written. Any application of them must rest upon this ground. It is not the writers' intention to set out the latest notions of radical scholars—English or foreign—nor even to describe the exact position at which the discussion of the various problems has arrived. The aim of the series is rather to put forward a constructive view of the books and their teaching, taking into consideration and welcoming results as to which there is a large measure of agreement among scholars.

In regard to form, subjects requiring comprehensive treatment are dealt with in Essays, whether forming part of the introduction or interspersed among the notes. The notes themselves are mainly concerned with the subject-matter of the books and the points of interest (historical, doctrinal, &c.) therein presented; they deal with the elucidation of words, allusions, and the like only so far as seems necessary to a proper comprehension of the author's meaning.

THOMAS STRONG.
HERBERT WILD.
GEORGE H. BOX.
General Editors.

TABLE OF CONTENTS

PREFACE 5

LIST OF ILLUSTRATIONS 8

INTRODUCTION:

A. How the Gospels came to be written 11

B. Church tradition as to the authorship of the Gospel . . 26

C. Internal evidence as to the sources of the Gospel . . 31

D. The picture of Jesus Christ in the Gospel 49

E. Marcan Authorship. Internal evidence 65

F. Place and date of composition of the Gospel . . . 68

Note 1. Mark's Christology 77

Note 2. Characteristics of Marcan style 79

Note 3. Bibliography 80

R.V. TEXT 83

COMMENTARY:

1^{1-13}. Introduction 133

1^{14}–3^{6}. The Beginning of the Ministry 142

3^{7}–6^{13}. The Twelve 160

6^{14}–8^{26}. Leaving Galilee 178

8^{27}–10^{45}. The Way of the Cross 195

10^{46}–13^{37}. The Appeal to Jerusalem 223

14^{1}–16^{8}. The Passion and Resurrection 242

16^{9-20}. The Epilogue 267

INDEX TO NOTES 271

LIST OF ILLUSTRATIONS

St. Mark in tradition. From an eighth-century Gospel-Book in Vienna . . . . *Frontispiece*

Map of Our Lord's Journeys in Palestine. Reproduced, by kind permission, from Burkitt, *The Gospel History and its Transmission* (T. & T. Clark, Edinburgh) 10

The mystery-religions of the Roman World. A fresco found in a tomb on the Appian Way, near Rome, illustrating the introduction of the dead person (through the doorway on the left) into the Elysian fields, to take part in the sacred banquet of the blessed. From Wilpert, *Le pitture delle Catacombe Romane* 15

Early Christianity at Rome. A fresco from the common grave of members of a Christian sect. Viale Manzoni, Rome . . . 17

A page of the famous *Codex Sinaiticus*, a Greek MS. of the fourth century. The part shown runs from Mark 6. 27 to 7. 1 . . 21

Medieval symbols of the Four Evangelists. The Angel for St. Matthew, the Eagle for St. John, the Lion for St. Mark, the Bull for St. Luke. From the tympanum over the West Door of Chartres Cathedral. Photograph, Giraudon 25

The Sea of Galilee, near Tiberias. Photograph by Mr. J. P. G. Finch 37

The Crucifixion. A miniature of the twelfth century in the Psalter of Queen Melisenda, representing the descent from the Cross. British Museum 39

A holy man of the East to-day. Photograph by Mr. R. Gorbold . 45

Preaching in a synagogue in Spain in the fourteenth century. From a Hebrew MS. in the British Museum 53

The Temple area at Jerusalem to-day. Photograph by Dr. M. J. Rendall 59

Caligula. Metropolitan Museum of Art, New York. 71

Jerusalem with the Mount of Olives in the background. Photograph by Dr. M. J. Rendall 73

The River Jordan. Photograph by Dr. M. J. Rendall 82

A model of the synagogue at Capernaum, probably built in the second century A. D., on the site of the synagogue in which Christ preached. From H. Kohl and C. Watzinger, *Antike Synagogen in Galilaea* 85

The courtyard of an Eastern house. Photograph by Dr. M. J. Rendall 87

Eastern leather-workers. Photograph by Mr. R. Gorbold . . 89

Sidon. Photograph, The American Colony, Jerusalem . . . 91

Ploughing in Palestine to-day. Photograph by Dr. M. J. Rendall 93

Carrying the harvest. Photograph by Mr. R. Gorbold 95

Nazareth. Photograph by Mr. J. P. G. Finch 99

The Death of John the Baptist. A brass panel on the font of Siena Cathedral, by Ghiberti. Photograph, Brogi 101
The Transfiguration. Below, the three apostles; above, Elijah and Moses. From a twelfth-century mosaic at Palermo. Photograph, Alinari 109
Camels grazing in the Hauran. Photograph by Dr. M. J. Rendall 111
The entry into Jerusalem. An ivory panel of the eleventh century in the British Museum 115
The Damascus Gate to-day. Photograph by Dr. M. J. Rendall . 115
The bazaar in the courtyard of the Holy Sepulchre. Photograph by Dr. M. J. Rendall 119
A housetop at dawn at Ramallah, near Jerusalem. Photograph by Dr. M. J. Rendall 121
Shepherds with their flocks of sheep and goats passing one of Solomon's Pools near Jerusalem. Photograph by Dr. M. J. Rendall 125
Courtyard of the Church of the Holy Sepulchre. Photograph by Dr. M. J. Rendall 129
Tomb with a rolling stone door. Photograph, The American Colony, Jerusalem 131
Mount Tabor, the traditional scene of the Transfiguration. Photograph by Dr. M. J. Rendall 207
Caesar's penny. A denarius of Tiberius. British Museum . . . 231
Palestine in the First Century A.D. . . . . . *Back endpaper*

NOTE TO MAP OF OUR LORD'S JOURNEYS

The map attempts to trace a consecutiveness in Our Lord's movements after 6^{39}, and to illustrate the theory that His movements at this time were directed by the wish to avoid Antipas' dominions, which consisted of Galilee and Peraea.

Starting from Capernaum, they set out for Bethsaida by boat (6^{45}), but arrived at Gennesareth (6^{53}), perhaps driven by the storm; thence they go 'through the borders of Tyre and Sidon (7^{24}), then through Decapolis to the Sea of Galilee (7^{31}), thence by boat to Dalmanutha (8^{10}) which is otherwise unknown, but is here placed at Tiberias (see note *ad loc.*); then to Bethsaida (8^{22}) and so to Caesarea Philippi (8^{27}).

The dotted line represents the journey from Caesarea Philippi, through Galilee in secret (9^{30}) to Capernaum (9^{33}), and so to 'the borders of Judaea and beyond Jordan' (10^{1}). For the suggestion of alternative routes from Galilee to Jericho see note on 10^{1}. From Jericho Jerusalem is reached (10^{46} 11^{1}).

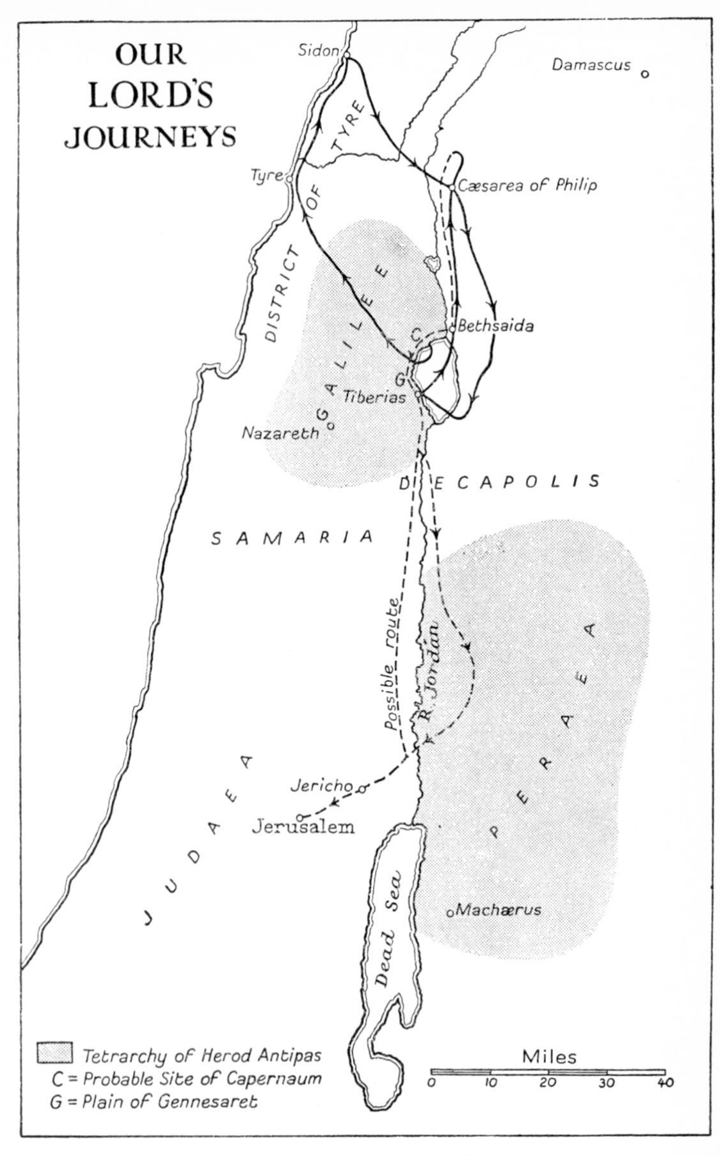

(See Note on page 9.)

INTRODUCTION

A. HOW THE GOSPELS CAME TO BE WRITTEN.

i

MANY people on first approaching the study of the gospels are, often unconsciously, under the influence of two preconceived ideas: (1) that the Church started with the gospels in its hand; (2) that these gospels were written freely by eye-witnesses, or were taken down directly from the reports of eye-witnesses.

Both these ideas are erroneous. The process by which the four gospels came to be written was not so simple as this. To trace that process must be our first task.

If we read carefully the first dozen chapters of Acts, it becomes clear that the Christians, at the outset, were not separated from the Jewish religion and the Jewish religious community. Like any other Jews, they frequented the Temple;[1] and though they had their own private meetings,[2] these were supplementary and not in opposition to the Temple-worship. The house of Mary, the mother of John Mark, which was the Christian centre,[3] was not a rival place of worship to the Temple. The Church had no churches. It was, in fact, a sect or party within the Jewish Church, and not yet a separate religious body. The Jews called it 'the sect of the Nazarenes'.[4] And this sect was by no means unpopular among the Jews or unsuccessful in its propaganda among them.[5]

The peculiar and distinctive tenet of this new sect was the belief that the Messiah, whom all the Jews had been taught to expect, had actually appeared on earth, in the person of Jesus of Nazareth. This belief had probably been held by some, at least, of His disciples before His Crucifixion.[6] His Resurrection was now taken as the seal of God's own authentication of it; it is

[1] Acts 2^{46}, 3^{1}, 5^{12}. [2] Acts 1^{13}, 2^{46}, 4^{23}. [3] Acts 12^{12}.

[4] Acts 24^{5}. The name 'Christian' was coined at Antioch. Ib. 11^{26}.

[5] Cf. Acts 2^{47}, 5^{13}, 21^{20}. We hear of 'priests' in 6^{7}, and 'Pharisees' in 15^{5}, as belonging to the Christian society.

[6] Peter's confession (Mk. 8^{29}) shows, at the least, a flash of temporary readiness to put this forward as the explanation of Our Lord's Personality.

the accepted view in all the speeches of Acts,[1] from Pentecost onwards.

In preaching this belief the Christians relied on (1) their personal testimony to Christ's Resurrection,[2] and on (2) the argument from prophecy. 'Testimonies', i.e. Old Testament texts, to which a Messianic bearing was or could be given, and which could be applied to the events of Christ's life,[3] were collected and used to support the Christian belief in argument with the Jews.[4] Very possibly the earliest specifically Christian book consisted of such a collection of proof-texts. Any one who decided to become a Christian was baptized 'into the Name of Jesus Christ'. He thus became a member of the society which believed in Jesus as 'the Christ' or 'Messiah',[5] and he shared in the spirit which permeated this society. The name given to this spirit was 'the Holy Spirit'.

In the earliest Christian preaching the chief emphasis was laid on Christ's Death and Resurrection. If the Messianic claim was to be justified, it had to be shown that Messiah's Death and Resurrection from death were foretold in the Old Testament. Further, if Jesus was the Messiah, then in God's time He would appear to judge the world.[6] This would be Messiah's '*Parousia*';[7] the present order of the world would be ended, and the new order of the Messianic Kingdom would be set up. The forecast of this Parousia was the Christian preacher's final warning to his hearers.

Thus the main practical interest of primitive Christianity was 'eschatological',[8] i.e. it was concerned with a future event when Christ would appear in glory, and a new world-order would take the place of the existing one. The Christian disciples lived in expectation of this event. The Parousia of Christ might happen at

[1] e.g. Acts 2^{36}, $3^{19f.}$ &c. [2] Acts 1^{22}.

[3] Often by straining or even perverting the literal sense: cf. Mt. $2^{15,23}$. But it was in keeping with the accepted methods of Jewish exegesis.

[4] e.g. Acts 2^{29}, 3^{22}, 8^{32}.

[5] 'Christ' is the Greek equivalent for the Hebrew 'Messiah'. It means 'anointed', and is thus an epithet, not a name. But 'Jesus Christ' soon came to be used as a name, as e.g. by Paul.

[6] Cf. Acts 3^{21}, 10^{42}, 17^{31}.

[7] = 'Presence' or 'Appearance'; usually translated, not quite correctly, 'Return' or 'Advent'.

[8] 'eschatology' = an account of the last things, i.e. doctrine as to the end of the present dispensation of human affairs.

any time and would, they believed, certainly happen soon. They had therefore no need for written records of His life on earth; and nobody thought it worth while to write one. The only sacred document of the Christians was the Jewish Old Testament. In it they could find all that would justify their declaration that the Messiah is Jesus; and that was the sum of what they had to say.

Such was the condition of primitive Christianity in Jerusalem. But in a short time the Christian message began to spread to non-Jewish cities; first to Antioch, and then beyond Syria; and Christian communities, in which non-Jews were a large element, began to arise. This meant a change of environment, and therefore a change of method in teaching. The declaration of Jesus the Christ's Death, Resurrection, and future Parousia must still of course be made; for it was in fact the Christian 'Gospel'. But it would need fuller exposition than was necessary in Jewish circles; and Paul's genius was fully employed in finding new language in which to expound the Christian truth in order to bring it home to his gentile hearers, and new applications of its meaning in order to make it effective in their lives.

The idea of the Messiah was not hard to explain to gentiles. It was, essentially, the simple idea of a great deliverer of mankind, and had obvious analogues in the heroes and demigods of heathen mythology (Hercules, Mithra, &c.). Moreover, many of the gentile converts to Christianity had previously been adherents in some sort of the Jewish synagogue,[1] and so were familiar with the Messianic hopes of Judaism. And the constant use of the Old Testament in the Christian meetings and preachings would soon teach a gentile convert the significance of calling Jesus 'the Christ'.

But in the gentile world another set of ideas was popular, namely those in vogue in the mystery-religions which were then

[1] In Acts they are called 'Godfearers', cf. 10², 13¹⁶,⁴³. They attended the synagogue services, and professed obedience to parts of the Mosaic law; but they were not circumcised. There had been for a long time a remarkably successful effort of Jewish propaganda in the countries of the 'Dispersion'; not only had many full proselytes been made, but the number of 'Godfearers' must have been very large. Judaism in fact had become one of the most influential religions in the Graeco-Roman world.

so strong and widespread an influence in Hellenistic society. These religions were all alike in being cults of a divine Lord (Mithra, Isis, or whatever the name might be), through whom Salvation (σωτηρία) was offered to the devotees. This idea Paul seized on; and, though he principally calls Jesus 'Christ', he yet speaks of Him as Lord (*Κύριος*) and Saviour (σωτήρ). He in fact sets Him forth as the One in whom men can really find the 'Salvation' which the mystery-religions professed to supply. No doubt to many gentiles Christianity, as preached by Paul, seemed to be only a new mystery-cult, and the Christian society to be only another circle of devotees to a new 'Lord'.[1]

But in the process of exposition the Christian 'Salvation' was found to be very different in meaning and implications from that of the mystery-religions. In them the conception is mythical, usually non-ethical (though Mithraism made some ethical demand on its votaries), almost magical. The world of mankind is conceived as being shut in by circles of existences, each of them under the control of its own demon or demons. The greatest of these demons are those who control the circles of the Seven Planets. These are the 'world-rulers',[2] whose spheres shut man in from the divine and eternal life beyond. The Saviour-Lord has taught the way to pass through those spheres. By initiation into and participation in his rites, the soul is enabled to make its way through the demon-controlled circles and to rise to the Divine.[3]

It is clear that Paul made much use of these ideas and of this language. Nevertheless, the difference between this conception of Salvation and that of Pauline thought is fundamental. In the mystery-cults Salvation is almost wholly non-ethical; the rites generally carry little moral implication and exercise little moral influence; and the Saviour is a mythical personage; no pretence is made that his life is historical.

But in Paul's conception of Salvation the ethical interest is immensely prominent. Pauline Christianity is not a mere theosophy or mysteriosophy. Like the Mysteries it proclaims the Death and

1 Cf. Acts 16[17].

2 *Κοσμοκράτορες*. The word is used in Eph. 6[12].

3 Cf. Bevan, *Hellenism and Christianity*, for a full account of these beliefs.

THE MYSTERY-RELIGIONS OF THE ROMAN WORLD. A fresco found in a tomb on the Appian Way, near Rome, illustrating the introduction of the dead person (through the doorway on the left) into the Elysian fields, to take part in the sacred banquet of the blessed

Resurrection of the Saviour-Lord; and it has its mystical rites of initiation and communion (Baptism and the Lord's Supper). But (1) Paul pins his faith to an historical Saviour, One Whose Life and Death and Resurrection are attested and dated facts; and (2) he insists that the test or proof of Salvation is to be found in a moral life of a special kind, that after the pattern of Jesus Christ.

It is often said, or even assumed as self-evident, by scholars that Paul was not interested in the details of Our Lord's life on earth.[1] The assertion is very difficult to believe. In his Epistles Paul makes, it is true, no direct reference to any events of Christ's life except His Death, Resurrection, and Ascension; these were, in fact, the crucial events which the Christians had to announce. But it is also beyond question that Paul sets up Jesus Christ as an example for human imitation.[2] Is it not almost inevitable then to suppose that some interest was taken in the particulars of Jesus' personal character?

Moreover, the distinctiveness of the Christian moral ideal as set out by Paul[3] has seldom been sufficiently recognized.[4] Of course it contains elements which are found in other ethical ideals, Jewish, Greek, Stoic &c. But the special 'flavour' of the Christian ideal, which results from the particular selection and proportion and blending of virtues, is absolutely distinctive and unique. The Pauline ideal man is quite certainly and unmistakably not the Greek gentleman, nor the Stoic sage, nor the Jewish righteous man. From where then did Paul derive his conception? Now it has always been acknowledged that if you want to explain what is meant by 'the imitation of Christ', you cannot do it better than by quoting one or other of the great Pauline summaries of moral duty. May this not be simply because Paul's ideal was drawn from the tradition of Jesus' personal character as preserved in the Church and illustrated by His remembered sayings and doings;

1 Of course 2 Cor. 5^{16}, which is often quoted in this connexion, in no way implies this.

2 e.g. Phil. $2^{5f.}$ (humility), 1 Cor. $10^{33f.}$ (benevolence).

3 In such passages as Gal. $5^{22f.}$, 1 Cor. 13, Col. $3^{12f.}$

4 Thus Lightfoot says that the 'mere ethical teaching . . . is . . . the least distinctive part of Christianity' (*Philippians*. Essay on St. Paul and Seneca, *ad fin.*). I venture to suggest that this is an injustice to the moral teaching of Christianity, which is as distinctive as its soteriology.

EARLY CHRISTIANITY AT ROME. A fresco from the common grave of members of a Christian sect. The scene may represent Christ 'the Good Shepherd' and his flock (the Twelve Apostles)

and that Paul's analysis, in e.g. 1 Cor. 13, is a 'reading-off' of features from a living portrait of Jesus, and not an accumulation of lines to form a fancy picture of a good Christian? At any rate there is no doubt of the strength of Paul's ethical interest. If he thinks of Christ as (1) an eschatological figure, the Messiah-Judge, and (2) as a mystical Saviour-Lord, he also regards Him (3) as a moral Ideal, the Pattern Man. His Epistles revolve round these three conceptions of Christ, and the applications of them.

These Epistles are the earliest Christian literature which we possess. It is therefore interesting to find that they give evidence (more than has always been recognized) of the existence in Pauline circles of some interest in Our Lord's character and some acquaintance with His life. More could hardly be expected from writings of so special and occasional a purpose.

No records of Christ's life were yet written; knowledge about it was handed on orally in the Christian society. This knowledge must of course go back to the primitive church of Jerusalem. No doubt, as was said above, eschatology was its chief interest, and its specific doctrine was the eschatological status of Jesus Christ. But the Jesus who was to come was the Jesus who had come;[1] and it is simply incredible that the earthly life of this Jesus was a matter of no concern to the primitive Christians. Even in the written records the impression of that life is overwhelming; is it possible that those who had personally experienced it *could* have kept silence about it? Or is it in the least likely that the earliest Christians would not have been interested in Jesus' sayings and doings? Acts gives us but scanty and not very intimate notices of the primitive Church; but even among these notices we can see in 2^{22}, 10^{38} a summary reference to Our Lord's miracles which makes it probable that narratives of His doings were in circulation; while the temper of the Church itself (cf. $2^{44f.}$, $4^{33f.}$) suggests that the spirit of His teaching and example was at work. If the 'Gospel' was the proclamation of Jesus the Messiah, of His Death, Resurrection, and Parousia, the sayings and doings of this Jesus must at any rate have been drawn upon to give life and colour and moral content and personal appeal to the announcement.

[1] Acts 1^{11}.

ii

As time went on and the Church grew the work of Christian teaching in the various churches required a larger number of teachers than could be supplied by eye-witnesses or by those who had learnt from eye-witnesses. Oral tradition was no longer sufficient. Besides, eye-witnesses might die; the tradition might be forgotten or adulterated. The Parousia still delayed to happen, and teachers were even warning the Church not to be too sure that it would come at once (cf. 2 Thess. 2^2). The need of written records of Jesus' life thus began to be felt. Perhaps, in different places, many tried to supply this need as far as they could, by writing down such scraps of gospel matter, incidents or sayings, as they knew. But in the older centres of Christianity, like Jerusalem, Antioch, Caesarea, or in a great centre of Church life like Rome, there would be more chance of collecting a more continuous story.

Of the more considerable of such early records scholars think that the existence of two (and perhaps a third) can be established:

(1) In the 1st and 3rd gospels, while there is a great deal which is derived from Mark, there is also a great deal which is not derived from Mark, and yet is found in both Matthew and Luke. This 'common matter' is conjectured to have been part of an original document, to which the label Q has been given.[1] The character of this document can be made out from the passages that are thought to have come from it.[2] It is generally agreed that (*a*) it was written by Jewish Christians in Palestine (or possibly at Antioch), perhaps within 15–20 years of Our Lord's Crucifixion (i.e. about A.D. 45); (*b*) if, as is possible, it was written in Aramaic, it was soon translated into Greek, and the Greek version was used for the 1st and 3rd gospels; (*c*) it contained mostly sayings, but also narratives connected with them; (*d*) it was written for the use of teachers to supplement the oral tradition of Christ's life, for a generation which had known Christ.[3]

[1] Short for *Quelle*, the German word for 'source'.

[2] There is nothing like general agreement among scholars as to the exact limits of the Q passages; but there is enough agreement to make certain generalizations possible.

[3] See *Oxford Synoptic Studies*, Essay VII.

(2) Streeter thinks that in the 3rd gospel can be found traces of an earlier and much shorter document, for which the name 'Proto-Luke' is suggested. This document has made use of Q but not of Mark; it may have been written (or the materials for it collected), by Luke or by some one else at Caesarea, perhaps at the time of Paul's imprisonment there (A.D. 56–8). A copy of Mark later came into Luke's hands, who used it in order to enlarge Proto-Luke into our present 3rd gospel. This theory was first suggested in 1921,[1] and has seemed attractive and possible to many scholars. It is, however, too soon yet to say if it will eventually establish itself. If it does, Proto-Luke would take its place by the side of Mark as an authority.

(3) The second gospel, as we possess it, was probably written at Rome shortly before A.D. 70 (or perhaps in the decade after that date). It is the writing-down of the traditional gospel-matter which was available at Rome, for a public which wanted to know the story of Christ's life. This traditional matter was partly oral and partly written. It seems to have consisted largely of Palestinian tradition, brought to Rome by Peter and others; but there is reason for believing that some gospel-matter (perhaps Q or a version of Q, and perhaps some of the narrative-matter too) already existed at Rome in written form, and was either used by, or at least known to, the writer of Mark. Indeed some scholars see in Mark a narrative intended to supplement Q.[2]

This, then, is the process by which gospel-literature began to be written. Before carrying on the story, let us realize some of the conditions which would affect the character of the books:

(1) The methods of book-producing were of course wholly

[1] Cf. Streeter, *The Four Gospels*, for an elaboration of the argument. The theory is worked out very thoroughly in Taylor's *Behind the Third Gospel*.

[2] The Synoptic problem is far too complicated for universal agreement to be claimed for any but very general conclusions. I have only stated briefly what seems to me the most probable view. Points of controversy in relation to the second gospel (some of which will be considered later) are: (1) does Mark show evidence of the use of documentary sources? (2) did Mark use or know Q? (3) is our Mark a Greek translation of an Aramaic original? (4) was it written first in Palestine, and earlier than 65, and translated when it was taken to Rome? (5) is our Mark an expansion of an originally shorter document?

A page of the famous *Codex Sinaiticus*, a Greek MS. of the fourth century. The part shown runs from Mark 6. 27 to 7. 1

different from ours. The author wrote one MS. (On the limitations set by the average size of the papyrus roll, cf. *Oxford Studies in the Synoptic Problem*, Essay I, by Sanday.) This could then be copied, by himself or by some one else, and so the number of copies would slowly multiply. But the author—or some one else—might produce a second version, revising the language, incorporating new material, correcting or omitting. This version might also be copied. Thus would arise different 'recensions'.

Then, again, copyists might make mistakes, or they might insert explanations, alter phrases or words, or even add paragraphs; and these copies might be re-copied. Thus would arise variations of text and 'families' of texts. It is the business of textual criticism to try to establish what most probably represents the original autograph of the writer.

We must remember, too, that for some time there were in existence other sources of gospel-matter, some oral, others written. The 'many' of Luke 1[1] seems to refer to general narratives; and we know that, after the four gospels had all been written, there were other gospels in existence, some of which for some time rivalled the four in popularity. Neither Mark nor Q was in any way an official production, written with Christendom in view. They were produced for the use of teachers and preachers in one local church; they spread from there only by the unofficial agency of Christian travellers taking copies with them on their journeys.

(2) The purpose for which the books were written makes it natural that they should show the influence of 'aetiology' (= the desire to give the reason of things). Thus, for instance, in his selection of what he did or did not write down, Mark would obviously be guided not only by his opinion of what was or was not important in itself, but also by his opinions as to what his readers would like to hear; he would not omit incidents or sayings which explained Church customs, such as Fasting or the Eucharist, or which reflected discredit on the Church's enemies the Jews, or which showed that the persecution which the Roman Church was suffering under Nero had been foretold by Our Lord. And this aetiological interest might not only affect his selection of incidents

but also the colouring of his record. By that it is not meant that he would deliberately invent or falsify, but that his interpretation of incidents and teaching might inevitably be influenced by the views of his Church environment. His gospel is not written as a biography, but as a text-book for teachers; and its purpose cannot help affecting its use of its material.

(3) We must realize also that a gulf both of time and of situation lies between the events recorded and the writing-down of them in Mark. The events took place in the environment of Herodian Palestine; Mark was written in the surroundings of a Gentile church in a Hellenistic city-society. There was obviously room for a certain amount of forgetfulness or misunderstanding of historical circumstances to operate.

How far these conditions have actually affected the historical value of Mark will have to be considered later, when we approach closer to the actual gospel. It should, however, be made quite clear (4) that the Christians were not prepared to receive *anything* that was given them as gospel-narrative. The story of Christ's life had often been told to them by word of mouth. Any gospel that they would be likely to welcome must tell them what they had heard; and, if it contained new information, they would expect it to have some guarantee of its authority. Fancy stories of Our Lord's life did come into being;[1] but they were all rejected from the New Testament Canon by the common sense of the Church; and the general soberness of the canonical gospels is excellent evidence that the Christians were not uncritical or indifferent to historical truth and credibility.

iii

The example of gospel-writing which had been set by Mark's work was in time followed by attempts at more complete records. Our first and third gospels are to be placed in this category; they are the product of a combination of written documents, though possibly with the addition in each case of fragments of oral tradition.

[1] See James, *Apocryphal New Testament*, for what remains of these early fictions.

The evidence for the use of Mark in Matthew and Luke is overwhelming.[1] Summarily stated, it is as follows: (1) Out of 661 verses in Mark, only about 50 do not reappear (in some shape) in Matthew or in Luke or in both. (2) The common *order* is Mark's. Where one of the two diverges from it, the other follows Mark. The occasions when the two agree in order against Mark are very few indeed. (3) The same is the case with the actual *language*. The two very seldom, and only in trifling respects, agree in wording different from Mark's. Both of them often alter, improve, &c. Mark's phraseology; but quite clearly Mark's language is the groundwork from which both of them start. (4) Moreover, this resemblance in order and language is so detailed, and extends to such unimportant points of language, that it cannot be ascribed to the use of a common oral tradition. The writers of Matthew and Luke had copies of the same written Greek source before them; and that source must be Mark.

Thus the following stages may be traced in the process of gospel-writing: (1) the time of oral tradition; (2) the writing-down of oral tradition (represented by Q); (3) a stage when oral and written tradition are both drawn on to make a consecutive narrative (represented by Mark and Proto-Luke; the former seems to be due partly to oral and partly to written authorities, while the latter is held to be a combination of a written Q with narrative-matter obtained orally);[2] (4) Matthew and Luke are books made out of books (Matthew out of Q and Mark, Luke out of Proto-Luke and Mark), though they also incorporate additional pieces of gospel-matter, which may have reached the writers either orally or in writing; (5) finally the fourth gospel, which stands apart from the three Synoptists and was certainly written

[1] The conclusion is the most assured result of Synoptic study. The first three Gospels are called 'the Synoptic gospels' or 'the Synoptists', and 'the Synoptic problem' is the problem of their relation to one another.

[2] If the theory of a Proto-Luke should not be accepted, the general scheme here given would not be substantially modified. Luke is certainly a combination of Q., Mark, and special matter. The problem is, (1) where was this special matter derived from? From oral tradition or a written document? (2) Was it incorporated with Q first, or were the three elements combined for the first time in the completed gospel? (3) Is Mark the groundwork of Luke? Or is some other document the groundwork, into which he fits extracts from Mark; and if so, what may that document have been?

after them, may have been intended, in part at least, to supplement, interpret, or correct the already familiar Synoptic narrative.

Mark's gospel, once written, must soon have begun to circulate among the churches, and it must have held a commanding position in the latter years of the first century. Any rival narratives

MEDIEVAL SYMBOLS OF THE FOUR EVANGELISTS
The Angel for St. Matthew, the Eagle for St. John, the Lion for St. Mark, the Bull for St. Luke. From the tympanum over the West Door of Chartres Cathedral

have disappeared. More remarkable still, the Marcan 'order' became as it were canonical; in Matthew and Luke the Marcan story is not the only authority, but neither evangelist dares tamper at all seriously with the main Marcan outline; and, when the fourth gospel, with its many divergences from the Synoptic sequence, became generally known, these divergences provided a puzzle for students from Tatian (A.D. 140) onwards, and disposed some to wish to deny the authority of 'John'.

But in the second century Mark fell from its high estate. Matthew and Luke supplanted it in popular esteem and use. To the writers of the middle of the century, such as Papias or Justin, the supreme gospel is Matthew. The Church eventually settled down to regard the four Gospels as a sacred quartette (we find this point of view in Irenaeus A.D. 180). But even then the uncultivated style of Mark, its comparative brevity and incompleteness, and its more primitive and antiquated point of view, caused it to be neglected by the Church; the oldest commentary on it is not earlier than the 5th or 6th century. It survived, however, in liturgical use; no doubt it was saved by (1) its one-time influence, (2) its traditional connexion with Peter, and (3) its origin in the Roman Church, which so soon became the leading church of Christendom. In modern times it has gained once more a primary importance in the eyes of historical students, as being the primordial narrative remaining to us of Our Lord's life.

B. CHURCH TRADITION AS TO THE AUTHORSHIP OF THE GOSPEL.

In any discussion of the authorship of this gospel, the starting-point must be the testimony of one Papias, who was bishop of Hierapolis in Phrygia in the first half of the second century A.D. He had met the daughters of Philip the Evangelist (of whom we hear in Acts 21^9), and was a friend of Polycarp, bishop of Smyrna, who had been a disciple of John and was martyred about A.D. 155. Thus Papias lived at a time when personal reminiscences of the apostolic age were not wholly at an end; he was probably born about A.D. 80. He wrote, perhaps about or soon after A.D. 140,[1] a book called 'Interpretation of the Lord's Precepts' (*κυριακῶν λογίων ἐξήγησις*) of which nothing but a few fragments survives. In one of these fragments he refers to the second gospel, professing to be giving information derived from a presbyter called John, who flourished about A.D. 100 and is thought by some scholars to have been the author of the fourth gospel. The relevant sentence is as follows:

'This also the Elder said: Mark, who had been Peter's interpreter, wrote down carefully, though not in order, the sayings and doings of Christ, so far as he remembered them. For he (i.e. Mark) was neither

[1] Some would place the date 20 or 25 years earlier.

a hearer nor a follower of the Lord, but was later a follower, as I said, of Peter, who (i.e. Peter) used to adapt his teachings to the needs (of his hearers), but not as if he were making a connected arrangement of the Lord's words. So that Mark committed no error in thus writing down some things as he remembered them. For he made it his one care to leave out nothing of the things he had heard and to falsify nothing in them.'[1]

The purpose of this passage may be inferred without much hesitation. Papias is trying to justify the fact that in writing an interpretation of the Lord's precepts he is going to make some use of Mark's gospel, though it is not a proper compendium of Christ's teaching, such as is found in Matthew,[2] which would be the main basis of his work. This use of Mark he justifies by quoting 'the Elder', in whom the tradition of an earlier age lived on, as his guarantee that Mark contains a trustworthy record of Christ's doings and sayings.

The quotation from the Elder probably extends only to the first sentence of the fragment from Papias. The rest seems to be Papias's own explanation and deduction; in any case the first sentence is the important one, containing the actual tradition.

Notice then (1) that it asserts that the Marcan gospel is connected with Peter. How close this connexion was is a problem which we shall have to discuss. The Elder may have regarded it as being closer and more direct than was the actual fact. But the tradition of *some* definite connexion with Peter is obviously one which cannot be lightly set aside.

[1] Papias *ap*. Eus. H.E. III. 39. *Καὶ τοῦθ' ὁ πρεσβύτερος ἔλεγε· Μάρκος μὲν, ἑρμηνευτὴς Πέτρου γενόμενος, ὅσα ἐμνημόνευσεν ἀκριβῶς ἔγραψεν, οὐ μέντοι τάξει, τὰ ὑπὸ τοῦ Χριστοῦ ἢ λεχθέντα ἢ πραχθέντα. οὔτε γὰρ ἤκουσε τοῦ κυρίου οὔτε παρηκολούθησεν αὐτῷ, ὕστερον δέ, ὡς ἔφην, Πέτρῳ, ὅς πρὸς τὰς χρείας ἐποιεῖτο τὰς διδασκαλίας, ἀλλ' οὐχ ὥσπερ σύνταξιν τῶν κυριακῶν ποιούμενος λόγων. ὥστε οὐδὲν ἥμαρτε Μάρκος, οὕτως ἔνια γράψας ὡς ἀπεμνημόνευσεν· ἑνὸς γὰρ ἐποιήσατο πρόνοιαν, τοῦ μηδὲν ὧν ἤκουσε παραλιπεῖν ἢ ψεύσασθαί τι ἐν αὐτοῖς.*

[2] Of Matthew Papias says that he 'wrote (or compiled) the oracles in the Hebrew tongue' (i.e. Aramaic). The Greek is *τὰ λόγια συνεγράψατο* (vl. *συνετάξατο*). He makes this statement on his own authority, and not on that of the Elder; and its value as evidence for the authorship of the first gospel is open to doubt. But it is at any rate clear that he regarded the first gospel as the standard compendium of Christ's teaching. Bacon's argument, that by this book of *Logia* (or 'oracles') he simply means the first gospel and not any lost Logia-document, appears to me convincing.

It is hard to be sure in what sense we are to take the statement that Mark was Peter's 'interpreter' (ἑρμηνευτής). We have no reason to suppose that Peter could only speak Aramaic and would need some one to turn his Aramaic into Greek. Greek was the *lingua franca* of the East, and Peter could probably speak Greek at least as well as Mark. Nor have we any reason to think that Peter would need an interpreter into Latin, or that Mark could have acted as such. The lower classes at Rome, from which the first Church of Rome was almost entirely drawn, were mainly Greeks or hellenized Orientals; all would speak Greek; many probably would know very little Latin. The Elder's phrase is better taken vaguely, as meaning either little more than 'servant' (ὑπηρέτης: Mark is called the 'servant' of Paul and Barnabas in Acts 13[5]), or at most something like 'amanuensis', i.e. he who writes down and so interprets Peter's teaching.

(2) The Papias-fragment makes it clear that in Papias's time the 'order' of Mark's gospel was criticized. We do not know whether in this respect it was unfavourably compared with Matthew or with John; but it is probable that the standard gospel was now Matthew; it was certainly so to Papias himself. Nor do we know whether the complaint was that Mark's sequence of events was insufficiently chronological or that his arrangement of his material was insufficiently literary. The Greek word for 'order' used by Papias (τάξις) might have either reference. Either complaint against Mark has ample justification. He does not group the teaching material artistically as Matthew does. And his chronological arrangement is defective and unsatisfactory; it is the best sequence available to us, however, and is followed by Matthew with little deviation. But the second-century Church had no special interest in exact historical details; its chief concern was with doctrine and with Our Lord's teaching. It is probable therefore that Mark was criticized as defective in literary arrangement rather than in chronological consecutiveness.

(3) The Elder's explanation of the defectiveness of Mark's order is that his gospel is a miscellany, built up out of the reminiscences of Peter's preaching, which are given, without any sustained effort at consecutive or literary arrangement, very much as they

are remembered. This may not be the complete explanation of the characteristics of Mark's gospel. We shall have to consider later whether it can be taken as the *mere* transcript of oral preaching. But that it is in the main a collection of catechetical [1] anecdotes may be accepted as a substantially correct account of the facts. The chief phenomena of the gospel which we possess in every way correspond with this tradition of its genesis.

Such then is the primary Church tradition about the authority of this gospel. It is reproduced in Church writers of later date with no alteration. We find it in Irenaeus (*circa* A.D. 180) in Tertullian (210), in Clement of Alexandria (210), in Origen (died 253), and in Jerome (400).

The tradition as to the date at which the gospel was written and the place of its writing is nearly as unanimous. Irenaeus III 1. says that it was written after the death (μετὰ τὴν ἔξοδον) of Peter and Paul; and, as he had visited Rome, he is probably recording the local tradition of the Roman Church. The Papias fragment, in connecting Mark with Peter, who was one of the martyr Apostles of the Roman Church, witnesses to the origin of the gospel in Rome. Clement of Alexandria, who also ascribes the gospel to Rome, suggests that Peter approved the project of its composition, though he does not definitely state that it was written before Peter's death. The story of Peter's approval may or may not be true. But Clement's ambiguous words certainly cannot weigh against Irenaeus's definite statement as to the date of the writing. The statement of Chrysostom (died 407) that the gospel was written in Egypt is probably a blunder, due to the tradition that Mark had preached at some time in Egypt. The question of the exact date and place of writing of the gospel will have to be more fully considered later. But the voice of tradition may be taken as placing the date after A.D. 64–5 and the place as Rome.

A minor detail relating to Mark is recorded by a Roman writer called Hippolytus (*Philosoph.* vii. 30, died 235), who says that

[1] 'catechetical', i.e. used in teaching. The early Christian form of teaching was regularly called κατήχησις, from which word are derived 'catechumen' = one being prepared for baptism, and 'catechism' = a manual of instruction.

Mark was known as 'the man with the stunted or docked finger' (ὁ κολοβοδάκτυλος). But we do not know the reason for this nickname. The preface to the Vulgate conjectures that Mark amputated a finger in order to disqualify himself for the Jewish priesthood; it is assumed that like his uncle (or cousin) Barnabas he was of Levitical descent. Another MS. more prosaically suggests that though he was tall, his fingers were short. The word seems originally to have meant a 'shirker', one who cut off a thumb to escape military service. Hence some connect the epithet with Mark's desertion of Paul and Barnabas, recorded in Acts 13[13], 15[38]; while others believe it to refer to the unfinished condition of the gospel. Fancy has a wide field here.

The New Testament references to Mark make it plain that he was a secondary figure in the apostolic Church. His Jewish name was probably John, Mark being his secondary name (like Saul, also called Paul, and others). The house of his mother Mary was the Christian centre in the early days of the Church at Jerusalem (Acts 12[12]); it has been conjectured that it was the house of the Last Supper. In Acts 12[25] he is taken as 'minister' by Paul and Barnabas on their first missionary journey. He left them at Perga (Acts 13[13]) for reasons that are not stated; it has been guessed that he shrank from an extension of the mission to predominantly Gentile countries. Paul was much incensed at this desertion, and the quarrel between him and Barnabas on the point (Acts 15[37-9]) led to their separation. Mark went with Barnabas to Cyprus. We do not hear of him again until the time of Paul's imprisonment. In Col. 4[10] Paul commends him to the friendly hospitality of the Colossian church; Mark is then in Paul's company, as he is found also in Philem. 24. In 2 Tim. 4[11] Paul desires his company and praises him as 'useful for ministering'. In 1 Pet. 5[13] he is in Rome and is called 'my son' by the author; [1] the Epistle may not be of Petrine authorship, but it bears witness to the existence of affectionate relations between Peter and Mark and to their association at Rome (which in the Epistle is called

[1] This is usually explained as meaning that he was Peter's pupil and spiritual child. But the word for such a relation is more usually *τέκνον*; here it is *υἱός*. It is conceivable that Mark was in fact Peter's son by blood.

'Babylon'). Finally, it may be said that there are plausible grounds for the conjecture that the 'young man' mentioned in Mark 14^{51} as being present at Our Lord's arrest was Mark himself (see note *ad loc.*).

Among extra-canonical notices of Mark we may note that the so-called *Acts of Barnabas* (4th or 5th century) state that Barnabas was martyred in Cyprus and that Mark then went to Egypt and evangelized Alexandria. Church tradition certainly connected Mark with Egypt, and the Egyptian Church claimed him as her first bishop.

C. INTERNAL EVIDENCE AS TO THE SOURCES OF THE GOSPEL.

We must now turn to examine the gospel itself for evidence as to its composition. Two questions are obviously raised by the Church tradition: (1) Does the gospel seem such as might reasonably be taken to be the work of the John Mark of the New Testament? (2) Does it seem such as might reasonably be held to be derived from Peter?

The second of these questions is much the more far-reaching. We cannot deal with the first until we have inquired into the alleged 'Petrinity' of the gospel. To this problem we shall now address ourselves.

i

The Papias-fragment seems to suggest that this gospel is nothing else but a direct transcript of the stories which Peter used to tell. This claim indeed is still very frequently made for the gospel; but not in works of balanced and careful scholarship. There are, in fact, too many signs of apparently 'secondary' matter in the gospel to make it easy to hold that it is entirely the mere report of first-hand oral reminiscence. Some of the more obvious of these *secondary traits* may here be noted:

(1) It is a patent fact that the story of Our Lord's ministry in Galilee is scanty and disjointed. The chronological sequence is vague and no definite indication of the length of time involved in the various episodes is supplied. The history does not become

really consecutive until Jerusalem is reached. Too much should not be made of this fact; for the catechetical character of the materials may sufficiently account for it. It is plain, however, that the author had not obtained from Peter any indications of the proper chronological relation of his anecdotes.

(2) It is more serious when we see reason for suspecting the presence in the gospel of genuine blunders, such as it seems unlikely that Peter would commit. Thus it is unquestionable that the story of Herod and John the Baptist in 6^{17-29} contains historical uncertainties, some of which appear to be real errors. Rawlinson suggests that this story in Mark may be the product of bazaar-rumour rather than of accurate record. The geographical difficulties involved in the apparent position of Gerasa in 5^{1-20} and in calling Bethsaida a 'village' in 8^{26} may be evaded, though not easily; but a journey 'from Tyre via Sidon through Decapolis to the Sea of Galilee' (7^{31}) is a geographical absurdity. So again it is admitted that in 7^{3} the ceremonial strictness of the Jews is greatly exaggerated, probably in the interests of the Church's later controversy with the Jews. The Marcan story of the Passion too seems to be incorrect in dating the Last Supper as the Passover-meal (14^{12}),[1] and appears to have been influenced by the Roman Church custom of observing Easter; while the actual story of Our Lord's public trials appears to many to be less satisfactory than that in e.g. the third gospel.[2] The cumulative impression of such details, few as they are, is that at least *some* redaction and some aetiological interest have been at work, which make the gospel story seem to be not *wholly* the transcript of an eye-witness's record.

(3) A few sections of the gospel suggest that some written sources have been used or consulted by the author. Of course the conclusion (16^{9-20}), which appears to be a compilation from the recorded appearances of Our Lord, cannot be cited here, as it is not a part of the original gospel. But the 'doom chapter' (13) strongly

[1] And is even inconsistent with itself, if the phrase in 15^{21} implies that Simon had been engaged in field-work. This, however, is not unavoidable. See further the note at c. 14 *ad init.*

[2] The commentary must be consulted *ad loc.* for a more detailed treatment of these points.

suggests a written document as its basis (though 13^{14} does not necessarily imply this). And it may be true that the parable in 4^{26-9} is to be taken as another version of the parable in 4^{3-9}; while it seems very probable that the two stories of the feeding of the multitude (in 6^{34-44} and 8^{1-9}) are two versions of the same event, and that the evangelist is therefore using at least one written source as well as his Petrine tradition, or is even using two parallel written accounts as if they dealt with two different incidents;[1] for it is unlikely that an eye-witness would give two divergent accounts of the same episode. Finally, we shall see later that there is reason to conjecture that Mark knew and made some use of the Q document. These evidences are not perhaps numerous, but they go to show that there has been *some* use of written sources, and that the gospel is therefore to some extent built out of previously-existing documents and is not the mere writing-down of oral reminiscence.

(4) The part played by Peter in the story is really remarkable. He seems almost singled out for condemnation, and is hardly once mentioned except in terms of rebuke. Cf. 8^{33} (even his confession of Christ's Messiahship in 8^{29} is not here, as in Matthew, noted for commendation), $9^{5,6}$, $10^{28,31}$, $14^{29,37,66f.}$. The slowness of the Twelve to apprehend their Master's meaning is repeatedly emphasized; and nothing is said about the Virgin Mary and Our Lord's brethren except to record their opposition and unbelief $3^{21,31f.}$, 6^{4}. These seem strange characteristics in a gospel which is alleged to be based on Peter's personal reminiscences. Nor does it entirely turn the edge of this criticism to say that none but Peter himself could thus be responsible for dilating on Peter's deficiencies; or to add (true as it may be) that by the time that the gospel was written, Peter's martyrdom had transfigured his reputation and that the story of his earlier failures had thus lost its sting. It still seems to us singular that Peter's preaching should have been so defective in its record with regard to the rest of the Twelve and our Lord's family circle. Certainly the story is not thereby proved to be *un*-Petrine. Probably none but ultimately Petrine authority could have sanctioned so disparaging a picture

[1] That Mark regarded the two incidents as different is plain from 8^{19-20}.

of the great Apostle's earlier years. But we find it hard not to think that the evangelist's *selection* of his material was to some extent influenced by some tendency which induced him thus to bring out the deficiencies of Peter and of the rest of the Twelve into prominence. What this tendency was it is hard to be certain. Was it loyalty to Paul, and the desire to show that if he in his young days 'persecuted the church of God', Peter in his young days had been a very fallible follower of Our Lord? The rivalry of the respective claims for Peter and Paul had played no little part in Church history; Mark had been associated with both of them and may have wished to reconcile the rivalry by showing that Peter had no advantage over Paul in virtue of his earlier acquaintance with Our Lord. Or he may have been a convinced 'Pauline'; though the tradition of his close association with Peter would not suggest that he was therefore necessarily hostile to Peter. But, however we explain the tendency, we do not find it easy to be sure that no such tendency is present; and if our feeling on this point is right, we must reckon this also as a 'secondary' trait which has at least coloured the mind of the evangelist in the use which he has made of his material.

ii

We must agree then that the gospel presents some secondary traits and some signs of the use of written sources. We must now note such evidences as it offers for the view that it is substantially derived from first-hand narrative (whether oral or written), and that the spirit in which it is told is not seriously influenced by the tendencies at work in the Church during and after the Apostolic age; that it is in general a narrative of *'primary' character*.

(1) First we may draw attention to the vivid and graphic style in which many of the narratives are told. Such passages as 1^{16-39}, 7^{24-30}, 10^{32}, $14^{32-52,66-72}$ exhibit a direct realism which strongly produces the impression that they come from an eye-witness; the same is the character of 4^{36-41}, $9^{5,6}$, however we care to explain the incidents there related. Graphic touches in the narrative are of constant occurrence. Cf. $1^{20,41}$, $3^{2,5,9,34}$, 4^{38}, 5^{43}, $6^{39,40}$, $7^{33,34}$, $8^{12,23-5}$, $10^{16,21}$, 11^{11}, $14^{40,51-2,54}$, 15^{21}. The degree to which this characteristic

appears to be the result of personal reminiscence on the part of one who was himself present at the scenes is a question of literary appreciation, which must be left to each reader to exercise for himself.[1]

(2) Until Jerusalem is reached, the gospel is only a series of anecdotes, indifferently connected with one another in sequence. But it is worth noting that the story does not even begin to be particularized until Peter appears (1^{16}), and that most of it from that point is such as Petrine recollections would well account for.

[1] But it really is not enough as an explanation to say, with Wernle and Bacon, that 'the characteristic belongs to the period rather than to the person. With the Gospel of Mark we stand nearer the time when freedom of descriptive detail was still permissible on the part of the narrator and was welcomed by the audience. It does not require that one should have sat among the "eating-companies" in Galilee (as admittedly Mark did not) to know how an outdoor group of Christians looks assembled for such a purpose on a green hillside. (The reference here is to the scene in $6^{39, 40}$.) Neither does it require that one should have been a companion of Apostles to know how "demoniacs" behave under the word of the exorcizer, or how paralytics and other afflicted people receive the healing act or word of the messenger of glad tidings. If one has spent a lifetime in "doing the work of an evangelist" such scenes are not difficult to reproduce.' (Bacon, *Gospel of Mark*, p. 300.) We may grant that the narrator was not blind to the symbolic or didactic uses to which some of the details might be put, e.g. those which picture Our Lord's power over the demons or His emotions when faced with human distress or unbelief. But many of the details cannot be so explained; they are pointless for any purpose save that of picturesqueness. Again, while we may allow that some of the picturesque details might have been noticed by the evangelist when he was present at church-gatherings, and might thus have been added by him as 'fancy touches', yet we must also recognize the fact that these details are always appropriate to the scene pictured, and that fancy picturesqueness is not often so artless and so naïve as it here appears. We have also to remember (a point of which Bacon makes much use in another context, and which presents a difficulty as to the authorship which we shall have to consider later) that the gospel is strangely deficient in elements which might appear to be due to Mark's own personal reminiscences. If he obtruded the fruits of his own observation on later occasions into his narrative of the gospel scenes, why did he not do it more thoroughly and obtrude also other personal notices (real or imaginary) of the actors in the gospel story? Bacon cannot have it both ways. If the evangelist sinks himself to such a degree that we may even hesitate (as Bacon does) to ascribe the gospel to Mark's authorship, we must not at the same time assume that he was ready to obtrude himself in order to make more picturesque the narratives which he was drawing from his sources. We are left therefore with the necessity of explaining the constant presence of graphic, yet appropriate, touches in the sources from which he drew; and it is hard to resist the impression that this characteristic is due to the fact that much of the narrative is ultimately derived from one who himself was present at the scenes depicted.

Furthermore, it must be admitted that the gospel exhibits a good deal of indifference to political detail; e.g. it is either careless or ignorant as to details of the Herodian Court, and it does not make clear the political divisions of the country, e.g. that Bethsaida or Gerasa are not in the tetrarchy of Antipas, that Phenicia was under the governor of Syria, while at Jericho Our Lord came into the sphere of the procurator of Judaea. None the less, the general sense of the political situation is correct. The gospel makes it plain that Jerusalem was more dangerous to Our Lord than Galilee. It is correct also in its witness that while in Galilee 'synagogue-rulers' were the religious authorities, in Jerusalem they were 'chief-priests', and that while Pharisees and scribes were met in both localities, Sadducees were found only at Jerusalem. There is moreover much to be said for Burkitt's theory [1] that after the incident in 3^{6} Our Lord was in some danger from Antipas, and that His frequent withdrawals—to the Lakeside (3^{7}, 4^{1}), to the other side of the Lake (4^{35}, 6^{45}, 8^{13}), to Tyre and Decapolis ($7^{24,31}$), to Caesarea Philippi (8^{27})—were due to the fact that Antipas's dominions were unsafe for Him (6^{14}) and that He was there exposed to the danger of public excitement and controversy (3^{20}, $7^{1f.}$, $8^{11f.}$. In 9^{30} he passes through Galilee but in secret). If this is a correct explanation of Our Lord's journeys, the gospel is right in its implied suggestion that Phenicia, Caesarea Philippi, and Bethsaida were relatively secure from Antipas. If then we realize that the gospel is neither a history nor a biography, but a set of catechetical anecdotes, there is nothing in its sense of the general situation to preclude the view that it is derived from a tradition of Palestinian origin; that, though recorded by a man who had little concern for a scrupulous exactitude in the details of the historical circumstances or of the political '*milieu*', it proceeds from one who was not ignorant of the general character of those circumstances.

(3) The gospel is not deficient in its doctrine of the Person of Christ.[2] But its Christology is artless and unobtrusive. No definite dogmatic tendency can be traced in it, such as would make

[1] *The Gospel History*, cap. III.

[2] The Christology of the gospel is dealt with in a more detailed manner in a separate Note to the Introduction.

THE SEA OF GALILEE, near Tiberias

us conclude that it had taken shape under the influence of systematic ecclesiastical formulation. Even the eschatological point of view (though it pervades the main story) is not directly and consciously emphasized except in the story of John the Baptist (1^{2-15}), i.e. in the part before Peter appears in the record; and though the phrase 'Kingdom of God' occurs in the gospel more than once, no special stress is laid, as is done in Matthew, upon the eschatological side of its significance. The doctrinal atmosphere is simple and primitive.

Some commentators have professed to find in the gospel such an abundance and definiteness of 'Pauline' conceptions as would make it impossible to believe that the gospel is to more than a slight degree a faithful record of Petrine tradition. This view will fall to be considered in greater detail later. At present we need only say (*a*) that there are in the gospel noticeable differences from the Pauline standpoint; in particular the limitation of the Gospel to the Jews is taken for granted, and no trace is discernible of that which was Paul's most characteristic doctrine, the equality of Jew and Gentile in Christ. (The story of the Syro-phenician woman 7^{26f}. is crucial on this point.) (*b*) The doctrine mainly emphasized in the gospel (from 8^{31} onwards) is the doctrine of the Cross; and this doctrine is unquestionably Pauline; i.e. in Paul's Epistles Jesus Christ is pre-eminently He Who died for men, and His Crucifixion is the climax of His revelation and the culminating event of His life. But what possible right have we to assume that this interpretation of His death was not within the compass of Jesus' own apprehension, that His death was not something which He could anticipate without needing any miraculous foresight, and that the idea of the redemptive possibilities of His death was not an idea that might have entered His mind? The gospel record, so far as this point is concerned, cannot be adjudged secondary, because a point of view which might well have been that of Jesus Himself was also that of His great Apostle.

What may have been Our Lord's 'programme' is a question that we shall have to discuss later. But we may be warned at once against a tendency which has been present in some schools of New Testament criticism, the tendency to draw a clear line between

THE CRUCIFIXION
A miniature of the twelfth century in the Psalter of Queen Melisenda, representing the descent from the Cross

Jesus and the Christian Church, and to reduce the contribution of Jesus Himself to the Christian religion, while increasing the contribution of Paul, the fourth gospel, and Church thought in general; to present Jesus as nothing but a great moral idealist, and a generous though finally ineffective enthusiast, while Christian doctrine is an idealistic theology built by men on the basis of this Jesus, which has coloured His somewhat limited life and personality with the colours of an ideal humanity and a divine incarnation. Of such a presentation it is almost not too rash to say that it is bound to be false; it rings hollow; it does not account for what has happened; it is a hypothesis which does not explain the facts. In relation to the Cross and the doctrine of the Atonement, which has been in all ages, and never more than now, the chief attractive force in Christianity and the very life-blood of Christian devotion, this theory asks us to believe that Jesus died without any glimpse of comprehension of the possible effectiveness for redemptive purposes of His death, that He was a mere victim and not a Priest of God offering Himself with intelligence for an end He envisaged; and that the spiritual originality of Paul fastened the atoning interpretation on Jesus' Crucifixion and so made Christianity that religion of the Crucified Christ which has changed the world. If we can really bring ourselves to believe this, we must have a more than common degree of credulity, of ability to accept results without asking for an adequate cause to produce them. It is after all the merest common sense to remember that the disciple is not greater than his lord.

(4) The miraculous element in the gospel story used to be regarded by many commentators of the last generation as an undeniably secondary trait. It was taken for granted that the miracles could not have happened, that no eye-witness could have recorded the incidents so, and that the stories must therefore be the product of the 'mythopoeic' fancy of a later generation. The tendency of more modern criticism is very different. (*a*) It is now admitted that many of the miracles, e.g. those of healing, are not incredible; that they are only more striking instances of a power seen in not a few modern and well-attested cures, the power of Mind over Body. (*b*) With regard to miracles in general, the

philosophy which treats 'Nature' as a closed system of mechanical necessity is now generally adjudged to be unsatisfactory. The rigid separation of the natural from the supernatural is no longer accepted as scientific. Thus it is not regarded as an irrational position to maintain that if Our Lord was such as Christian belief claims Him to be, we cannot exactly limit His power of influencing the natural order of things. This does not mean that we believe Him to be divine *because* He wrought miracles; the miracles are no longer evidential to us in this sense, as they were to the early Church and to the Church of even fifty years ago. But, having learnt to accept Him as divine on moral and spiritual grounds, we go on to say that such a Being might be expected to be able to exercise powers which ordinary imperfect humanity can neither compass nor explain.

(*c*) Furthermore, critics now generally agree that in Mark's gospel there are no traces of a desire to heighten the element of marvel in the story by the addition of legendary colouring (such as is seen in the Apocryphal Gospels). Men will of course speculate about the miracles where 'power over inanimate nature' is displayed, such as the walking on the water, the blasting of the fig-tree, or the feeding of the multitude; suggestions are made to explain one or other of such marvels in such a way as to remove from the story the miraculous element. But such speculations are perhaps more curious than useful. It need not be denied that if the incidents had been witnessed by modern observers, some or all of them might have been seen to conform to the 'natural order' as we now understand it. But it cannot also be denied that the mental attitude of men in Our Lord's time was such as to make them give a miraculous interpretation to strange or striking events. The presence of such stories is at least no argument against their character as primary records. The miracles are told simply and directly, and are such as are not unbecoming to Christ's Personality; the evangelist shows no desire to multiply prodigies for their own sake.

With regard to the exorcisms of demoniacs in particular, it is to be recognized that the world of those days was one in which the power and activity of diabolical agencies was an accepted idea, and the power of exorcizing these agencies was as readily believed to reside in special individuals. The striking fact in the records of Our Lord's exorcisms is only that He, being an unofficial person, was yet credited with ability to exorcize. This at least witnesses to the impression which He made, and is evidence for the belief that He showed wonderful effectiveness in dealing with and healing people whom we perhaps would regard as lunatic or epileptic, but who were then regarded as devil-possessed. The ascription to Him of such miracles need in no way shake the view that the record is the product of an eye-witness.

iii

It is not easy to draw from the internal evidence of the gospel any very clear-cut conclusion as to its sources. The problem is certainly not met by light-heartedly accepting Papias's statement as literal truth, and by regarding Mark's gospel as if it were almost a verbatim report of Peter's preaching. *That* at least is not a sufficient theory. *Some* written material seems to have been used in the composition of the gospel. *Some* of its sections are not easy to credit to Peter's testimony; e.g. the story of Herod and John the Baptist (already alluded to), and the story of the Gerasene demoniac (5^{1-20}) which reads like a local tale. The bulk of the gospel is certainly best understood as based on catechetical anecdotes. But it is likely that these anecdotes had been often related and had assumed something of a stereotyped form even in oral tradition. Some of them may have already been put into written form. It is not likely that all of them, nor even perhaps that most of them, had been so written. Most critics will probably share Burkitt's[1] feeling that the gospel gives the impression of being a first attempt at a continuous story. If that is so, its written sources were only fragmentary in character, the sequence and scheme of the narrative are Mark's own arrangement. But we seem driven to conclude that the gospel is not entirely the compilation of oral material. It is a book made out of written as well as oral sources, and it is possible that written sources are

[1] *Earliest Sources for the Life of Jesus*, p. 83.

responsible for a larger area of the story than we saw reason to suggest above.[1]

This, however, we may say with some confidence, that in the main substance of it the gospel is based on material which, whether oral or written, is primary in character; and that its record is not greatly coloured by later tendencies, whether dogmatic or devotional. We may then still call it the Petrine gospel in this sense that it is based on the primitive tradition of the Palestinian Church which, no doubt, Peter and others brought with them and stood sponsors for at Rome. Its core is good eye-witness's work. It tells the sort of story that Peter used to tell.

iv

It is probably a waste of labour to go any further and to make experiments at any more definite source-analysis than this. Some commentators do this very elaborately. Thus Wendling sees in our present gospel the work of at least three hands. The first is that of a sober historian, whom he calls M^1, who wrote a plain tale in Aramaic. This was then translated into Greek by M^2, who was a dramatic poet and revised the tale in the interests of dramatic impressiveness. And finally M^3, who was a theologian, gave it a further edition in the interests of dogmatic adequacy. Bacon, on the other hand, attempts to distinguish three sources behind the gospel, viz. the Petrine tradition which he calls P, the teaching-document Q, and an otherwise unknown source X; these three sources have been compiled by an editor, who is responsible for the connexion and sequence in which the anecdotes are joined together.

Such analyses are exercises in ingenuity, but they never seem to be very convincing. Wendling's is obviously too subjective and artificial, and is fatally exposed to Stanton's query 'Might not the same man have a little in him of all three (historian, poet, and theologian), at least to the degree that would be required for the putting together of this record?'[2] Bacon's theory is less subjective, but it has the defects of being unnaturally complicated and

[1] See later for a discussion as to the possible dependence of Mark on Q.
[2] *Gospels as Historical Documents*, II, p. 177.

of making no allowance for 'the personal equation', i.e. for the idiosyncrasies which might have characterized the writer; while his grounds of differentiation between the sources are connected with his theories about Our Lord's purpose in His mission, and are seriously weakened if, as we shall try to show, those theories are gravely inadequate.

Two questions, however, which are raised by such criticism, are important enough to deserve special consideration. The first is, did Mark know or use Q? The second is, is there any good ground for the suggestion that the gospel was originally written in a shorter form, and that the gospel as we have it is a later recension of this shorter original? To these two questions we must now address ourselves.[1]

(1) *Did Mark use Q?*

The theory that Q is of later date than Mark has the support of Wellhausen and Meyer. But even their great authority has been insufficient to win common acceptance for this view. It is on general grounds far more probable that Our Lord's teaching should have been written down before any narrative of His life; the need of a written record would obviously be sooner felt for the accurate preservation of teaching than for the narrative of incidents. We may therefore assume that the general view of scholars, that Q is earlier than Mark, is correct.

The phenomena are these: Mark contains little of Our Lord's teaching. But some of the sections of teaching which he gives in brief form are found in Matthew and Luke in a form so much fuller that these evangelists must clearly have derived their material at these points from Q and not from Mark. Such sections are:

(*a*) 1^{4-13}; the story of the Baptist's preaching and of the Temptation; recorded in Matthew 3–4^{11}, Luke $3^{1-17,21-2}$.

(*b*) 3^{22-30}; the Beelzebub controversy; in Matthew 9^{34}, 12^{24-37}, Luke 11^{15-26}.

[1] The cognate question, whether the gospel was originally written in Aramaic, will be considered later in connexion with a discussion of its date. This question is in itself not bound up with the theory of an *Ur-Marcus* (i.e. an original shorter Mark).

THE PREACHING OF JOHN THE BAPTIST
A holy man of the East to-day

(*c*) 6^{7-11}; the instructions to the Twelve; in Matthew $10^{1,5-15}$; Luke 9^{1-5}, 10^{4-12}.

(*d*) 12^{38-40}; the woes on the Pharisees; in Matthew 23^{1-36}, Luke 20^{45-7}, (cf. 11^{39}, $16^{14f.}$).

If then these sections are represented in both Q and Mark, are we to hold that Mark had read Q and that his version is an abbreviation of that which the other two gospels have preserved from Q in fuller form? It is easy to be too certain of this inference. Bacon declares [1] that Mark's use of Q 'is susceptible of critical demonstration'. But this scholar, learned and stimulating as he is, can only be followed with great caution. His conclusions are too often stated with a dogmatic positiveness that refuses to take any account of alternative possibilities. It is perfectly possible that the Petrine tradition may have overlapped the Q tradition in certain respects, and that Mark's teaching-material in these sections may therefore not be derived from Q. But, if we stop short of claiming demonstrative certainty for the inference, we may at least feel that the easiest and most obvious inference in this case is that Mark was acquainted with Q (or at least with a version of Q, though not necessarily the same as that used by Matthew and Luke), and the conclusion, so stated, is accepted by many scholars. Mark may even have written his gospel to supplement a teaching-document with which his readers were already familiar; and this may be an explanation of the paucity of teaching-material in his gospel. It is certain, however, that, if Mark's version of Q was the same as that used by the other two evangelists, he must have used it sparingly and perhaps only from memory; he does not seem to have consulted it at all carefully or systematically in the writing of his own story. Finally, we may note that our inference here, if it is correct, gives another evidence that Mark made some use of written sources, for which view we have already contended.

(2) *Was there an 'Ur-Marcus'?*

Is our gospel the last of successive recensions of a shorter original? We have seen the form in which Wendling put forward this

[1] *Beginnings of Gospel Story*, p. xx.

theory. Williams, who criticized and rejected Wendling's views, himself put forward[1] another version, suggesting that the gospel had circulated at first without caps. 6^{45}–8^{27} and 13, that in the next recension cap. 13 had been inserted, and that in the final recension caps. 6^{45}–8^{27} had also been added.

The reasons for these suggestions are instructive though the suggestions themselves are unconvincing; these reasons are:

(1) Some 31 verses of Mark do not appear at all in either Matthew or Luke; the most notable of these omissions are Mk. 4^{26-9} (the seed growing secretly), 8^{22-6} (the cure of the blind man at Bethsaida). These omissions are, however, so few that it is very precarious to build on them a theory that these verses did not exist in the copy of Mark which was known to Matthew and Luke. Other reasons may easily be imagined for the omissions; e.g. the first of the two passages cited above might be considered but another version of the parable of the Sower, and the second might be thought to imply a gradualness in the effect of Our Lord's healing power, which was incompatible with the usual idea of its immediacy.

(2) The passages where Matthew and Luke agree in phraseology which varies from Mark's account of the same incident are, it is suggested, due to the fact that the later two used an edition of Mark, into which a certain number of corrections of style had been introduced. But this is certainly an unnecessary theory. The phenomena may as easily be accounted for as due in some cases to independent correction of Mark's grammar by the two later evangelists, in others to a textual assimilation which caused scribes in the act of copying to bring Matthew and Luke into verbal identity with one another; while in some cases the agreement seems to be due to actual textual error.

(3) The entire omission by Luke of Mark 6^{45}–8^{27} has prompted the theory that Luke's copy of Mark did not possess this section. But other explanations are as possible: thus (*a*) the omission may be deliberate,[2] each part of the section being in turn rejected because Luke for one or another reason had no use for it; or (*b*) it

[1] *Oxford Studies in the Synoptic Problem*, p. 389 f.
[2] Sir John Hawkins in *Oxford Studies in the Synoptic Problem*, p. 66 f.

may be accidental, due to the fact that 6^{44} and 8^{21} each conclude a story of the feeding of a multitude, and that 6^{45} and 8^{22} each mention a journey to Bethsaida; or (*c*) Luke's copy may have been mutilated at this point. Against the explanation of a shorter recension used by Luke are the arguments (*a*) that this section is in the same style as the rest of the gospel, and so must be the work of the same author; (*b*) that [1] any editor who produced a new recension of Mark, inserting two chapters in the middle, would surely have supplied an ending to the gospel after 16^{8}, if the original ending was already lost; but if the ending was not yet lost, how does it happen that Luke deserts Mark's narrative exactly at Mark 16^{8}, at the exact point where the gospel is now mutilated or defective? When the whole case is weighed up, we see that there is no sufficient ground for doubting that Matthew and Luke used a Mark which was substantially the same as our gospel.[2]

We have then decided to conclude on literary grounds of internal evidence that the gospel is based in the main on good primitive Palestinian tradition, which we may call Petrine; that much of this tradition *may* have been oral, before Mark recorded it; but that he certainly made some, and may have made much, use of written sources. We have now to consider whether on historical grounds the same conclusion can be supported; in particular, whether the picture of Jesus Christ drawn in the gospel is such that we can reasonably ascribe it to primitive tradition and call it Petrine. The matter is obviously vital. But in considering it, it is important to remember at the outset that we have no right to judge Mark's picture by preconceived ideas of our own as to what Jesus ought to have been or would have been, if our theories could have dictated matters. We have to see what Mark's picture actually is, and then to ask whether it is not a possible picture to

[1] Streeter, *The Four Gospels*, p. 175 f.

[2] The suggestion that cap. 13 is not a part of the original gospel is due to the character of its contents and to its apparent isolation in the general atmosphere of the gospel. This chapter will be considered in somewhat greater detail later. In relation to the hypothesis of an *Ur-Marcus* it plays very little part and is only brought into consideration tentatively by Williams.

be drawn by His disciples of One Who is too big and many-sided a Personality to fit wholly into the canvas of any single painter who is of smaller spiritual dimensions than Himself.

D. THE PICTURE OF JESUS CHRIST IN THE GOSPEL.

Most of us have been to some extent familiar from our childhood with the New Testament picture of Jesus Christ. That picture, as we have it in our minds, is a composite picture; all the four gospels and some of Paul's writings have contributed lines and colours to make up the composition. One of the first of our difficulties in studying a single gospel is therefore to isolate for the time being its testimony from that of the other New Testament writings, in order to realize what particular lines and colours are specially to be found in the one gospel under study. This is what we must now try to do with Mark. We must take his book by itself and see what picture of Jesus he has drawn.

i

Jesus is presented as beginning His public career after the imprisonment of John the Baptist; He is, so to speak, John's successor; and His first message is to announce that the Kingdom of God is at hand; men therefore are to repent and believe in the gospel.

This idea of a coming Kingdom of God was, of course, not new to Jewish ears. For nearly two centuries the Jews fed their souls, in the political and religious distresses and humiliations to which they had been subjected, on the hopes of a great divine event, when God would end the present dispensation of human affairs and inaugurate a new era of the world. Such a hope, in one form or another, was the staple of that 'apocalyptic' literature, which from the book of Daniel (*circa* 160 B. C.) onwards through books like the books of Enoch, of Jubilees, &c., had been the popular reading of the nation. Preliminary to this new era was to come some one to announce its advent. Different books pictured him in different ways, as a returning Elijah, as a son of David reviving the Davidic glory, as a supernatural Man from heaven (so the book of Enoch, which calls him 'the Son of Man').

This expectation had both its political and its spiritual elements. To some it was the hope of a spiritually regenerated world; to others the hope of an organized theocratic Kingdom; to others the hope of a time of Jewish liberty, prosperity, and dominion.

Jesus then, according to Mark, alined Himself at the outset with the apocalyptic hopes of the nation. The character of His public preaching of the Kingdom is, however, given in very little detail in this gospel. In incidental pieces of teaching in 2^{21} and 9^{35} it is seen to imply a new principle of religious duty and a new relationship between men. In cap. 4 we have three parables of its growth; and in $7^{1f.}$ ritual laws are abrogated in favour of inner purity. Beyond this, we are told nothing of what Jesus taught about the Kingdom. But the effectiveness of His ministry in the synagogues of Galilee is repeatedly exhibited ($1^{24f.}$, $2^{1,13}$, 3^{20}). The preaching was combined with and rendered more effective by works of healing and exorcism; though it is suggested also that the stir caused by such works was found by Jesus to be an interruption to the main task which He had at heart ($1^{35,45}$).

But the opposition of the religious authorities is aroused; first by His claim to forgive sins (2^{6}), and by His readiness to consort with publicans and sinners (2^{16}); then by His unconventional attitude towards Jewish customs such as fasting (2^{18}); and finally by His indifference to Sabbatarian regulations (2^{24}, 3^{2}). The incidents provoking this opposition are few in number, and can only be taken as a selection of those which occurred. But in 3^{6} a rupture with the Pharisees clearly results. They go out and complain to the secular authorities of the Herodian government.

From this point till 8^{26} we are given a series of anecdotes, arranged on no consecutive plan that we can discern, and seemingly observing no chronological sequence. But the main strands of the story can, perhaps, be disentangled, if we note that henceforth Jesus is never represented as preaching again in a synagogue except once in His own town of Nazareth (6^{2}), where His preaching is a failure. The continuance and hardening of opposition from the Pharisees is clearly indicated in $7^{1f.}$; and though Herod is only mentioned in 6^{14}, and is not represented as taking any overt action against Jesus, the mere mention of his name is significant. Obviously Jesus no longer finds His ministry so free as it was. True, He evangelizes the Lake-side and the villages of Galilee (3^{7}, 4^{1}, 5^{21}, 6^{6}). But His career is marked by journeys and withdrawals, which seem to be due to the fact that Antipas's dominions are felt to be insecure to Him. Thus He retires to the other side of the Lake in 4^{35}, to 'the desert' in 6^{31}, to Bethsaida in 6^{45} and 8^{22} (the latter journey being apparently so hurried that the party had no time to procure food, 8^{14}), to Phenicia in 7^{24}, to Decapolis in 7^{31}. Thus hampered in His public work, He appoints and sends out the Twelve as His substitutes to preach and exorcise (3^{14}, 6^{7}) and seems to concentrate His efforts on their special instruction ($4^{10,34}$). Fear of the Pharisees and Herodians appears to be the main clue to the labyrinth of this section.

At last at Caesarea Philippi (8^{27}) He seems to decide on a fresh development. His position as Messiah, of which so far we have had nothing but hints (in the recognition of the demons and perhaps in the use of the title 'Son of Man'), is now openly confessed by Peter. Henceforth this is treated as the main aspect of Jesus' work (cf. $9^{7,12-13}$); and the narrative at once becomes more closely knit. His Messianic claim is admitted by Him to His disciples, but not in public, and is at once connected by Him with the idea of suffering and death, though His eventual Resurrection is foretold (8^{31}, 9^{31}, $10^{30,45}$). The Way of the Cross now looms clearly before Him.

Passing secretly (9^{30}) through Galilee to Capernaum, He goes down into Judaea (10^{1}), with His future apparently clear before Him (10^{32-4}). His thoughts are revealed for us in the parable of 12^{1-11}. He is going to Jerusalem to challenge His fate, and through His death to introduce the new age.

At Jerusalem He makes His challenge as public as possible. He effects a Messianic entry into the city ($11^{1f.}$), He cleanses the Temple (11^{15}) and publicly affronts the religious authorities ($12^{12,38}$), He meets the questions of those authorities with something like defiance (11^{27}). He is arrested and tried and put to death for assuming the Messianic character (14^{61}); to Pilate He is a mere disturber of the peace (15^{4}). The conclusion of the gospel is lost, if it was ever written. But in its last authentic section the fact of Jesus' Resurrection is simply stated. How much farther the author took or intended to take his story we cannot say. But 16[7] makes it likely that at least an appearance in Galilee would have been included.

This then is the Marcan picture of Jesus. When we view it thus in isolation, it strikes us at once as being a very meagre story. The chronological notices are so sparse and vague that one year might be taken as the duration of Our Lord's public ministry; and even of that year large parts are unaccounted for. The arrangement of the anecdotes in the Galilean section seems confused. The story gives no explanation of the way in which Jesus' Name had become known in Jerusalem (there is no trace of an early Ministry in Jerusalem such as the fourth gospel records). Jesus is presented as beginning as a teacher, but of his teaching in Galilee (and even later too) very little is recorded, and that little is mostly incidental. It is a story about Jesus, but it does not give us much idea of what Jesus actually preached. If this were a biography, it would be a very defective one.

Not only is the story meagre, but it is extraordinarily parsimonious of colour in its portraiture of Jesus. If we compare Mark with Matthew, we see that (*a*) very little ethical teaching is ascribed in Mark to Our Lord, and (*b*) very little of that teaching which treats the Kingdom as a growing society. Mark contains neither (*a*) the Sermon on the Mount, the parables of the unforgiving servant and of the sheep and the goats, nor (*b*) the parables of the tares, the net, the treasure, the pearl, the labourers in the vineyard, the marriage feast, or the ten virgins. Compared with Luke, Mark contains neither the detailed teaching on prayer, the mission-instructions of the Seventy, nor the teaching inculcating a friendly attitude to the gentile, the poor, and the outcast, such as Luke records in the Sermons on the Plain or at Nazareth, or in the parable of the Prodigal Son, of Dives and Lazarus, of the good Samaritan, of the Pharisee and the publican. Thus the Marcan Jesus is neither, as in Matthew, the giver of a new Law, nor, as in Luke, the preacher of a catholic fraternity. The Marcan Jesus is an austere figure, mysterious, stormy, imper-

Preaching in a synagogue in Spain in the fourteenth century.
From a Hebrew MS.

ious. His portrait is drawn with the utmost economy of line and colour. Practically all is subordinated to the emphasizing of His Messianic intention. First He announces the Messianic Kingdom, then He admits His Messianic position, then He publicly assumes the Messianic role, goes up to Jerusalem to die, and dies for His Messianic claim.

ii

Now it cannot be denied that in primitive Christianity the vital principle was eschatological. The sermons in the Acts are full of the thought of Christ's Parousia; the early Pauline epistles are also full of it, and Paul built his Christology on the basis of Jesus Christ's Messianic status. Thus the Marcan picture is undoubtedly that which the early Church drew. That of Matthew became the dominant conception after A.D. 100, that of Luke has never till our own more humanitarian times been the peculiar inspiration of any but a few elect Christian souls like Francis of Assisi, though in certain respects its influence can be traced in the monastic movement. But our problem is, Is the Marcan picture so much an ecclesiastically coloured picture as to be unfaithful to what Jesus actually was; or was Jesus such, even if He was also more? Granted that Mark shows Jesus in one light, does that light distort the real Jesus, or does it reveal at least one element which was actually strong and prominent in His Ministry? This is obviously a question which can only be answered by a consideration of our personal impressions about Jesus Himself. We have no evidence at all about Him save that which the gospels themselves give us, and that derived from a realization of the part that Christianity has played in human history. Does the Marcan picture in any way commend itself to us as not untrue to our idea of Jesus, or does it seem to us to be a picture which has so disfigured His lineaments that we can only accept it as a picture of what the Church of (say) A.D. 70 thought about Him, but not as anything but a caricature of what He really was?

There is not much doubt that the picture of Jesus can be spoilt, if its Messianic character is exaggerated. This seems to be the main fault in Schweitzer's epoch-making book *The Quest of the Historical Jesus*. In that book Schweitzer presses the Marcan point of view with a one-sidedness that lands him in extravagance. There is little ethical or social teaching in Mark; therefore he concludes that Jesus had no notion of spiritualizing the Messianic idea. Jesus' whole purpose was crassly eschatological. His secret, prematurely discovered by Peter, was that He was the Messiah to come and that His death was to be the signal for the coming of the Messianic Kingdom. He went to Jerusalem with the conscious purpose of dying, and He died disappointed because the Kingdom did not come (so Schweitzer interprets Mk. 15^{34}; the Resurrection he omits from his story). He gave no moral rules for permanent use, only moral precepts for observance in the short interim before the new age should begin. He did not intend to found a Church, and He did not appoint the Twelve to continue His work.

This striking interpretation seems obviously to press the eschatological element in Jesus' work to such an extent that the resultant picture of Jesus becomes a caricature. It is impossible to believe that Jesus did not spiritualize any idea that He touched. Even in Mark His eschatological proclamation (in 1^{15}) is coupled with a call to repent which implies some moral claim; and the parables of the sower and of the seed (in cap. 4), even if (as Schweitzer says) they mainly teach the idea of unseen causation, also imply the idea of gradual development. That Jesus demanded sincerity and charity, that He preached trust in God and indifference to riches, that He encouraged prayer and self-sacrifice, and these not as interim moral duties but as permanent moral imperatives, is a view which can only be rejected if we regard both Q and Luke's Special Source (? Proto-Luke) as untrustworthy; and to do that is a violent rejection of good evidence.

Schweitzer then over-states his case. But still he *has* a case. If Mark is right—and Mark's evidence is also good—the eschatological idea was very strong in Jesus. Can we really believe that He could not have used the title 'Son of Man' of Himself, and could not have used it in a Messianic signification? Can we really believe that the Church's Christology, however much it may be the result of building-up by Christian thought and devotion, is built on no foundation at all; and that the eschatology which provided the foundation had no place in Jesus' mind and was merely a fancy theory which the early Church imported with no justification into the story of Jesus?

Let us consider an alternative, if we reject the Marcan picture. We can take it from Bacon's stimulating study of Mark in *The Beginnings of the Gospel Story*. According to him Jesus' purpose was to champion the 'disinherited masses' of the Jewish people, the publicans, women, Samaritans, outcasts from the Synagogue, the scattered sheep, the lost sons, 'in other words, people who did not scrupulously observe the ceremonial Law, and were despised and condemned by orthodox Rabbis and Pharisees'.[1] He came to Galilee where these masses were most numerous, and preached their value to God. Driven out of Galilee, He went to Jerusalem to challenge the ecclesiastical hierocracy at the centre. He went not to die but to pursue His reforming movement, and His death marked the failure of the movement. Bacon acknowledges that in Mark the Ministry assumes a Messianic colour from Caesarea Philippi on; but he does not know if Jesus repudiated this personally or accepted the conception only to transfigure it. In any case Jesus' principal role was not that of Messiah but that of champion of religious catholicity. The eschatological idea was not His main idea, but is due to the unintelligent colouring of a Church agog with apocalyptic expectations. The 'Son of Man' view of Jesus is superposed in Mark on a Person Who did not claim in any sense a Christological Sonship of God but Who preached an 'ethico-religious' Sonship of God open to all men.

It is clear how Bacon got his picture. He has concentrated his attention on Luke's Special Source and holds that here only do you find the real Jesus. Now nobody will deny that Bacon's picture may be a true picture of one side of Jesus. But we are again driven to ask, Is it the only side which He showed, or has Bacon also pressed one element to exaggeration One thing is certain, that if Bacon's picture is the whole truth, Mark's picture is a bad one; Mark may have had eye-witness record to go on, but he has spoilt the picture there drawn by the colouring which he has given to it.

[1] Montefiore, *Synoptic Gospels*, vol. i, p. lxxxiii.

In criticizing Bacon's theory it is legitimate to raise the question whether there is any good evidence of the existence of such 'masses' of unchurched people as his theory supposes. Montefiore, who discusses this question fully, considers the evidence very questionable. 'It has been supposed', he says, 'that the number of "outcasts and sinners" ... was proportionately greater in Galilee than in Judaea. This, however, is by no means certain. Nor does much good evidence exist for what Professor Cheyne has called their imperfect legal orthodoxy. In fact, another scholar observes that "upon the whole they are said to have been strict in their religious observances".'[1] 'Even the Gospels scarcely imply that the *masses* had no religion which they cared for or brought them comfort, or that the Rabbis were not their teachers or their friends.'[2] 'The Rabbis were drawn from the people, and were emphatically of the people. Many of them were extremely poor; working with their hands in the daytime, studying, discussing, and teaching in the evenings and on Sabbaths and festivals. An habitual antagonism between them and the 'multitude' is out of the question. ... The people who did not observe the Law were the rich rather than the poor; the tax-gatherers were rich ... and so in all probability were the "sinners". ... If there really *did* exist a "submerged tenth", who neglected the Law, disliked the Rabbinic teachers and were disliked by them in return, we may feel fairly sure that it was a *small* tenth and no more. The mass of the nation at any rate, both women and men, held with keenness and affection to the Rabbinical religion, and the leaders of the Pharisees were the leaders of the people.'[3]

But even if we allow that there were enough of these outcasts to need a champion, and that Jesus might have taken up their cause, is that all that He was and did? Is it after all not likely that He would link up His message with the Messianic idea, which was the chief religious aspiration of His people? He *did* go to Jerusalem and challenge the religious leaders. If He went in order to put forward at the centre a programme of peaceful reform in the interests of the 'masses', the Paschal week is far too short for such a propaganda to have excited feeling to such a fury that his

[1] *op. cit.*, p. lxxxiii. [2] *op. cit.*, p. xcix. [3] *op. cit.*, p. lxxvi.

murder was contemplated, let alone executed. If He went, as Mark suggests, for a Messianic demonstration, we can understand that even one public declaration might have been sufficient to precipitate the catastrophe.

It is worth asking if we are right in regarding Jesus as a man with a clear-cut programme at all. Are we not nearer the truth if we hold that He conceived His one purpose as being *to be Himself*; and that, whether His preaching was couched in ethical, religio-social, or eschatological conceptions, it was still always and only the simple expression of what He was in Himself? And are we sure that any one category is sufficient to include Him? Grant that Mark's picture is inadequate, and that, to understand what Jesus was, we must supplement it from the evidence of Q and Proto-Luke; yet is the Marcan picture, so far as it goes, such as we cannot take as substantially true? Grant even that Mark has over-pressed the Messianic element in Our Lord's idea, yet can we confidently affirm that this element was not there at all? (*a*) Is there any convincing reason why we should hold it to be impossible, or even unlikely, that Jesus should have conceived of Himself as the Messiah? Is it so very incredible that, in a nation thrilling with Messianic hope, a great spiritual genius should have felt a vocation to be Himself the fulfilment of this hope? (*b*) The Messianic idea in its Christian form and the hope of Jesus' Parousia as Messiah in triumph fired the early Church and captured the world; and we know something of what this enthusiasm thus kindled has done in human history. Is it really credible that the starting-point of such an energy is nothing else but, to put it candidly, an ecclesiastical 'fake'? Illusions often live long, do wonders, and die hard. But does the history of Christianity really seem to bear the marks of being but the history of another such illusion?

iii

We turn to another point (to which brief allusion has already been made), the 'Paulinism' which is said by not a few scholars to infect this gospel to such an extent that it cannot be considered as uncoloured record of fact; it is said to exhibit the 'Paulinizing of

THE TEMPLE AREA AT JERUSALEM TO-DAY

Petrine tradition'. Let us examine the chief definite arguments adduced to support this judgement.

(1) The gospel is said to be consistently anti-Jewish in its tone. The 'hardening of heart' which had befallen the Jews is repeatedly emphasized (cf. Mk. 4^{12}, 6^{3}, 8^{11}, 9^{13}, $10^{2,5}$, $12^{1-12,13}$, 14^{49}). This is compared with the language of Paul in Romans 10^{21}, $11^{8,25}$. So, too, the ritualism of the Pharisees and 'all the Jews' is exaggerated in Mk. $7^{1\,f.}$; and the general intention of the gospel seems to be unduly disparaging to the Jews.

It is true enough that the gospel seems to lay emphasis on the Jewish opposition to Our Lord. But that opposition was after all a fact. It is true also that Paul accounts for it by the theory that a 'judicial blindness' has been inflicted on them. But are we entitled to suppose, is it even likely, that Paul was the only man who thus speculated as to the cause of the Jewish repudiation of Christ? Is it not more probable that such speculation was rife in the circles of Jerusalem Christianity in the early days of the Church, and may even have been audible in the circle of Our Lord's disciples before His Crucifixion? And the theory of a divine 'hardening' of the people's heart would not be far to fetch to any Jew who had read Isaiah and the story of Moses in Egypt. A theory of Paul's need not have been his exclusive monopoly; it need not be 'Pauline', i.e. peculiar to Paul, merely because it is in Paul. As for Mark's alleged exaggeration of Jewish ritualism, it is not certain that there is any (see note, *ad loc.*), but if there is, it seems not to go further than a certain looseness of statement which may well be due to the influence of the Church's controversy with the Jews. And the general depreciation of the Jews in the gospel is at any rate not unmitigated. For the gospel contains in 7^{27} a definite admission that the Jews are specially God's 'children', and in 12^{34} a definite commendation of a scribe who answered 'discreetly' and showed more capacity of appreciating the spiritual bearing of our Lord's teaching.

(2) It is said that the gospel shows ignorance or contemptuous indifference concerning Our Lord's Mother and brethren, and only mentions them to show their opposition to Him; and that its attitude towards the Twelve, and especially towards Peter is consistently disparaging.

The force of this argument has already been admitted. The attitude towards the Twelve and Our Lord's family is more 'Paulinist' than 'Pauline', i.e. it would perhaps be the attitude among some of Paul's adherents. We may, if we like, acknowledge it as a sign of 'Paulinism'. Of this, however, we may feel confident, that a story which *overtly* and *deliberately* depreciated Peter would not be likely either to originate in, or to be welcomed by, the church of Rome in about A.D. 70. By the time when Mark wrote, Peter and Paul had both earned at Rome their titles as martyrs, and the veneration of the Roman Church for both of them must have begun. In their deaths they were not divided, even if for a time they had been at variance in their lives. Mark's gospel may indeed have no more controversial aim than that of showing that in their early hardness to Christ they were not so dissimilar, though one had been the disciple of Jesus and the other the persecutor of the saints. If so, it reflects not so much anti-Petrine feeling as what was probably the average feeling of the average members of a Petro-Pauline church.

The gospel's neglect to tell us much about Our Lord's family seems the more strange to us, because we have learnt to look for personal details in historical narratives. It is to be noted that James, the brother of Our Lord, seems to have been much more officially antagonistic to Paul than Peter ever was (cf. Gal. 2^{12}); all that we hear of James shows us that he was an intensely and avowedly Judaistic Christian, to whom Paul's views and methods must probably have been most uncongenial; and we need not suppose that Pauline circles thought or spoke more admiringly about James than James's circle thought or spoke of Paul. But, so far as this gospel is concerned, we can only say that it is not exuberant in depreciation of Our Lord's family, but only that it gives them but one mention, though that is disparaging; and the reason may possibly be merely that the Roman Christians took no special interest in them. The brethren of the Lord, and James in particular, were no doubt very important people in the Christian community at Jerusalem before A.D. 70; but what would that matter to the Church of Rome? These brethren of Our Lord had not played any leading part in the events of His life, so what would be the purpose in gossiping about them in a series of catechetical anecdotes? It is not really surprising that in this gospel, planned as it is, the only connexion in which they are introduced is designed to show that Jesus' 'foes' were not only of his own nation but even 'of his own household'. It is even possible that the story in question was only related at all in order to illustrate our Lord's mournful prediction of the divisions that His coming would cause (Mt. 10^{36}). True, that prediction is only cited in Matthew (though there is something like it in John 13^{18}) and is not in Mark (though Mark 6^{4} is similar in its thought). But its very nature is such as to make it likely that it was frequently in Christian mouths, especially in times of persecution, such as had befallen the Roman Church at Nero's hands.

As to Mark's candour with regard to the slowness of the Twelve to understand their Master, it is absurd to see in this anything specially unnatural, and it is purely fanciful to see in it anything distinctively 'Pauline'. They *had* been slow; but their subsequent fidelity had taken any sting out of the recollection.

(3) The chief argument, however, upon which those scholars rely who desire to establish the 'Paulinism' of Mark is that drawn from the alleged relation between the Christology of Paul and that of the gospel. We have already dealt to some extent with this in our study of the Marcan picture of Jesus, and need not go over that ground again. It need not, and indeed cannot, be denied that Mark in some respects exhibits traces of Pauline influence in his view of Christ. It would be strange if he did not, since for years he must have been moving in the atmosphere of Pauline Christianity. But these traces are not sufficient to establish a direct affiliation of Mark to Paul,[1] or to justify the view that Pauline conceptions have seriously affected the authentic lines in the Marcan portrait.

There is, as even Bacon admits, this vital difference between the two men, that Paul's Christology is 'incarnational'—i.e. that to him Christ is the pre-existent Son of God Who was made man—whereas Mark has nothing explicit or implicit in this sense; he

[1] Bacon's arguments on this point in his *Gospel of Mark* part IV seem to me wiredrawn and unconvincing in the extreme.

gives no account of a miraculous conception, and his account has even been read in an 'adoptionist' sense, i.e. it has been taken to support the view that Christ's divine status began with God's adoption of Him at His baptism (Mk. 1[11]). A greater divergence could not exist.

Other divergences between the views of the two writers are also worth noting; thus (1) The title 'Son of Man' which is common in Mark is not used by Paul at all. (2) Mark gives much attention to Our Lord's miracles and exorcisms, Paul does not even mention them, and his disparagement of 'signs' (e.g. in 1 Cor. 12) might imply that he regarded them as of little evidential value. (3) Paul's theory of Our Lord's Resurrection Appearances is in no direct way connected with the Empty Tomb (1 Cor. 15), whereas Mark's is. Of course, the absence of Mark's conclusion leaves us ignorant whether Mark was acquainted with, or gave attention to, Appearances such as Paul enumerates. (4) As has been said, Mark nowhere declares the Pauline doctrine that the Gentiles are as admissible as the Jews to the benefits of Christ's death. It is true that his comment in 7[19] on Our Lord's teaching about clean meats implies this inference. That comment is in fact the most specifically 'Pauline' statement in the whole gospel. It is only the more striking that Mark does not explicitly draw this inference there or anywhere else, and does not connect it with the death of Christ.

When all is considered, we are disposed to feel that Werner's conclusion[1] that 'there cannot be the slightest idea of an influence of Pauline theology in the Gospel of Mark', though it seems too positive and unqualified, is so far true that no *radical Paulinism* can be found in the gospel.

As to Mark's doctrine of the Cross, which is certainly the same as Paul's, we have already questioned whether we have any justification for supposing that Jesus could not have foreseen His fate. From the death of John the Baptist at least He can have been under no illusion as to the risk of a similar end being in store for Him. Nor do we see any ground for doubting that Jesus was able to foresee the redemptive possibilities of His

[1] Quoted in Bacon, *op. cit.*, p. 247.

Death. We are told that He foretold His Resurrection. We may, if we like, doubt whether His forecast was so definite as the Christians after the event represented it to have been. But that He foretold that His Death would lead to God's Victory—is that not very like what many of the Old Testament prophets did, who foretold a theocratic triumph as following on the disaster of God's people? With Isaiah 53 before Him, would not the thought of Victory through Death suggest itself to Jesus, even if we will not agree that He might have thought spontaneously of such a result? That chapter of Isaiah was prominent in the thought of the early Christians after the event (cf. Acts 8^{32}). Is there anything unlikely in supposing that its teaching was familiar to Our Lord before the event?

In truth this idea that the doctrine of the Cross, because it is Pauline, was only or specially Pauline, that nobody could think of a martyr fate as leading to triumph, that in particular Jesus could not do so—this idea seems to imply that Jesus was obtuse to the bearing of the noblest teaching in the Old Testament; and such a notion needs no refutation other than the mere statement of it immediately provokes.

There then we must leave the subject. In the nature of the case no completely demonstrative proof is possible on one side or the other. We must judge for ourselves from our data, and from our idea of the general verisimilitude of the picture which they give of what Jesus was. But our own conclusion may be briefly stated. Though Mark's picture is inadequate and needs supplementing from Q and Proto-Luke (as well as from the fourth gospel), yet it is a true and lifelike picture of one side of Jesus' Personality, and of a side which was prominent in Him and which indubitably first fired the Church. (1) Jesus did present Himself as the Messiah of Jewish hopes; He deepened, moralized, and spiritualized that conception; but the Messianic role was one which He adopted. (2) Jesus did foresee His own Death, and believed it would lead to God's Victory. Thus the Marcan picture of Jesus Christ records facts which are vital to our true understanding of what Jesus was.

E. THE MARCAN AUTHORSHIP. INTERNAL EVIDENCE

We have still to examine the internal evidence of the gospel to see if it supports the tradition that the gospel was written by Mark. Let us first recall some of the facts that we know about John Mark. If the Mark who is credited with this gospel is not the John Mark of the New Testament, it is useless to discuss any further the authorship of this gospel; for we know of no other Mark who might possibly be intended.

The house of Mark's mother was the central meeting-place of the early church at Jerusalem. Thus Mark must have had abundant chances of meeting the Christian leaders during the years A.D. 30–42, if he was at home. He was in the company of Paul and Barnabas during part of the missionary journey which they took together. After he had left them at Perga, he is not heard of again until Acts 15^{37}, when he is found at Antioch. He then accompanied Barnabas, we do not know for how long. Thus he must have been in close contact with Paul and Barnabas, one or both of them, between A.D. 47 and 50. Later on he is found in association with Paul at Rome (A.D. 59–61); and he is said to have been a close companion of Peter, probably also at Rome.

This being his record, we cannot but notice with some surprise that the gospel is totally destitute of anything that looks like personal reminiscences (with the possible exception of the incident in 14^{51-52}, and the hint given in 15^{21} that the author was personally acquainted with Alexander and Rufus). We are told nothing about most of the Twelve, nothing about Our Lord's Ministry in Jerusalem save what is contained in the Passion story, almost nothing about Our Lord's family, though one of His brethren, James, was the head of the Christian Church at Jerusalem at the time when Mark's mother's house was the Christian centre there. One feels that Bacon[1] has some grounds for putting the questions 'Had Mark never met Andrew, Peter's brother? Could he tell nothing whatever about James the Lord's brother, or about Mary His Mother? If he knew James and John, the sons of Zebedee, why has he nothing whatever to tell about the former, nothing

[1] *Gospel of Mark*, p. 301.

about the latter save that he incurred Jesus' rebuke for voicing the intolerance of the Twelve ($9^{38\text{ f.}}$)? Why has he nothing to tell about the pair save the sobriquet Boanerges (which he renders 'Sons of Thunder', but without explaining its application), and the martyr fate which befell them according to the prediction of Jesus? Why has he nothing to tell about Peter himself of any personal character, and nothing about the rest of the Twelve, some of whom must have frequented his mother's house during those twelve years while it was still their headquarters? . . . First and last, the son of Mary of Jerusalem and cousin of Barnabas must have enjoyed unusual knowledge of the eye-witnesses and their story.'

So, too, we cannot help feeling some surprise at the apparent blunders with regard to Palestinian conditions which are found in the gospel. No doubt some of them may be explained away without much strain, and others might be explicable if we knew the circumstances better ourselves. But, again, Bacon [1] does not seem to be unreasonable in expressing surprise 'that a resident of Jerusalem from boyhood to maturity should not be able to convey a clearer idea of the journeys he wished to describe, or the historical conditions of his own time'.

Indeed, we may wonder why Mark should have used any documents at all in writing his work. From the circles he had moved in, he must surely have derived sufficient personal knowledge of the Gospel story to have been able to write a very direct gospel of his own, without any resort to documents.

We need not make too much of such difficulties. But they are puzzling enough to call for an admission that the question of authorship is not so easy as it is often assumed to be, and that the Papias tradition must not be taken offhand as making any discussion superfluous.

It is merely slapdash to say that the gospel is not Marcan; no reputable scholar goes so far as this. The tradition connects Mark with the gospel, and that tradition is the sole evidence which we possess. If we reject it downright, we must simply confess that we are absolutely ignorant who wrote the gospel and provided the

[1] *op. cit.*, p. 304.

connecting link between the Petrine tradition and the completed work.

But the theory is possible that something less than actual authorship by Mark may better correspond with the phenomena which the gospel presents. Bacon suggests that this gospel is the Petrine story *as Mark used to preach it* in public, i.e. that an unknown author wrote down the record of what Mark used to say as being Peter's story, and combined this record with other documents, so producing this gospel. Thus would be explained the absence of personal colouring such as we might have expected Mark to give, if he was writing the book himself.

We cannot, however, say that this suggestion is more than possible. For against accepting it as conclusive must be entered two caveats:

(1) Whoever wrote the gospel was not, like the writers of the first and third gospels, a practised author and a literary artist, nor, like Luke, a competent historian. The second gospel is not in an historical or literary aspect a well-written story. It gives an impression of carelessness, and it is not fanciful to conjecture that it was put together in a hurry. It was a new venture in its kind; and it may be that it was the best which Mark could do under the circumstances and within the limits of his capacity for literary composition.

(2) The writer, let us again remember, was not writing with Christendom in view. He had no reason to anticipate the importance which was subsequently to attach to his work. He was only writing a catechetical manual for one church. It is therefore quite possible that, if Mark was this writer, he felt that he was only entitled to give that which was officially sponsored. His purpose was not to write a biography, but only to preserve the Petrine tradition, with which the Roman Church was already familiar, though with this tradition he incorporated some other traditional material whose authority was probably also established in the Church. In such a work his own personal reminiscences might seem out of place, especially as he was still alive to recount them. He uses documents, then, because he is not writing an independent book of his own, but is compiling materials which have a sort of

official authority. The gospel is Petrine tradition; it is not the story which Mark himself might have been able to tell from his own experiences. The value of the gospel rests not on its Marcan authorship but on the Petrine tradition which it preserves; and it survived and became authoritative because of its connexion with Peter's and not with Mark's name.

F. PLACE AND DATE OF COMPOSITION OF THE GOSPEL

i

So far we have assumed that this gospel was written in the Church of Rome. This view is so generally accepted by all scholars that the arguments for it need only be briefly set forth.

The tradition on which the gospel is based must, of course, have originated in Palestine. But that the gospel was not written in Palestine is indicated by (1) the fact that it in some places supplies a Greek translation of Aramaic phrases which are given in Aramaic (e.g. Boanerges 3^{17}, Talitha cumi 5^{41}, Corban 7^{11}, Ephphatha 7^{34}, Eloi Eloi 15^{34}. Cf. also the explanation of 'Preparation' in 15^{42}). This would not have been necessary if the evangelist had been writing for a Church in which every one spoke Aramaic. (2) The blunders as to Palestinian conditions, to which we have already referred, are anyhow hard enough to account for; they become inexplicable if we suppose not only that the tradition originated in Palestine, but also that the gospel was written there.

Mark's Greek, it is true, abounds in Aramaisms (see later), like the Greek of the Septuagint. This has led certain oriental scholars like Wellhausen, Torrey, and Allen to maintain that the Greek Mark is the translation of an Aramaic document which was written in Palestine. The force of this view can only be estimated by an Aramaic scholar. But students of the gospels in general do not accept Wellhausen's conclusions on this point. Some of Mark's sources, it is admitted, may have been written in Aramaic. Most of the tradition must have been first delivered orally in Aramaic. But it is more generally agreed that Mark's style is sufficiently explained by the fact that the gospel is written by a man who thinks in Aramaic and writes in a Greek already affected with Aramaisms. Aramaic and Greek were both much spoken in Palestine, and the spoken Greek was affected by the spoken Aramaic. Mark's Greek is certainly very rough and uncouth. It is at best the Greek of a foreigner who could speak it but was not accustomed to the literary use of it. But while it certainly shows the presence of an Aramaic background to the gospel, it need not be taken to demonstrate the presence of an Aramaic document of which it is a translation.

If, then, the gospel was not written in Palestine, the only other candidate for the honour is Rome. The tradition which says so in no way conflicts with the phenomena in the gospel. In particular (1) the gospel's dating of the Last Supper is possibly best explained as reflecting the custom of Easter observance which obtained in the Roman Church (see note *ad loc.*); (2) the use of Latin technical words may be some evidence in the same direction (for a list of such passages see the note on Mark's style later); (3) the influence of the gospel in subsequent literature is best explained by supposing that it had behind it the connexion with Peter and with a great centre of Christianity; and Christian tradition always connected Peter with Rome.

ii

The date usually given by scholars for the writing of the gospel is between A.D. 65 and 67. The reasons for this precision are succinctly given by Rawlinson. The tradition which says that the gospel was written after the death of Peter is probably correct; it is hard to think that the gospel was written when Peter was directly accessible. Peter was martyred in the Neronic persecution which broke out in A.D. 64. Therefore the gospel can scarcely have been written earlier than A.D. 65. The fact that cap. 13 contains no direct allusion to the siege of Jerusalem (as is found in Luke 21[20]) nor to the outbreak of the Jewish War, and that it speaks of persecution and distress as the 'beginning of travail' (verse 8) and as 'not the end' (verse 7) seems to place the book before A.D. 70, and probably before the final campaign began, i.e. before A.D. 68.

These seem strong arguments. Nevertheless there are scholars who claim that the gospel is earlier. Harnack sought to support the view that Acts was written before Paul's death, i.e. before A.D. 65–8, and that as Luke preceded Acts and Mark preceded Luke, a date nearer A.D. 50 for the writing of Mark was indicated. But his proposed date for Acts has not been accepted by any competent scholars, in spite of his great authority. So early a date for Mark is very unlikely, unless it be held that Mark is a translation of an Aramaic document, in which case the Aramaic original might be dated even as early as A.D. 40. Torrey in fact proposed this date, basing his view on the argument that Mark 13^{14} refers to Caligula's intention to set up his own statue in the Holy of Holies, an intention only finally frustrated by his assassination in A.D. 41. We shall hear more of this interpretation in a moment. As regards the date of the gospel, however, the proposal cannot hold, if we are right in repudiating the view that the gospel as a whole is the translation of an Aramaic original.

There is more to be said for the converse argument of some scholars that the gospel was not written till after A.D. 70, and is to be dated nearer A.D. 80. Two grounds for this suggestion call for special notice: (1) the Church of Rome observed Easter on a different system from that of the churches of the East. The Roman usage is reflected in Mark's dating of the Last Supper. This divergence can scarcely have arisen while Peter and Paul were both alive, for the eastern custom based itself on immemorial usage. Some time must therefore be allowed for the divergent usage of Rome to arise; we can hardly allow less than ten years, or even more. This, however, is an argument so full of conjectures that it can scarcely be held to be conclusive by itself. It may be doubted whether the exact date for the observance of Easter was regarded as a matter of such importance in Paul's lifetime as it was regarded in A.D. 120. Local convenience or even local accident might easily cause a divergent custom to arise at Rome at once, and we do not feel so sure that either Paul or Peter would have considered the divergence so momentous as to be worth opposing.

(2) Bacon (*Gospel of Mark,* Part II) elaborates an argument based on cap. 13, and more particularly on the wording of 13^{14}, an argument which is so ingenious and suggestive that, whether

we agree with his conclusion or not, it will be instructive to examine the process by which he reaches it.

He begins by urging that the chapter as a whole can hardly be taken as an authentic prediction of Our Lord's. With this view many will agree gladly. We need not go so far as those who describe

CALIGULA

the eschatology of this chapter as 'gross and grotesque'. We modern westerns are not good judges of eschatological language, for it is wholly alien from our mentality. The extent to which Jesus might have couched some of His teaching in current apocalyptic form is a vexed question to which only subjective tests can be applied. That He at any rate foresaw doom for Judaism and the Temple (as in Mk. 13^2) is in no way improbable; in this respect He would be wholly in a line with much Old Testament prophecy; and His prediction of the destruction of the Temple was a charge against Him at His trial (Mk. 14^{58}, 15^{29}; cf. Acts 6^{14}). But that He indulged in the elaborate and fantastic predictions of cap. 13 is not easily credible. It is not, we may say, at all in Jesus' style, and is inconsistent with the undeniably authentic utterance in Mk. 13^{32}. Bacon has good ground for saying,[1] 'If we were asked to name a passage which by its contradiction of authentic utterances, as well as by its manifest inferiority to the moral plane of the Master, might be set down as the least worthy of acceptance within the limits of Synoptic tradition, it might well be the section which includes this verse (13^{14}) as its climax.' Many scholars indeed hold that this chapter incorporates a Jewish or Jewish-Christian apocalypse which may have circulated independently in oral or written-leaflet form and may have been current in Christian circles as 'a word of the Lord' at the time of the impending doom of Jerusalem or earlier.

This being premised, Bacon begins by accepting Torrey's view that the revival of the Daniel prophecy (Dan. 9^{27}, 11^{31}, 12^{11}) of a great Profanation (which in Daniel referred to the erection, by Antiochus Epiphanes, of an altar of Zeus in the desecrated Temple) must have arisen in connexion with Caligula's threat to place his own statue in the Holy of Holies. This threat aroused the excited fears and fury of the whole Jewish world. Till Caligula's murder in 41 the whole people shivered and raged lest it should be carried out. The effect of the mere threat was that the Jews never again felt towards the Roman Empire as they had felt before. It sowed the seed of the revolutionary spirit. Torrey then suggests that at this time a 'word of the Lord' began to circulate in Jerusalem which saw in this menace a new form of the Profanation of which Daniel had spoken; and that in Jewish-Christian circles such a 'word of the Lord' would infallibly have been represented as a word of Jesus. This revival of the Daniel prophecy of an 'abomination that maketh desolate' must be dated about A.D. 40, after the threat had matured, but before the murder of Caligula had averted its fulfilment.

Bacon himself then takes up the tale. He maintains that this prophecy continued to circulate in Christian circles, though it was

[1] *op. cit.*, p. 63.

JERUSALEM, with the Mount of Olives behind

adapted both to suit events of a later date and in accordance with the spiritual capacities of each adapter. He notes the process of successive adaptation as follows:

(1) Paul changes the idea of an abomination into that of a personal Antichrist (2 Thess. $2^{2,4}$, written in A.D. 50). The Daniel prophecy is still the basis of his language; thus his prediction of an apostasy looks back to Dan. 11^{30}, and his description of the lawless king is in the language of Dan. 11^{36}. But the great profanation which he descries is the growth of Emperor-worship; he foresees a great struggle between this and the spiritual Israel.

(2) Matthew (24^{15}), looking back on the Jewish War and the fall of Jerusalem, recurs definitely to the Danielic idea of an 'abomination' and speaks of it as standing (neuter ἑστός) in a holy place (ἐν τόπῳ ἁγίῳ without the article). This has usually been taken to refer to the destruction of the Temple. But Bacon insists that the omission of the article is intentional, and that the Profanation which Matthew has in mind is that of a synagogue at Caesarea, the event which in Josephus' opinion caused the actual breaking out of the Jewish rebellion. According to Josephus (*Bell. Jud.* II. xiv. 5) some riotous person (no doubt a member of the anti-Jewish section of the populace) turned an earthen vessel bottom upward at the entrance of the Synagogue and sacrificed birds on it. Josephus adds that this thing terribly exasperated the Jews, because their laws were affronted and the place was polluted.

(3) Finally, Luke, a Gentile and an historian and no willing eschatologist, takes up the prophecy and makes it a definite prediction of the siege of Jerusalem (Lk. 21^{20}); the 'abomination' disappears, to be replaced by the compassing of Jerusalem with armies, which presages its 'desolation'.

Where, then, in this series are we to fit Mark in? Mark's words are: 'When ye see the abomination of desolation (τὸ βδέλυγμα τῆς ἐρημώσεως: the word for "abomination" is neuter) standing (ἑστηκότα, masculine) where it ought not (ὅπου οὐ δεῖ).' Why, asks Bacon, does not Mark say 'in the holy place'? Why does he use a phrase so vague as 'where it ought not'? The reason, he replies, is because the Temple was already destroyed, and Mark felt uneasy as to the phrase which should accordingly be used instead of the definite note of place. He solves his difficulty by a vagueness, but his uneasiness reveals the fact that he is writing after the fall of Jerusalem. The date of the gospel must therefore be after A.D. 70. How far after that date it should be placed is a question which Bacon seeks to answer by a very finely drawn attempt to prove that other features in Mark's chapter show Mark in writing it to be drawing, not only on Q (that is generally agreed) but also on Luke's Special Source. Bacon dates this Special Source soon after 70; he thus reaches A.D. 75 as the earliest possible date for Mark. But we need not go into these arguments here. They are in themselves very far from convincing, and they seem to be at variance with the latest trend of criticism with regard to the composition of Luke's gospel. We may take the choice presented to us for Mark's date as being between 'before and after A.D. 70'.

Bacon's discussion is extraordinarily ingenious and is in some respects really illuminating. But it is as fragile as a card-castle. Every step is conjectural, and each conjecture by itself is not conclusive. Our own feeling is (1) that Torrey's argument for the year 40 as the date for the revival of the Daniel prophecy is very strong; (2) that it is very likely that this revived prophecy circulated among the Christians as a word of Jesus, for Paul certainly adapts it; (3) that it is difficult to deny that Matthew and Luke look back on the fall of Jerusalem and shape their wording of the prophecy according to the event. The theory of Matthew's reference to the outrage at Caesarea builds a great deal on the omission of an article; but his language seems to imply that the profanation consisted of some *thing erected*, and is not so easily referred to the destruction of the Temple. (The same applies to Mark's phrase.)

But the real fragility of Bacon's argument seems to us to lie in his inference from Mark's wording in 13^{14}. All that Mark actually says is that a Profanation (an abomination standing where it ought not) will be a beginning of travail-pangs which will end in the Parousia. Is his language not sufficiently explained as mere apocalyptic vagueness? If the Temple had been destroyed when he wrote, why should he not have kept the definite mention of it? We often note instances both in the Old and in the New Testaments where predictions, though unfulfilled, have yet been preserved. It would be strange that Mark should feel any uneasiness at a phrase which, if kept, would show Jesus to have uttered a prediction which was literally fulfilled. Why should Mark have thrown away such a chance?

But if the gospel was written during the Neronic persecution, we may see a real and sensible purpose in his vagueness. That which the Roman Christians were then mightily concerned with was Nero's savage attack on the Church of Rome. Nero appeared to be very Antichrist, as the Christians continued for long to call him after his death. Is it not possible that Mark, in thus modifying the Danielic prediction into vagueness, intended to make his language such as might cover by implication such a profanation as Nero was then committing? 'Nero's persecution is terrible', he would in effect be saying, 'but its outcome will be the Parousia.' It is worth noting that Mark uses the masculine form (ἑστηκότα) for 'standing'; he has therefore a personal Profaner in view. This would not be very applicable to the destruction of the Temple; Matthew evidently felt this. But it would be applicable to the personal hatred of Nero.

It seems, then, that Mark must be interpolated in Bacon's series after Paul, no doubt, but nearer to Paul (to whom also the abomination is a personal Antichrist) than to Matthew and Luke. There is nothing to convince us that the case for the date after 70 is proved, or that we need abandon the usual dating. We may finally note, if the point will not seem fanciful, that the language of Mark 13[13] suggests, at any rate, an interesting parallel to that of Tacitus, who in reference to the Neronic persecution accuses the victims of being afflicted with 'hatred of the human race'. Rawlinson's commentary is specially helpful for its continual notice of the appropriateness of the gospel to the conditions of a persecuted church.

NOTE I

MARK'S CHRISTOLOGY

Of all the four gospels, Mark is the most 'familiar' in its references to Our Lord. It frequently draws attention to His glance and His personal gestures. It records His personal emotions, grief (3^{5}), surprise (6^{6}), compassion (6^{34}, 7^{34}, 8^{12}), indignation (10^{14}), affection (10^{21}), spiritual trouble (14^{33}). It represents Him under human limitations of knowledge (5^{32}, $9^{16,21}$, 13^{32}). It says on one occasion that He 'could' do no mighty work (6^{5}. Contrast Mt. 13^{58}). It records His refusal of the epithet 'good', as being God's prerogative (10^{18}; contrast Mt. 19^{17}).

But nevertheless there is a definite Christology in Mark's gospel. It is artless and in some respects primitive, but it clearly embodies a supernatural conception of our Lord's person. Thus:

(1) His miracles and exorcisms, and the wonder they aroused are frequently noticed (2^{12}, 4^{41}, 5^{42}, 7^{37}). His power to read men's hearts (2^{8}, 3^{4-5}) and to foretell the future (9^{31}, 10^{34}, 13^{2}, $14^{27,30}$) is illustrated.

(2) His own claims are unique. He claims authority to forgive sins (2^{10}); lordship of the sabbath (2^{28}); to be a fulfilment of Scripture (9^{12}, $14^{27,49}$). He is to rise again from the dead ($9^{9,31}$, 10^{34}). His death will be a ransom for many (10^{45}). He is the destined Judge of mankind ($13^{26,27}$, 14^{62}).

The Marcan Jesus is thus One who stands in a unique relation both to God and to man. He is called 'Lord' (*κύριος*) in 5^{19}, 7^{28}, 11^{3}, and 'Son of God' in $1^{1,11}$, 3^{11}, 5^{7}, 9^{7}. The demons acknowledge Him as Son of God or 'the Holy One of God' ($1^{24,34}$, 3^{11}, 5^{7}).

It is to be noted, however, that no trace is to be found in Mark of the Pauline doctrine of a pre-existent Being who became incarnate, nor of the Johannine doctrine of the Word of God made flesh. Mark says nothing about Our Lord's conception, birth, or infancy. He begins at Jesus' baptism by John the Baptist; and, whether Mark deserves the treatment or not, it is a fact that among both early heretics and modern scholars are some who consider Mark's Christology to be Adoptionist, i.e. (as has already been explained) Jesus' divine status is not held to begin till His baptism. The phrase in 1^{11} (Gk. *εὐδόκησα*) implies probably not pre-existence but present election.

Nor does Mark seem to be much attracted by the Christological view of which Matthew makes much, that expressed in the term 'Son of David', according to which our Lord is the scion of the royal line and his pedigree is a matter of importance. No genealogy is given in Mark. The title 'Son of David' is only applied to Our Lord twice in the gospel, once by blind Bartimaeus (10^{47}) openly, and once by obvious implication in the acclamations of the crowd at the entry into Jerusalem [1] ($11^{9,10}$). And Our Lord's question in 12^{35-37} would seem to imply a repudiation of the view that physical descent from David is the real basis of Messiah's authority. It points out that David himself refers that authority to God's exaltation of Messiah to His own right hand; the stress on Davidic pedigree is something that 'the scribes say'.

The Christological view which sees in Our Lord the fulfilment of the prophecy of the Suffering Servant in Isaiah 53 was, as we have noted, prominent in the early Church. In Mark it is taken for granted. No direct reference to Isaiah 53 is given, nor is Jesus ever called the 'Servant' (παῖς) of God, as He is called in Acts 3^{13}, $4^{27,30}$. But the purpose of His coming is declared to be 'to minister', and the value of His sufferings is set forth as 'a ransom for many' (Mk. 10^{45}). Mark's view of Jesus is one which presupposes, if it does not overtly proclaim, the recognition of Him as the Man of Sorrows, who by suffering wins the deliverance of His people.

There is no doubt that the aspect in which Mark predominantly thinks of Jesus' work is that Jesus is the supernatural Messiah (the Christ), sent by God to fulfil the Messianic hope of the Jews, and exalted at last to heaven at God's right hand, where He is to sit as Judge, when the Kingdom of God shall come. The Messianic conception is the Christological idea which figures most prominently in Mark. The title 'Son of Man' is nowhere explained, any more than the title 'Christ'. It is assumed that Mark's readers will know the significance of such titles. We may be confident that they were used from the very infancy of the Church; and we have tried to give reason for believing that the Messianic conception comes from Our Lord Himself.

This, then, is the summary of Mark's Christological views: Jesus

[1] Bacon suggests on these two passages: 'The people who welcome Jesus to Jerusalem with their hosannas to "the Son of David" . . . are to Mark's view as blind as Bartimaeus, who both stands among them and is representative of them.' I am not sure that this is not a purely fanciful exegesis; nor am I sure that Mark himself saw the full purpose of Our Lord's question in 12^{35-37}; Paul would have seen it. But Bacon's discussion of the Marcan Christology (*Gospel of Mark*, Pt. IV, cap. 1) is very suggestive and I owe much to it, though I cannot agree to many of his conclusions.

is the Son of God, unique in His relation to God; He is Son of Man, the Christ, the fulfilment of the Messianic hope; and He is the Redeemer of His people, who by His sufferings wins God's triumph, who is exalted to heaven, and who will come again to judge the world.

NOTE 2

CHARACTERISTICS OF MARCAN STYLE

Nothing but an enumeration of some of the most decided characteristics, with a few references, need here be given: a fuller list will be found in Allen's commentary.

Duplication of phrase and redundancy of expression: 1^{32}, 2^{25}, 6^{35}, 13^{20}.
The verb 'to be' with a participle: $1^{13,22}$, 2^{18}, 4^{38}, 5^{5}. (24 times.)
Accumulation of participles before a verb: 1^{41}, 5^{25}, 12^{28}.
Harsh constructions: 4^{31}, $6^{8,9}$, 8^{28}.
Asyndeton: 10^{27-29}.
εὐθύς = straightway (41 times).
πάλιν = again (26 times).
πολλά adverbial = much (13 times).
ὅτι introducing *oratio recta* (50 times).
Narrative present (151 times).
Rare words or uses of words:

σχίζω 1^{10} | ἐκβάλλω 1^{12} | ἀμφιβάλλω 1^{16}
ἐπιράπτω 2^{21} | προσκαρτερέω 3^{9}
ἐπιπίπτω 3^{10} | ἀναπίπτω 6^{40}
στίλβω 9^{3} | τρυμαλιά 10^{25} | ἄμφοδον 11^{4}
στιβάς 11^{8} | κεφαλιόω 12^{4} | ἐπιβαλών 14^{72}
ἐνειλέω 15^{46}.

Diminutives: θυγάτριον 5^{23}, 7^{25}; παιδίον $5^{39,40}$; πλοιάριον 3^{9}; κοράσιον $5^{41,42}$; κυνάριον $7^{27,28}$; ἰχθύδια 8^{7}.
Latin words: κράββατος 2^{4}; κοδράντης 12^{42}; δηνάριον 12^{15}; κεντυρίων 15^{39}; Λεγιών 5^{9}; ξέστης 7^{4}; σπεκουλάτωρ 6^{27}.

Aramaic words: 3^{17}, 5^{41}, $7^{11,34}$, 11^{10}, 14^{36}, 15^{34}.
Aramaic idioms and phrases (the following are derived from the list in Wellhausen's *Einleitung*):
Verb before subject, e.g. εἶπεν ὁ Ἰησοῦς: frequent.
Subject of subordinate clause taken out and governed by principal verb: 7^{2}, 11^{32}, 12^{34}.

Weak participle to open sentence: *ἰδών, λαβών*, &c.
Relative as conjunction: 1^{7}, 7^{25}.
Periphrastic conjugation in active: 10^{22} *al.*
Historic present: 151 times.
Αὐτός to define: $6^{17,22}$.
Over-use of *αὐτός*: $3^{31,32,34}$.
εἰ μή = only: 8^{14}.
εἰ as used in 8^{12}.

Words like *σκανδαλίζειν, βαπτίζειν, πειράζειν, ἀναστῆναι, περιπατεῖν* (of a way of life), *πειρασμός, σκάνδαλον, πλήρωμα* (2^{21}).

Phrases like *ὁδὸς θεοῦ, υἱοὶ νυμφῶνος, ἐν μιᾷ τῶν σαββάτων, ἐν δυνάμει* or *ἐν ἐξουσίᾳ*.

Distributive phrases of number, as in 4^{8}, $6^{7,39,40}$, 14^{19}.

Internal accusative like *ἐφοβοῦντο φόβον*.

Note 3

BIBLIOGRAPHY

Literature on the Gospels is so abundant that nothing but a selection of important books for the present study can here be given.

Editions.

SWETE. *The Gospel according to St. Mark. Commentary on the Greek text*, 1902. Very scholarly, representing the most sane of cautious conservatism. In some respects modern discussion has, however, gone beyond the problems which were to the fore when this commentary was written.

BACON. *Beginnings of the Gospel Story*: a commentary on the English text, 1909. Stimulating and provocative, but to be read with questioning discrimination.

ALLEN. *Oxford Church Biblical Commentary*, 1915. Ultra-conservative; regards the Gospel as a translation from the Aramaic.

RAWLINSON. *Westminster Commentary*, 1925. The latest and most helpful edition on the English text.

GOULD. *International Critical Commentary*, 1897. Somewhat old-fashioned, but still serviceable.

WELLHAUSEN. *Das Evangelium Marci*, 1909. Short and crisp and suggestive notes.

MONTEFIORE. *Synoptic Gospels*, vol. i, 2nd ed. revised, 1927. A valuable commentary on the English text by a leader of Liberal Judaism.

BARTLET. *St. Mark*, in the revised Century Bible, 1922. A useful short commentary.

Introductions and treatises.

MOFFATT. *Introduction to the New Testament*, 1911. A good *résumé* of Synoptic study.

WELLHAUSEN. *Einleitung in die drei ersten Evangelien*, 1911. A stimulating piece of work.

LOISY. *Les évangiles synoptiques*, 1894. Represents the extreme critical standpoint.

BURKITT. *The Gospel history and its transmission*, 1907.
Earliest sources for the life of Jesus, 1910.
Christian beginnings, 1924.
Burkitt's work is interesting and very helpful. His view on the Petrine authority of the Gospel is perhaps rather too much in favour of wholesale acceptance.

BACON. *The Gospel of Mark*, 1925.
Is Mark a Roman gospel? 1919.
Bacon forces one to face problems. His treatment of them is often exposed to criticism, but his learning is immense and his point of view is always suggestive.

SANDAY. *Outlines of the life of Christ*, 1905.
The life of Christ in recent research, 1907.
These possess Sanday's qualities of scholarly caution and judicious appreciation. But since their date some new questions have been raised by later scholarship.

STANTON. *The Gospels as historical documents*. Parts I and II, 1903 and 1909. Full of careful scholarship.

Oxford Studies in the Synoptic Problem, by various writers, edited by Sanday, 1911. Invaluable for the discussion of critical points in the relation of the Synoptic Gospels to one another.

STREETER. *The Four Gospels*. A book of recent date (1924), which has marked an epoch in the study of Luke and of the *provenance* of the Gospels.

SCHWEITZER. *Von Reimarus zu Wrede*. E.T. 'The Quest of the historical Jesus', 1910. An epoch-making study of the gospel eschatology; it exaggerates, however, the point of view which it supports.

EMMET. *The eschatological question in the Gospels*, 1911. Provides a helpful criticism of Schweitzer's views.

ABRAHAMS. *Studies in Pharisaism and the Gospels*. 1st series, 1917; 2nd series, 1924. A very useful and careful treatise from the Jewish point of view.

MENZIES. *The earliest Gospel*, 1901. Very helpful.

THE RIVER JORDAN

THE

GOSPEL ACCORDING TO ST. MARK

INTRODUCTION

John the Baptist

1 THE beginning of the gospel of Jesus Christ, [1]the Son of God.
2 Even as it is written [2]in Isaiah the prophet,
Behold, I send my messenger before thy face,
Who shall prepare thy way;
3 The voice of one crying in the wilderness,
Make ye ready the way of the Lord,
Make his paths straight;
4 John came, who baptized in the wilderness and preached the
5 baptism of repentance unto remission of sins. And there went out unto him all the country of Judæa, and all they of Jerusalem; and they were baptized of him in the river Jordan, con-
6 fessing their sins. And John was clothed with camel's hair, and *had* a leathern girdle about his loins, and did eat locusts and
7 wild honey. And he preached, saying, There cometh after me he that is mightier than I, the latchet of whose shoes I am not
8 [3]worthy to stoop down and unloose. I baptized you [4]with water; but he shall baptize you [4]with the [5]Holy Ghost.

The Baptism and Temptation of Jesus

9 And it came to pass in those days, that Jesus came from Nazareth of Galilee, and was baptized of John [6]in the Jordan.
10 And straightway coming up out of the water, he saw the heavens rent asunder, and the Spirit as a dove descending upon
11 him: and a voice came out of the heavens, Thou art my beloved Son, in thee I am well pleased.
12 And straightway the Spirit driveth him forth into the wilder-
13 ness. And he was in the wilderness forty days tempted of Satan; and he was with the wild beasts; and the angels ministered unto him.

[1] Some ancient authorities omit *the Son of God.* [2] Some ancient authorities read *in the prophets.* [3] Gr. *sufficient.* [4] Or, *in* [5] Or, *Holy Spirit*: and so throughout this book. [6] Gr. *into.*

F 2

SCENES IN GALILEE

The Beginning of the Ministry

First message and call of first disciples

14 Now after that John was delivered up, Jesus came into 15 Galilee, preaching the gospel of God, and saying, The time is fulfilled, and the kingdom of God is at hand: repent ye, and believe in the gospel.

16 And passing along by the sea of Galilee, he saw Simon and Andrew the brother of Simon casting a net in the sea: for they 17 were fishers. And Jesus said unto them, Come ye after me, and 18 I will make you to become fishers of men. And straightway 19 they left the nets, and followed him. And going on a little further, he saw James the *son* of Zebedee, and John his brother, 20 who also were in the boat mending the nets. And straightway he called them: and they left their father Zebedee in the boat with the hired servants, and went after him.

Preaching and signs and their effect

21 And they go into Capernaum; and straightway on the sab- 22 bath day he entered into the synagogue and taught. And they were astonished at his teaching: for he taught them as having 23 authority, and not as the scribes. And straightway there was in their synagogue a man with an unclean spirit; and he cried out, 24 saying, What have we to do with thee, thou Jesus of Nazareth? art thou come to destroy us? I know thee who thou art, the 25 Holy One of God. And Jesus rebuked [1]him, saying, Hold thy 26 peace, and come out of him. And the unclean spirit, [2]tearing 27 him and crying with a loud voice, came out of him. And they were all amazed, insomuch that they questioned among themselves, saying, What is this? a new teaching! with authority he 28 commandeth even the unclean spirits, and they obey him. And the report of him went out straightway everywhere into all the region of Galilee round about.

29 And straightway, [3]when they were come out of the synagogue, they came into the house of Simon and Andrew, with James 30 and John. Now Simon's wife's mother lay sick of a fever; and 31 straightway they tell him of her: and he came and took her by the hand, and raised her up; and the fever left her, and she ministered unto them.

[1] Or, *it* [2] Or, *convulsing* [3] Some ancient authorities read *when he was come out of the synagogue, he came, &c.*

A MODEL OF THE SYNAGOGUE AT CAPERNAUM, probably built in the second century A.D. on the site of the synagogue in which Christ preached

32 And at even, when the sun did set, they brought unto him all
33 that were sick, and them that were [1]possessed with devils. And
34 all the city was gathered together at the door. And he healed many that were sick with divers diseases, and cast out many [2]devils; and he suffered not the [2]devils to speak, because they knew him[3].

35 And in the morning, a great while before day, he rose up and went out, and departed into a desert place, and there prayed.
36 And Simon and they that were with him followed after him;
37 and they found him, and say unto him, All are seeking thee.
38 And he saith unto them, Let us go elsewhere into the next towns, that I may preach there also; for to this end came I
39 forth. And he went into their synagogues throughout all Galilee, preaching and casting out [2]devils.

40 And there cometh to him a leper, beseeching him, [4]and kneeling down to him, and saying unto him, If thou wilt, thou canst
41 make me clean. And being moved with compassion, he stretched forth his hand, and touched him, and saith unto him, I will; be
42 thou made clean. And straightway the leprosy departed from
43 him, and he was made clean. And he [5]strictly charged him, and
44 straightway sent him out, and saith unto him, See thou say nothing to any man: but go thy way, shew thyself to the priest, and offer for thy cleansing the things which Moses commanded,
45 for a testimony unto them. But he went out, and began to publish it much, and to spread abroad the [6]matter, insomuch that [7]Jesus could no more openly enter into [8]a city, but was without in desert places: and they came to him from every quarter.

Opposition

2 And when he entered again into Capernaum after some days,
2 it was noised that he was [9]in the house. And many were gathered together, so that there was no longer room *for them*, no, not even about the door: and he spake the word unto them.
3 And they come, bringing unto him a man sick of the palsy, borne
4 of four. And when they could not [10]come nigh unto him for the crowd, they uncovered the roof where he was: and when they

[1] Or, *demoniacs* [2] Gr. *demons.* [3] Many ancient authorities add *to be Christ.* [4] Some ancient authorities omit *and kneeling down to him.* [5] Or, *sternly* [6] Gr. *word.* [7] Gr. *he.* [8] Or, *the city* [9] Or, *at home* [10] Many ancient authorities read *bring him unto him.*

THE COURTYARD OF AN EASTERN HOUSE

had broken it up, they let down the bed whereon the sick of the
5 palsy lay. And Jesus seeing their faith saith unto the sick of
6 the palsy, [1]Son, thy sins are forgiven. But there were certain
7 of the scribes sitting there, and reasoning in their hearts, Why
doth this man thus speak? he blasphemeth: who can forgive
8 sins but one, *even* God? And straightway Jesus, perceiving in
his spirit that they so reasoned within themselves, saith unto
9 them, Why reason ye these things in your hearts? Whether is
easier, to say to the sick of the palsy, Thy sins are forgiven; or
10 to say, Arise, and take up thy bed, and walk? But that ye may
know that the Son of man hath [2]power on earth to forgive sins
11 (he saith to the sick of the palsy), I say unto thee, Arise, take
12 up thy bed, and go unto thy house. And he arose, and straightway took up the bed, and went forth before them all; insomuch
that they were all amazed, and glorified God, saying, We never
saw it on this fashion.

13 And he went forth again by the sea side; and all the multitude
14 resorted unto him, and he taught them. And as he passed by,
he saw Levi the *son* of Alphæus sitting at the place of toll, and
he saith unto him, Follow me. And he arose and followed him.
15 And it came to pass, that he was sitting at meat in his house,
and many publicans and sinners sat down with Jesus and his
16 disciples: for there were many, and they followed him. And the
scribes [3]of the Pharisees, when they saw that he was eating with
the sinners and publicans, said unto his disciples, [4]He eateth
17 [5]and drinketh with publicans and sinners. And when Jesus
heard it, he saith unto them, They that are [6]whole have no
need of a physician, but they that are sick: I came not to call
the righteous, but sinners.

18 And John's disciples and the Pharisees were fasting: and
they come and say unto him, Why do John's disciples and the
19 disciples of the Pharisees fast, but thy disciples fast not? And
Jesus said unto them, Can the sons of the bride-chamber fast,
while the bridegroom is with them? as long as they have the
20 bridegroom with them, they cannot fast. But the days will
come, when the bridegroom shall be taken away from them,
21 and then will they fast in that day. No man seweth a piece of
undressed cloth on an old garment: else that which should fill

[1] Gr. *Child.* [2] Or, *authority* [3] Some ancient authorities read *and the Pharisees.* [4] Or, How is it *that he eateth . . . sinners?* [5] Some ancient authorities omit *and drinketh.* [6] Gr. *strong.*

it up taketh from it, the new from the old, and a worse rent is
22 made. And no man putteth new wine into old [1]wine-skins: else the wine will burst the skins, and the wine perisheth, and the skins: but *they put* new wine into fresh wine-skins.

23 And it came to pass, that he was going on the sabbath day through the cornfields; and his disciples [2]began, as they went,
24 to pluck the ears of corn. And the Pharisees said unto him, Behold, why do they on the sabbath day that which is not

'They put new wine into fresh wine-skins.' Eastern leather-workers

25 lawful? And he said unto them, Did ye never read what David did, when he had need, and was an hungred, he, and they that
26 were with him? How he entered into the house of God [3]when Abiathar was high priest, and did eat the shewbread, which it is not lawful to eat save for the priests, and gave also to them
27 that were with him? And he said unto them, The sabbath was
28 made for man, and not man for the sabbath: so that the Son of man is lord even of the sabbath.

3 And he entered again into the synagogue; and there was a
2 man there which had his hand withered. And they watched

[1] That is, *skins used as bottles.* [2] Gr. *began to make* their *way plucking.*
[3] Some ancient authorities read *in the days of Abiathar the high priest.*

him, whether he would heal him on the sabbath day; that they
3 might accuse him. And he saith unto the man that had his
4 hand withered, [1]Stand forth. And he saith unto them, Is it
lawful on the sabbath day to do good, or to do harm? to save
5 a life, or to kill? But they held their peace. And when he had
looked round about on them with anger, being grieved at the
hardening of their heart, he saith unto the man, Stretch forth
thy hand. And he stretched it forth: and his hand was restored.
6 And the Pharisees went out, and straightway with the Herodians took counsel against him, how they might destroy him.

THE TWELVE

The separation of the Twelve

7 And Jesus with his disciples withdrew to the sea: and a great
8 multitude from Galilee followed: and from Judæa, and from
Jerusalem, and from Idumæa, and beyond Jordan, and about
Tyre and Sidon, a great multitude, hearing [2]what great things
9 he did, came unto him. And he spake to his disciples, that a
little boat should wait on him because of the crowd, lest they
10 should throng him: for he had healed many; insomuch that as
many as had [3]plagues [4]pressed upon him that they might touch
11 him. And the unclean spirits, whensoever they beheld him, fell
down before him, and cried, saying, Thou art the Son of God.
12 And he charged them much that they should not make him
known.

13 And he goeth up into the mountain, and calleth unto him
14 whom he himself would: and they went unto him. And he appointed twelve,[5] that they might be with him, and that he
15 might send them forth to preach, and to have authority
16 to cast out [6]devils: [7]and Simon he surnamed Peter; and
17 James the *son* of Zebedee, and John the brother of James;
and them he surnamed Boanerges, which is, Sons of thunder:
18 and Andrew, and Philip, and Bartholomew, and Matthew, and
Thomas, and James the *son* of Alphæus, and Thaddæus, and
19 Simon the [8]Cananæan, and Judas Iscariot, which also betrayed
him.

20 And he cometh [9]into a house. And the multitude cometh

[1] Gr. *Arise into the midst.* [2] Or, *all the things that he did* [3] Gr. *scourges.*
[4] Gr. *fell.* [5] Some ancient authorities add *whom also he named apostles.*
[6] Gr. *demons.* [7] Some ancient authorities insert *and he appointed twelve.*
[8] Or, *Zealot* [9] Or, *home*

SIDON

together again, so that they could not so much as eat bread.
21 And when his friends heard it, they went out to lay hold on
22 him: for they said, He is beside himself. And the scribes which
came down from Jerusalem said, He hath Beelzebub, and, [1]By
23 the prince of the [2]devils casteth he out the [2]devils. And he
called them unto him, and said unto them in parables, How can
24 Satan cast out Satan? And if a kingdom be divided against
25 itself, that kingdom cannot stand. And if a house be divided
26 against itself, that house will not be able to stand. And if
Satan hath risen up against himself, and is divided, he cannot
27 stand, but hath an end. But no one can enter into the house
of the strong *man*, and spoil his goods, except he first bind the
28 strong *man*; and then he will spoil his house. Verily I say unto
you, All their sins shall be forgiven unto the sons of men, and
29 their blasphemies wherewith soever they shall blaspheme: but
whosoever shall blaspheme against the Holy Spirit hath never
30 forgiveness, but is guilty of an eternal sin: because they said,
He hath an unclean spirit.

31 And there come his mother and his brethren; and, standing
32 without, they sent unto him, calling him. And a multitude was
sitting about him; and they say unto him, Behold, thy mother
33 and thy brethren seek for thee. And he answereth them, and
34 saith, Who is my mother and my brethren? And looking round
on them which sat round about him, he saith, Behold, my
35 mother and my brethren! For whosoever shall do the will of
God, the same is my brother, and sister, and mother.

The teaching of the Twelve

4 And again he began to teach by the sea side. And there is
gathered unto him a very great multitude, so that he entered
into a boat, and sat in the sea; and all the multitude were by
2 the sea on the land. And he taught them many things in
3 parables, and said unto them in his teaching, Hearken: Behold,
4 the sower went forth to sow: and it came to pass, as he sowed,
some *seed* fell by the way side, and the birds came and devoured
5 it. And other fell on the rocky *ground*, where it had not much
earth; and straightway it sprang up, because it had no deepness
6 of earth: and when the sun was risen, it was scorched; and
7 because it had no root, it withered away. And other fell among
the thorns, and the thorns grew up, and choked it, and it

[1] Or, *In* [2] Gk. *demons*.

PLOUGHING IN PALESTINE TO-DAY

The form of the wooden plough has not changed in two thousand years

8 yielded no fruit. And others fell into the good ground, and yielded fruit, growing up and increasing; and brought forth, 9 thirtyfold, and sixtyfold, and a hundredfold. And he said, Who hath ears to hear, let him hear.

10 And when he was alone, they that were about him with the 11 twelve asked of him the parables. And he said unto them, Unto you is given the mystery of the kingdom of God: but unto 12 them that are without, all things are done in parables: that seeing they may see, and not perceive; and hearing they may hear, and not understand; lest haply they should turn again, 13 and it should be forgiven them. And he saith unto them, Know ye not this parable? and how shall ye know all the parables? 14 The sower soweth the word. And these are they by the way 15 side, where the word is sown; and when they have heard, straightway cometh Satan, and taketh away the word which 16 hath been sown in them. And these in like manner are they that are sown upon the rocky *places*, who, when they have 17 heard the word, straightway receive it with joy; and they have no root in themselves, but endure for a while; then, when tribulation or persecution ariseth because of the word, straight-18 way they stumble. And others are they that are sown among 19 the thorns; these are they that have heard the word, and the cares of the [1]world, and the deceitfulness of riches, and the lusts of other things entering in, choke the word, and it be-20 cometh unfruitful. And those are they that were sown upon the good ground; such as hear the word, and accept it, and bear fruit, thirtyfold, and sixtyfold, and a hundredfold.

21 And he said unto them, Is the lamp brought to be put under the bushel, or under the bed, *and* not to be put on the stand? 22 For there is nothing hid, save that it should be manifested; neither was *anything* made secret, but that it should come to 23 light. If any man hath ears to hear, let him hear. And he said 24 unto them, Take heed what ye hear: with what measure ye mete it shall be measured unto you: and more shall be given 25 unto you. For he that hath, to him shall be given: and he that hath not, from him shall be taken away even that which he hath.

26 And he said, So is the kingdom of God, as if a man should 27 cast seed upon the earth; and should sleep and rise night and day, and the seed should spring up and grow, he knoweth not

[1] Or, *age*

28 how. The earth [1]beareth fruit of herself; first the blade, then 29 the ear, then the full corn in the ear. But when the fruit [2]is ripe, straightway he [3]putteth forth the sickle, because the harvest is come.

30 And he said, How shall we liken the kingdom of God? or in 31 what parable shall we set it forth? [4]It is like a grain of mustard seed, which, when it is sown upon the earth, though it be less 32 than all the seeds that are upon the earth, yet when it is sown,

Carrying the harvest

groweth up, and becometh greater than all the herbs, and putteth out great branches; so that the birds of the heaven can lodge under the shadow thereof.

3 And with many such parables spake he the word unto them, 4 as they were able to hear it: and without a parable spake he not unto them: but privately to his own disciples he expounded all things.

'arious Miracles

5 And on that day, when even was come, he saith unto them, 6 Let us go over unto the other side. And leaving the multitude, they take him with them, even as he was, in the boat. And

[1] Or, *yieldeth* [2] Or, *alloweth* [3] Or, *sendeth forth* [4] Gr. *As unto.*

37 other boats were with him. And there ariseth a great storm of wind, and the waves beat into the boat, insomuch that the 38 boat was now filling. And he himself was in the stern, asleep on the cushion: and they awake him, and say unto him, [1]Master, 39 carest thou not that we perish? And he awoke, and rebuked the wind, and said unto the sea, Peace, be still. And the wind 40 ceased, and there was a great calm. And he said unto them, 41 Why are ye fearful? have ye not yet faith? And they feared exceedingly, and said one to another, Who then is this, that even the wind and the sea obey him?

5 And they came to the other side of the sea, into the country 2 of the Gerasenes. And when he was come out of the boat, straightway there met him out of the tombs a man with an 3 unclean spirit, who had his dwelling in the tombs: and no man 4 could any more bind him, no, not with a chain; because that he had been often bound with fetters and chains, and the chains had been rent asunder by him, and the fetters broken in pieces: 5 and no man had strength to tame him. And always, night and day, in the tombs and in the mountains, he was crying out, and 6 cutting himself with stones. And when he saw Jesus from afar, 7 he ran and worshipped him; and crying out with a loud voice, he saith, What have I to do with thee, Jesus, thou Son of the 8 Most High God? I adjure thee by God, torment me not. For he said unto him, Come forth, thou unclean spirit, out of the man. 9 And he asked him, What is thy name? And he saith unto him, 10 My name is Legion; for we are many. And he besought him much that he would not send them away out of the country. 11 Now there was there on the mountain side a great herd of swine 12 feeding. And they besought him, saying, Send us into the 13 swine, that we may enter into them. And he gave them leave. And the unclean spirits came out, and entered into the swine: and the herd rushed down the steep into the sea, *in number* 14 about two thousand; and they were choked in the sea. And they that fed them fled, and told it in the city, and in the country. And they came to see what it was that had come to 15 pass. And they come to Jesus, and behold [2]him that was possessed with devils sitting, clothed and in his right mind, 16 *even* him that had the legion: and they were afraid. And they that saw it declared unto them how it befell [2]him that was 17 possessed with devils, and concerning the swine. And they

[1] Or, *Teacher* [2] Or, *the demoniac*

18 began to beseech him to depart from their borders. And as he was entering into the boat, he that had been possessed with 19 [1]devils besought him that he might be with him. And he suffered him not, but saith unto him, Go to thy house unto thy friends, and tell them how great things the Lord hath done for 20 thee, and *how* he had mercy on thee. And he went his way, and began to publish in Decapolis how great things Jesus had done for him: and all men did marvel.

21 And when Jesus had crossed over again in the boat unto the other side, a great multitude was gathered unto him: and he 22 was by the sea. And there cometh one of the rulers of the synagogue, Jaïrus by name; and seeing him, he falleth at his 23 feet, and beseecheth him much, saying, My little daughter is at the point of death: *I pray thee*, that thou come and lay thy 24 hands on her, that she may be [2]made whole, and live. And he went with him; and a great multitude followed him, and they thronged him.

25 And a woman, which had an issue of blood twelve years, 26 and had suffered many things of many physicians, and had spent all that she had, and was nothing bettered, but rather 27 grew worse, having heard the things concerning Jesus, came in 28 the crowd behind, and touched his garment. For she said, If 29 I touch but his garments, I shall be [2]made whole. And straightway the fountain of her blood was dried up; and she felt in her 30 body that she was healed of her [3]plague. And straightway Jesus, perceiving in himself that the power *proceeding* from him had gone forth, turned him about in the crowd, and said, 31 Who touched my garments? And his disciples said unto him, Thou seest the multitude thronging thee, and sayest thou, 32 Who touched me? And he looked round about to see her that 33 had done this thing. But the woman fearing and trembling, knowing what had been done to her, came and fell down before 34 him, and told him all the truth. And he said unto her, Daughter, thy faith hath [4]made thee whole; go in peace, and be whole of thy [3]plague.

35 While he yet spake, they come from the ruler of the synagogue's *house*, saying, Thy daughter is dead: why troublest 36 thou the [5]Master any further? But Jesus, [6]not heeding the word spoken, saith unto the ruler of the synagogue, Fear not,

[1] Gr. *demons.* [2] Or, *saved* [3] Gr. *scourge.* [4] Or, *saved thee*
[5] Or, *Teacher* [6] Or, *overhearing*

37 only believe. And he suffered no man to follow with him, save 38 Peter, and James, and John the brother of James. And they come to the house of the ruler of the synagogue; and he be- 39 holdeth a tumult, and *many* weeping and wailing greatly. And when he was entered in, he saith unto them, Why make ye a 40 tumult, and weep? the child is not dead, but sleepeth. And they laughed him to scorn. But he, having put them all forth, taketh the father of the child and her mother and them that 41 were with him, and goeth in where the child was. And taking the child by the hand, he saith unto her, Talitha cumi; which 42 is, being interpreted, Damsel, I say unto thee, Arise. And straightway the damsel rose up, and walked; for she was twelve years old. And they were amazed straightway with a great 43 amazement. And he charged them much that no man should know this: and he commanded that *something* should be given her to eat.

The mission of the Twelve

6 And he went out from thence; and he cometh into his own 2 country; and his disciples follow him. And when the sabbath was come, he began to teach in the synagogue: and [1]many hearing him were astonished, saying, Whence hath this man these things? and, What is the wisdom that is given unto this man, and *what mean* such [2]mighty works wrought by his 3 hands? Is not this the carpenter, the son of Mary, and brother of James, and Joses, and Judas, and Simon? and are not his 4 sisters here with us? And they were [3]offended in him. And Jesus said unto them, A prophet is not without honour, save in his own country, and among his own kin, and in his own 5 house. And he could there do no [4]mighty work, save that he 6 laid his hands upon a few sick folk, and healed them. And he marvelled because of their unbelief.

And he went round about the villages teaching.

7 And he called unto him the twelve, and began to send them forth by two and two; and he gave them authority over the un- 8 clean spirits; and he charged them that they should take nothing for *their* journey, save a staff only; no bread, no wallet, no [5]money 9 in their [6]purse; but *to go* shod with sandals: and, *said he*, put 10 not on two coats. And he said unto them, Wheresoever ye

[1] Some ancient authorities insert *the*. [2] Gr. *powers*. [3] Gr. *caused to stumble*. [4] Gr. *power*. [5] Gr. *brass*. [6] Gr. *girdle*.

NAZARETH

11 enter into a house, there abide till ye depart thence. And whatsoever place shall not receive you, and they hear you not, as ye go forth thence, shake off the dust that is under your feet 12 for a testimony unto them. And they went out, and preached 13 that *men* should repent. And they cast out many [1]devils, and anointed with oil many that were sick, and healed them.

Leaving Galilee

Herod and John the Baptist

14 And king Herod heard *thereof*; for his name had become known: and [2]he said, John [3]the Baptist is risen from the dead, 15 and therefore do these powers work in him. But others said, It is Elijah. And others said, *It is* a prophet, *even* as one of the 16 prophets. But Herod, when he heard *thereof*, said, John, whom 17 I beheaded, he is risen. For Herod himself had sent forth and laid hold upon John, and bound him in prison for the sake of 18 Herodias, his brother Philip's wife: for he had married her. For John said unto Herod, It is not lawful for thee to have thy 19 brother's wife. And Herodias set herself against him, and 20 desired to kill him; and she could not; for Herod feared John, knowing that he was a righteous man and a holy, and kept him safe. And when he heard him, he [4]was much perplexed; and 21 he heard him gladly. And when a convenient day was come, that Herod on his birthday made a supper to his lords, and the 22 [5]high captains, and the chief men of Galilee; and when [6]the daughter of Herodias herself came in and danced, [7]she pleased Herod and them that sat at meat with him; and the king said unto the damsel, Ask of me whatsoever thou wilt, and I will 23 give it thee. And he sware unto her, Whatsoever thou shalt 24 ask of me, I will give it thee, unto the half of my kingdom. And she went out, and said unto her mother, What shall I ask? And 25 she said, The head of John [3]the Baptist. And she came in straightway with haste unto the king, and asked, saying, I will that thou forthwith give me in a charger the head of John [3]the 26 Baptist. And the king was exceeding sorry; but for the sake of his oaths, and of them that sat at meat, he would not reject 27 her. And straightway the king sent forth a soldier of his guard, and commanded to bring his head: and he went and beheaded

[1] Gr. *demons*. [2] Some ancient authorities read *they*. [3] Gr. *the Baptizer*. [4] Many ancient authorities read *did many things*. [5] Or, *military tribunes* Gr. *chiliarchs*. [6] Some ancient authorities read *his daughter Herodias*. [7] Or, *it*

'And he went and beheaded him in the prison, and brought his head in a charger.' The death of John Baptist, a brass panel on the font of Siena cathedral, by Ghiberti

28 him in the prison, and brought his head in a charger, and gave
29 it to the damsel; and the damsel gave it to her mother. And
when his disciples heard *thereof*, they came and took up his
corpse, and laid it in a tomb.

The feeding of the 5,000 *and other miracles*

30 And the apostles gather themselves together unto Jesus; and
they told him all things, whatsoever they had done, and what-
31 soever they had taught. And he saith unto them, Come ye
yourselves apart into a desert place, and rest a while. For
there were many coming and going, and they had no leisure so
32 much as to eat. And they went away in the boat to a desert
33 place apart. And *the people* saw them going, and many knew
them, and they ran there together [1]on foot from all the cities,
34 and outwent them. And he came forth and saw a great
multitude, and he had compassion on them, because they were
as sheep not having a shepherd: and he began to teach them
35 many things. And when the day was now far spent, his disciples came unto him, and said, The place is desert, and the day
36 is now far spent: send them away, that they may go into the
country and villages round about, and buy themselves some-
37 what to eat. But he answered and said unto them, Give ye
them to eat. And they say unto him, Shall we go and buy two
38 hundred pennyworth of bread, and give them to eat? And he
saith unto them, How many loaves have ye? go *and* see. And
39 when they knew, they say, Five, and two fishes. And he commanded them that all should [2]sit down by companies upon the
40 green grass. And they sat down in ranks, by hundreds, and by
41 fifties. And he took the five loaves and the two fishes, and
looking up to heaven, he blessed, and brake the loaves; and he
gave to the disciples to set before them; and the two fishes
42 divided he among them all. And they did all eat, and were
43 filled. And they took up broken pieces, twelve basketfuls, and
44 also of the fishes. And they that ate the loaves were five
thousand men.

45 And straightway he constrained his disciples to enter into
the boat, and to go before *him* unto the other side to Bethsaida,
46 while he himself sendeth the multitude away. And after he had
taken leave of them, he departed into the mountain to pray.
47 And when even was come, the boat was in the midst of the sea,

[1] Or, *by land* [2] Gr. *recline*.

48 and he alone on the land. And seeing them distressed in rowing, for the wind was contrary unto them, about the fourth watch of the night he cometh unto them, walking on the sea; and he 49 would have passed by them: but they, when they saw him walking on the sea, supposed that it was an apparition, and 50 cried out: for they all saw him, and were troubled. But he straightway spake with them, and saith unto them, Be of good 51 cheer: it is I; be not afraid. And he went up unto them into the boat; and the wind ceased: and they were sore amazed in 52 themselves; for they understood not concerning the loaves, but their heart was hardened.

53 And when they had [1]crossed over, they came to the land unto 54 Gennesaret, and moored to the shore. And when they were come out of the boat, straightway *the people* knew him, and ran 55 round about that whole region, and began to carry about on 56 their beds those that were sick, where they heard he was. And wheresoever he entered, into villages, or into cities, or into the country, they laid the sick in the marketplaces, and besought him that they might touch if it were but the border of his garment: and as many as touched [2]him were made whole.

Teaching about cleanness

7 And there are gathered together unto him the Pharisees, and certain of the scribes, which had come from Jerusalem, 2 and had seen that some of his disciples ate their bread with 3 [3]defiled, that is, unwashen, hands. For the Pharisees, and all the Jews, except they wash their hands [4]diligently, eat not, 4 holding the tradition of the elders: and *when they come* from the marketplace, except they [5]wash themselves, they eat not: and many other things there be, which they have received to hold, 5 [6]washings of cups, and pots, and brasen vessels[7]. And the Pharisees and the scribes ask him, Why walk not thy disciples according to the tradition of the elders, but eat their bread with 6 [3]defiled hands? And he said unto them, Well did Isaiah prophesy of you hypocrites, as it is written,

This people honoureth me with their lips,
But their heart is far from me.

[1] Or, *crossed over to the land, they came unto Gennesaret* [2] Or, *it*
[3] Or, *common* [4] Or, *up to the elbow* Gr. *with the fist.* [5] Gr. *baptize.* Some ancient authorities read *sprinkle themselves.* [6] Gr. *baptizings.*
[7] Many ancient authorities add *and couches.*

7 But in vain do they worship me,
Teaching *as their* doctrines the precepts of men.

8 Ye leave the commandment of God, and hold fast the tradition 9 of men. And he said unto them, Full well do ye reject the com- 10 mandment of God, that ye may keep your tradition. For Moses said, Honour thy father and thy mother; and, He that 11 speaketh evil of father or mother, let him [1]die the death: but ye say, If a man shall say to his father or his mother, That wherewith thou mightest have been profited by me is Corban, 12 that is to say, Given *to God*; ye no longer suffer him to do aught 13 for his father or his mother; making void the word of God by your tradition, which ye have delivered: and many such like 14 things ye do. And he called to him the multitude again, and 15 said unto them, Hear me all of you, and understand: there is nothing from without the man, that going into him can defile him: but the things which proceed out of the man are those 17 that defile the man.[2] And when he was entered into the house from the multitude, his disciples asked of him the parable. 18 And he saith unto them, Are ye so without understanding also? Perceive ye not, that whatsoever from without goeth into the 19 man, *it* cannot defile him; because it goeth not into his heart, but into his belly, and goeth out into the draught? *This he* 20 *said*, making all meats clean. And he said, That which pro- 21 ceedeth out of the man, that defileth the man. For from within, out of the heart of men, [3]evil thoughts proceed, fornications, 22 thefts, murders, adulteries, covetings, wickednesses, deceit, 23 lasciviousness, an evil eye, railing, pride, foolishness: all these evil things proceed from within, and defile the man.

Miracles outside Galilee.

24 And from thence he arose, and went away into the borders of Tyre [4]and Sidon. And he entered into a house, and would 25 have no man know it: and he could not be hid. But straightway a woman, whose little daughter had an unclean spirit, having 26 heard of him, came and fell down at his feet. Now the woman was a [5]Greek, a Syrophœnician by race. And she besought him 27 that he would cast forth the [6]devil out of her daughter. And he said unto her, Let the children first be filled: for it is not meet

[1] Or, *surely die* [2] Many ancient authorities insert ver. 16. *If any man hath ears to hear, let him hear.* [3] Gr. *thoughts that are evil.* [4] Some ancient authorities omit *and Sidon.* [5] Or, *Gentile* [6] Gr. *demon.*

28 to take the children's [1]bread and cast it to the dogs. But she answered and saith unto him, Yea, Lord: even the dogs under 29 the table eat of the children's crumbs. And he said unto her, For this saying go thy way; the [2]devil is gone out of thy 30 daughter. And she went away unto her house, and found the child laid upon the bed, and the [2]devil gone out.

31 And again he went out from the borders of Tyre, and came through Sidon unto the sea of Galilee, through the midst of the 32 borders of Decapolis. And they bring unto him one that was deaf, and had an impediment in his speech; and they beseech 33 him to lay his hand upon him. And he took him aside from the multitude privately, and put his fingers into his ears, and he 34 spat, and touched his tongue; and looking up to heaven, he sighed, and saith unto him, Ephphatha, that is, Be opened. 35 And his ears were opened, and the bond of his tongue was 36 loosed, and he spake plain. And he charged them that they should tell no man: but the more he charged them, so much the 37 more a great deal they published it. And they were beyond measure astonished, saying, He hath done all things well: he maketh even the deaf to hear, and the dumb to speak.

8 In those days, when there was again a great multitude, and they had nothing to eat, he called unto him his 2 disciples, and saith unto them, I have compassion on the multitude, because they continue with me now three days, and have 3 nothing to eat: and if I send them away fasting to their home, they will faint in the way; and some of them are come from 4 far. And his disciples answered him, Whence shall one be able 5 to fill these men with [3]bread here in a desert place? And he asked them, How many loaves have ye? And they said, Seven. 6 And he commandeth the multitude to sit down on the ground: and he took the seven loaves, and having given thanks, he brake, and gave to his disciples, to set before them; and they 7 set them before the multitude. And they had a few small fishes: and having blessed them, he commanded to set these also 8 before them. And they did eat, and were filled: and they took 9 up, of broken pieces that remained over, seven baskets. And 10 they were about four thousand: and he sent them away. And straightway he entered into the boat with his disciples, and came into the parts of Dalmanutha.

11 And the Pharisees came forth, and began to question with

[1] Or, *loaf* [2] Gr. *demon.* [3] Gr. *loaves.*

12 him, seeking of him a sign from heaven, tempting him. And he sighed deeply in his spirit, and saith, Why doth this generation seek a sign? verily I say unto you, There shall no sign be given
13 unto this generation. And he left them, and again entering into *the boat* departed to the other side.

14 And they forgot to take bread; and they had not in the boat
15 with them more than one loaf. And he charged them, saying, Take heed, beware of the leaven of the Pharisees and the leaven
16 of Herod. And they reasoned one with another, [1]saying, [2]We
17 have no bread. And Jesus perceiving it saith unto them, Why reason ye, because ye have no bread? do ye not yet perceive,
18 neither understand? have ye your heart hardened? Having eyes, see ye not? and having ears, hear ye not? and do ye not
19 remember? When I brake the five loaves among the five thousand, how many [3]baskets full of broken pieces took ye up?
20 They say unto him, Twelve. And when the seven among the four thousand, how many [3]basketfuls of broken pieces took ye
21 up? And they say unto him, Seven. And he said unto them, Do ye not yet understand?

22 And they come unto Bethsaida. And they bring to him a
23 blind man, and beseech him to touch him. And he took hold of the blind man by the hand, and brought him out of the village; and when he had spit on his eyes, and laid his hands
24 upon him, he asked him, Seest thou aught? And he looked up,
25 and said, I see men; for I behold *them* as trees, walking. Then again he laid his hands upon his eyes; and he looked stedfastly,
26 and was restored, and saw all things clearly. And he sent him away to his home, saying, Do not even enter into the village.

THE WAY OF THE CROSS

First Prediction. Cross and Crown.

27 And Jesus went forth, and his disciples, into the villages of Cæsarea Philippi: and in the way he asked his disciples, saying
28 unto them, Who do men say that I am? And they told him, saying, John the Baptist: and others, Elijah; but others, One
29 of the prophets. And he asked them, But who say ye that I am? Peter answereth and saith unto him, Thou art the Christ.

[1] Some ancient authorities read *because they had no bread.* [2] Or, It is *because we have no bread.* [3] *Basket* in ver. 19 and 20 represents different Greek words.

30 And he charged them that they should tell no man of him. And 31 he began to teach them, that the Son of man must suffer many things, and be rejected by the elders, and the chief priests, and 32 the scribes, and be killed, and after three days rise again. And he spake the saying openly. And Peter took him, and began to 33 rebuke him. But he turning about, and seeing his disciples, rebuked Peter, and saith, Get thee behind me, Satan: for thou 34 mindest not the things of God, but the things of men. And he called unto him the multitude with his disciples, and said unto them, If any man would come after me, let him deny himself, 35 and take up his cross, and follow me. For whosoever would save his [1]life shall lose it; and whosoever shall lose his [1]life 36 for my sake and the gospel's shall save it. For what doth it 37 profit a man, to gain the whole world, and forfeit his [1]life? For 38 what should a man give in exchange for his [1]life? For whosoever shall be ashamed of me and of my words in this adulterous and sinful generation, the Son of man also shall be ashamed of him, when he cometh in the glory of his Father with the holy angels.

9 And he said unto them, Verily I say unto you, There be some here of them that stand *by*, which shall in no wise taste of death, till they see the kingdom of God come with power.

2 And after six days Jesus taketh with him Peter, and James, and John, and bringeth them up into a high mountain apart by 3 themselves: and he was transfigured before them: and his garments became glistering, exceeding white; so as no fuller on 4 earth can whiten them. And there appeared unto them Elijah 5 with Moses: and they were talking with Jesus. And Peter answereth and saith to Jesus, Rabbi, it is good for us to be here: and let us make three [2]tabernacles; one for thee, and one 6 for Moses, and one for Elijah. For he wist not what to answer; 7 for they became sore afraid. And there came a cloud overshadowing them: and there came a voice out of the cloud, This 8 is my beloved Son: hear ye him. And suddenly looking round about, they saw no one any more, save Jesus only with themselves.

9 And as they were coming down from the mountain, he charged them that they should tell no man what things they had seen, save when the Son of man should have risen again 10 from the dead. And they kept the saying, questioning among

[1] Or, *soul* [2] Or, *booths*

themselves what the rising again from the dead should mean.
11 And they asked him, saying, [1]The scribes say that Elijah must
12 first come. And he said unto them, Elijah indeed cometh first, and restoreth all things: and how is it written of the Son of man, that he should suffer many things and be set at nought?
13 But I say unto you, that Elijah is come, and they have also done unto him whatsoever they listed, even as it is written of him.

14 And when they came to the disciples, they saw a great multi-
15 tude about them, and scribes questioning with them. And straightway all the multitude, when they saw him, were greatly
16 amazed, and running to him saluted him. And he asked them,
17 What question ye with them? And one of the multitude answered him, [2]Master, I brought unto thee my son, which hath
18 a dumb spirit; and wheresoever it taketh him, it [3]dasheth him down: and he foameth, and grindeth his teeth, and pineth away: and I spake to thy disciples that they should cast it
19 out; and they were not able. And he answereth them and saith, O faithless generation, how long shall I be with you? how
20 long shall I bear with you? bring him unto me. And they brought him unto him: and when he saw him, straightway the spirit [4]tare him grievously; and he fell on the ground, and
21 wallowed foaming. And he asked his father, How long time is it since this hath come unto him? And he said, From a child.
22 And oft-times it hath cast him both into the fire and into the waters, to destroy him: but if thou canst do anything, have
23 compassion on us, and help us. And Jesus said unto him, If thou canst! All things are possible to him that believeth.
24 Straightway the father of the child cried out, and said[5], I
25 believe; help thou mine unbelief. And when Jesus saw that a multitude came running together, he rebuked the unclean spirit, saying unto him, Thou dumb and deaf spirit, I command
26 thee, come out of him, and enter no more into him. And having cried out, and [4]torn him much, he came out: and *the child* became as one dead; insomuch that the more part said, He is
27 dead. But Jesus took him by the hand, and raised him up;
28 and he arose. And when he was come into the house, his disciples asked him privately, [6]*saying*, We could not cast it out.

[1] Or, How is it *that the scribes say . . . come?* [2] Or, *Teacher* [3] Or, *rendeth him* [4] Or, *convulsed* [5] Many ancient authorities add *with tears.* [6] Or, How is it *that we could not cast it out?*

THE TRANSFIGURATION

Below, the three apostles; above, Elijah and Moses. From a twelfth-century mosaic at Palermo

29 And he said unto them, This kind can come out by nothing, save by prayer[1].

Second Prediction. Qualities in the Kingdom.

30 And they went forth from thence, and passed through Galilee; and he would not that any man should know it. 31 For he taught his disciples, and said unto them, The Son of man is delivered up into the hands of men, and they shall kill him; 32 And when he is killed, after three days he shall rise again. But they understood not the saying, and were afraid to ask him.

33 And they came to Capernaum: and when he was in the house 34 he asked them, What were ye reasoning in the way? But they held their peace: for they had disputed one with another in the 35 way, who *was* the [2]greatest. And he sat down, and called the twelve; and he saith unto them, If any man would be first, 36 he shall be last of all, and minister of all. And he took a little child, and set him in the midst of them: and taking him in his 37 arms, he said unto them, Whosoever shall receive one of such little children in my name, receiveth me: and whosoever receiveth me, receiveth not me, but him that sent me.

38 John said unto him, [3]Master, we saw one casting out [4]devils in thy name: and we forbade him, because he followed not us. 39 But Jesus said, Forbid him not: for there is no man which shall do a [5]mighty work in my name, and be able quickly to speak 40 evil of me. For he that is not against us is for us. For whoso- 41 ever shall give you a cup of water to drink, [6]because ye are Christ's, verily I say unto you, he shall in no wise lose his 42 reward. And whosoever shall cause one of these little ones that believe [7]on me to stumble, it were better for him if [8]a great millstone were hanged about his neck, and he were cast into 43 the sea. And if thy hand cause thee to stumble, cut it off: it is good for thee to enter into life maimed, rather than having thy 45 two hands to go into [9]hell, into the unquenchable fire.[10] And if thy foot cause thee to stumble, cut it off: it is good for thee to enter into life halt, rather than having thy two feet to be 47 cast into [9]hell. And if thine eye cause thee to stumble, cast it out: it is good for thee to enter into the kingdom of God with

[1] Many ancient authorities add *and fasting*. [2] Gr. *greater*. [3] Or, *Teacher* [4] Gr. *demons*. [5] Gr. *power*. [6] Gr. *in name that ye are*. [7] Many ancient authorities omit *on me*. [8] Gr. *a millstone turned by an ass*. [9] Gr. *Gehenna*. [10] Ver. 44 and 46 (which are identical with ver. 48) are omitted by the best ancient authorities.

one eye, rather than having two eyes to be cast into [1]hell;
48 where their worm dieth not, and the fire is not quenched. For
49 every one shall be salted with fire.[2] Salt is good: but if the salt
50 have lost its saltness, wherewith will ye season it? Have salt
in yourselves, and be at peace one with another.

Camels grazing in the Hauran, east of the Jordan

10 And he arose from thence, and cometh into the borders of Judæa and beyond Jordan: and multitudes come together unto him again; and, as he was wont, he taught them
2 again. And there came unto him Pharisees, and asked him, Is
3 it lawful for a man to put away *his* wife? tempting him. And
he answered and said unto them, What did Moses command
4 you? And they said, Moses suffered to write a bill of divorce-
5 ment, and to put her away. But Jesus said unto them, For
6 your hardness of heart he wrote you this commandment. But
from the beginning of the creation, Male and female made he
7 them. For this cause shall a man leave his father and mother,

[1] Gr. *Gehenna* [2] Many ancient authorities add *and every sacrifice shall be salted with salt.*

8 [1]and shall cleave to his wife; and the twain shall become one 9 flesh: so that they are no more twain, but one flesh. What therefore God hath joined together, let not man put asunder. 10 And in the house the disciples asked him again of this matter. 11 And he saith unto them, Whosoever shall put away his wife, 12 and marry another, committeth adultery against her: and if she herself shall put away her husband, and marry another, she committeth adultery.

13 And they brought unto him little children, that he should 14 touch them: and the disciples rebuked them. But when Jesus saw it, he was moved with indignation, and said unto them, Suffer the little children to come unto me; forbid them not: 15 for of such is the kingdom of God. Verily I say unto you, Whosoever shall not receive the kingdom of God as a little 16 child, he shall in no wise enter therein. And he took them in his arms, and blessed them, laying his hands upon them.

17 And as he was going forth [2]into the way, there ran one to him, and kneeled to him, and asked him, Good [3]Master, what 18 shall I do that I may inherit eternal life? And Jesus said unto unto him, Why callest thou me good? none is good save one, 19 *even* God. Thou knowest the commandments, Do not kill, Do not commit adultery, Do not steal, Do not bear false witness, 20 Do not defraud, Honour thy father and mother. And he said unto him, [3]Master, all these things have I observed from my 21 youth. And Jesus looking upon him loved him, and said unto him, One thing thou lackest: go, sell whatsoever thou hast, and give to the poor, and thou shalt have treasure in heaven: and 22 come, follow me. But his countenance fell at the saying, and he went away sorrowful: for he was one that had great possessions.

23 And Jesus looked round about, and saith unto his disciples, How hardly shall they that have riches enter into the kingdom 24 of God! And the disciples were amazed at his words. But Jesus answereth again, and saith unto them, Children, how hard is it [4]for them that trust in riches to enter into the kingdom of 25 God! It is easier for a camel to go through a needle's eye, than 26 for a rich man to enter into the kingdom of God. And they were astonished exceedingly, saying [5]unto him, Then who can be

[1] Some ancient authorities omit *and shall cleave to his wife* [2] Or, *on his way* [3] Or, *Teacher* [4] Some ancient authorities omit *for them that trust in riches* [5] Many ancient authorities read *among themselves*.

27 saved? Jesus looking upon them saith, With men it is impossible, but not with God: for all things are possible with God.
28 Peter began to say unto him, Lo, we have left all, and have
29 followed thee. Jesus said, Verily I say unto you, There is no man that hath left house, or brethren, or sisters, or mother, or father, or children, or lands, for my sake, and for the gospel's
30 sake, but he shall receive a hundredfold now in this time, houses, and brethren, and sisters, and mothers, and children, and lands,
31 with persecutions; and in the [1]world to come eternal life. But many *that are* first shall be last; and the last first.

Third Prediction. Rank in the Kingdom.

32 And they were in the way, going up to Jerusalem; and Jesus was going before them: and they were amazed; [2]and they that followed were afraid. And he took again the twelve, and began to tell them the things that were to happen unto him, *saying*,
33 Behold, we go up to Jerusalem; and the Son of man shall be delivered unto the chief priests and the scribes; and they shall condemn him to death, and shall deliver him unto the Gentiles:
34 and they shall mock him, and shall spit upon him, and shall scourge him, and shall kill him; and after three days he shall rise again.

35 And there come near unto him James and John, the sons of Zebedee, saying unto him, [3]Master, we would that thou
36 shouldest do for us whatsoever we shall ask of thee. And he said unto them, What would ye that I should do for you?
37 And they said unto him, Grant unto us that we may sit, one
38 on thy right hand, and one on *thy* left hand, in thy glory. But Jesus said unto them, Ye know not what ye ask. Are ye able to drink the cup that I drink? or to be baptized with the
39 baptism that I am baptized with? And they said unto him, We are able. And Jesus said unto them, The cup that I drink ye shall drink; and with the baptism that I am baptized withal
40 shall ye be baptized: but to sit on my right hand or on *my* left hand is not mine to give: but *it is for them* for whom it hath
41 been prepared. And when the ten heard it, they began to be
42 moved with indignation concerning James and John. And Jesus called them to him, and saith unto them, Ye know that they which are accounted to rule over the Gentiles lord it over
43 them; and their great ones exercise authority over them. But

[1] Or, *age* [2] Or, *but some as they followed were afraid* [3] Or, *Teacher*

it is not so among you: but whosoever would become great
44 among you shall be your [1]minister: and whosoever would be
45 first among you, shall be [2]servant of all. For verily the Son of man came not to be ministered unto, but to minister, and to give his life a ransom for many.

THE MINISTRY IN JERUSALEM

The Appeal to Jerusalem

The approach.

46 And they come to Jericho: and as he went out from Jericho, with his disciples and a great multitude, the son of Timæus,
47 Bartimæus, a blind beggar, was sitting by the way side. And when he heard that it was Jesus of Nazareth, he began to cry
48 out, and say, Jesus, thou son of David, have mercy on me. And many rebuked him, that he should hold his peace: but he cried out the more a great deal, Thou son of David, have mercy upon
49 me. And Jesus stood still, and said, Call ye him. And they call the blind man, saying unto him, Be of good cheer: rise, he
50 calleth thee. And he, casting away his garment, sprang up, and
51 came to Jesus. And Jesus answered him, and said, What wilt thou that I should do unto thee? And the blind man said unto
52 him, Rabboni, that I may receive my sight. And Jesus said unto him, Go thy way; thy faith hath [3]made thee whole. And straightway he received his sight, and followed him in the way.

The Entry and the Challenge.

11 And when they draw nigh unto Jerusalem, unto Bethphage and Bethany, at the mount of Olives, he sendeth
2 two of his disciples, and saith unto them, Go your way into the village that is over against you: and straightway as ye enter into it, ye shall find a colt tied, whereon no man ever yet sat;
3 loose him, and bring him. And if any one say unto you, Why do ye this? say ye, The Lord hath need of him; and straight-
4 way he [4]will send him [5]back hither. And they went away, and found a colt tied at the door without in the open street; and
5 they loose him. And certain of them that stood there said unto
6 them, What do ye, loosing the colt? And they said unto them
7 even as Jesus had said: and they let them go. And they bring

[1] Or, *servant* [2] Gr. *bondservant.* [3] Or, *saved thee* [4] Gr. *sendeth.*
[5] Or, *again*

THE ENTRY INTO JERUSALEM
An ivory panel of the eleventh century

'And He entered into Jerusalem.' One of the gates of the city (the Damascus Gate) to-day

the colt unto Jesus, and cast on him their garments; and he sat
8 upon him. And many spread their garments upon the way;
9 and others [1]branches, which they had cut from the fields. And
they that went before, and they that followed, cried, Hosanna;
10 Blessed *is* he that cometh in the name of the Lord: Blessed *is*
the kingdom that cometh, *the kingdom* of our father David:
Hosanna in the highest.

11 And he entered into Jerusalem, into the temple; and when
he had looked round about upon all things, it being now eventide, he went out unto Bethany with the twelve.

12 And on the morrow, when they were come out from Bethany,
13 he hungered. And seeing a fig tree afar off having leaves, he
came, if haply he might find anything thereon: and when he
came to it, he found nothing but leaves; for it was not the
14 season of figs. And he answered and said unto it, No man eat
fruit from thee henceforward for ever. And his disciples
heard it.

15 And they come to Jerusalem: and he entered into the temple,
and began to cast out them that sold and them that bought in
the temple, and overthrew the tables of the money-changers,
16 and the seats of them that sold the doves; and he would not
suffer that any man should carry a vessel through the temple.
17 And he taught, and said unto them, Is it not written, My house
shall be called a house of prayer for all the nations? but ye have
18 made it a den of robbers. And the chief priests and the scribes
heard it, and sought how they might destroy him: for they
feared him, for all the multitude was astonished at his teaching.

19 And [2]every evening [3]he went forth out of the city.

20 And as they passed by in the morning, they saw the fig tree
21 withered away from the roots. And Peter calling to remembrance saith unto him, Rabbi, behold, the fig tree which thou
22 cursedst is withered away. And Jesus answering saith unto
23 them, Have faith in God. Verily I say unto you, Whosoever
shall say unto this mountain, Be thou taken up and cast into
the sea; and shall not doubt in his heart, but shall believe that
24 what he saith cometh to pass; he shall have it. Therefore I say
unto you, All things whatsoever ye pray and ask for, believe
25 that ye have received them, and ye shall have them. And
whensoever ye stand praying, forgive, if ye have aught against

[1] Gr. *layers of leaves.* [2] Gr. *whenever evening came.* [3] Some ancient authorities read *they*.

any one; that your Father also which is in heaven may forgive you your trespasses.[1]

27 And they come again to Jerusalem: and as he was walking in the temple, there come to him the chief priests, and the 28 scribes, and the elders; and they said unto him, By what authority doest thou these things? or who gave thee this au- 29 thority to do these things? And Jesus said unto them, I will ask of you one [2]question, and answer me, and I will tell you 30 by what authority I do these things. The baptism of John, was 31 it from heaven, or from men? answer me. And they reasoned with themselves, saying, If we shall say, From heaven; he will 32 say, Why then did ye not believe him? [3]But should we say, From men—they feared the people: [4]for all verily held John 33 to be a prophet. And they answered Jesus and say, We know not. And Jesus saith unto them, Neither tell I you by what authority I do these things.

12 And he began to speak unto them in parables. A man planted a vineyard, and set a hedge about it, and digged a pit for the winepress, and built a tower, and let it out 2 to husbandmen, and went into another country. And at the season he sent to the husbandmen a [5]servant, that he might 3 receive from the husbandmen of the fruits of the vineyard. And 4 they took him, and beat him, and sent him away empty. And again he sent unto them another [5]servant; and him they 5 wounded in the head, and handled shamefully. And he sent another; and him they killed: and many others; beating some, 6 and killing some. He had yet one, a beloved son: he sent him 7 last unto them, saying, They will reverence my son. But those husbandmen said among themselves, This is the heir; come, let 8 us kill him, and the inheritance shall be ours. And they took him, and killed him, and cast him forth out of the vineyard. 9 What therefore will the lord of the vineyard do? he will come and destroy the husbandmen, and will give the vineyard unto 10 others. Have ye not read even this scripture;

The stone which the builders rejected,
The same was made the head of the corner:
11 This was from the Lord,
And it is marvellous in our eyes?

[1] Many ancient authorities add ver. 26 *But if ye do not forgive, neither will your Father which is in heaven forgive your trespasses.* [2] Gr. *word.* [3] Or, *But shall we say, From men?* [4] Or, *for all held John to be a prophet indeed.* [5] Gr. *bondservant.*

12 And they sought to lay hold on him; and they feared the multitude; for they perceived that he spake the parable against them: and they left him, and went away.

Counter-Challenges.

13 And they send unto him certain of the Pharisees and of the
14 Herodians, that they might catch him in talk. And when they were come, they say unto him, [1]Master, we know that thou art true, and carest not for any one: for thou regardest not the person of men, but of a truth teachest the way of God: Is it
15 lawful to give tribute unto Cæsar, or not? Shall we give, or shall we not give? But he, knowing their hypocrisy, said unto them, Why tempt ye me? bring me a penny, that I may see it.
16 And they brought it. And he saith unto them, Whose is this image and superscription? And they said unto him, Cæsar's.
17 And Jesus said unto them, Render unto Cæsar the things that are Cæsar's, and unto God the things that are God's. And they marvelled greatly at him.
18 And there come unto him Sadducees, which say that there
19 is no resurrection; and they asked him, saying, [1]Master, Moses wrote unto us, If a man's brother die, and leave a wife behind him, and leave no child, that his brother should take his wife,
20 and raise up seed unto his brother. There were seven brethren:
21 and the first took a wife, and dying left no seed; and the second took her, and died, leaving no seed behind him; and the
22 third likewise: and the seven left no seed. Last of all the
23 woman also died. In the resurrection whose wife shall she be
24 of them? for the seven had her to wife. Jesus said unto them, Is it not for this cause that ye err, that ye know not the
25 scriptures, nor the power of God? For when they shall rise from the dead, they neither marry, nor are given in marriage;
26 but are as angels in heaven. But as touching the dead, that they are raised; have ye not read in the book of Moses, in *the place concerning* the Bush, how God spake unto him, saying, I *am* the God of Abraham, and the God of Isaac, and the God of
27 Jacob? He is not the God of the dead, but of the living: ye do greatly err.
28 And one of the scribes came, and heard them questioning together, and knowing that he had answered them well, asked
29 him, What commandment is the first of all? Jesus answered,

[1] Or, *Teacher*

The first is, Hear, O Israel; [1]The Lord our God, the Lord is one:
30 and thou shalt love the Lord thy God [2]with all thy heart, and [3]with all thy soul, and [2]with all thy mind, and [2]with all thy
31 strength. The second is this, Thou shalt love thy neighbour as thyself. There is none other commandment greater than these.

'Salutations in the marketplaces.' The bazaar in the courtyard of the Holy Sepulchre

32 And the scribe said unto him, Of a truth, [3]Master, thou hast
33 well said that he is one; and there is none other but he: and to love him with all the heart, and with all the understanding, and with all the strength, and to love his neighbour as himself,
34 is much more than all whole burnt offerings and sacrifices. And when Jesus saw that he answered discreetly, he said unto him, Thou art not far from the kingdom of God. And no man after that durst ask him any question.

35 And Jesus answered and said, as he taught in the temple,

[1] Or, *The Lord* is *our God*; *the Lord is one* [2] Gr. *from*. [3] Or, *Teacher*

36 How say the scribes that the Christ is the son of David? David himself said in the Holy Spirit,

The Lord said unto my Lord,
Sit thou on my right hand,
Till I make thine enemies [1]the footstool of thy feet.

37 David himself calleth him Lord; and whence is he his son? And [2]the common people heard him gladly.

38 And in his teaching he said, Beware of the scribes, which desire to walk in long robes, and *to have* salutations in the 39 marketplaces, and chief seats in the synagogues, and chief 40 places at feasts: they which devour widows' houses, [3]and for a pretence make long prayers; these shall receive greater condemnation.

41 And he sat down over against the treasury, and beheld how the multitude cast [4]money into the treasury: and many that 42 were rich cast in much. And there came [5]a poor widow, and 43 she cast in two mites, which make a farthing. And he called unto him his disciples, and said unto them, Verily I say unto you, This poor widow cast in more than all they which are 44 casting into the treasury: for they all did cast in of their superfluity; but she of her want did cast in all that she had, *even* all her living.

The Doom.

13 And as he went forth out of the temple, one of his disciples saith unto him, [6]Master, behold, what manner 2 of stones and what manner of buildings! And Jesus said unto him, Seest thou these great buildings? there shall not be left here one stone upon another, which shall not be thrown down.

3 And as he sat on the mount of Olives over against the temple, Peter and James and John and Andrew asked him 4 privately, Tell us, when shall these things be? and what *shall be* the sign when these things are all about to be accomplished? 5 And Jesus began to say unto them, Take heed that no man 6 lead you astray. Many shall come in my name, saying, I am *he*; 7 and shall lead many astray. And when ye shall hear of wars and rumours of wars, be not troubled: *these things* must needs 8 come to pass; but the end is not yet. For nation shall rise

[1] Some ancient authorities read *underneath thy feet* [2] Or, *the great multitude* [3] Or, *even while for a pretence they make* [4] Gr. *brass.* [5] Gr. *one.* [6] Or, *Teacher*

'Let him that is on the housetop not go down.' A housetop at dawn at Ramallah, near Jerusalem

against nation, and kingdom against kingdom: there shall be earthquakes in divers places; there shall be famines: these things are the beginning of travail.

9 But take ye heed to yourselves: for they shall deliver you up to councils; and in synagogues shall ye be beaten; and before governors and kings shall ye stand for my sake, for a testimony 10 unto them. And the gospel must first be preached unto all the 11 nations. And when they lead you *to judgement*, and deliver you up, be not anxious beforehand what ye shall speak: but whatsoever shall be given you in that hour, that speak ye: for it 12 is not ye that speak, but the Holy Ghost. And brother shall deliver up brother to death, and the father his child; and children shall rise up against parents, and [1]cause them to be put 13 to death. And ye shall be hated of all men for my name's sake: but he that endureth to the end, the same shall be saved.

14 But when ye see the abomination of desolation standing where he ought not (let him that readeth understand), then let 15 them that are in Judæa flee unto the mountains: and let him that is on the housetop not go down, nor enter in, to take any-16 thing out of his house: and let him that is in the field not 17 return back to take his cloke. But woe unto them that are with 18 child and to them that give suck in those days! And pray ye 19 that it be not in the winter. For those days shall be tribulation, such as there hath not been the like from the beginning of the creation which God created until now, and never shall be. 20 And except the Lord had shortened the days, no flesh would have been saved: but for the elect's sake, whom he chose, he 21 shortened the days. And then if any man shall say unto you, 22 Lo, here is the Christ; or, Lo, there; believe [2]*it* not: for there shall arise false Christs and false prophets, and shall shew signs 23 and wonders, that they may lead astray, if possible, the elect. But take ye heed: behold, I have told you all things beforehand.

24 But in those days, after that tribulation, the sun shall be 25 darkened, and the moon shall not give her light, and the stars shall be falling from heaven, and the powers that are in the 26 heavens shall be shaken. And then shall they see the Son of 27 man coming in clouds with great power and glory. And then shall he send forth the angels, and shall gather together his elect from the four winds, from the uttermost part of the earth to the uttermost part of heaven.

[1] Or, *put them to death* [2] Or, *him*

28 Now from the fig tree learn her parable: when her branch is now become tender, and putteth forth its leaves, ye know that 29 the summer is nigh; even so ye also, when ye see these things coming to pass, know ye that [1]he is nigh, *even* at the doors. 30 Verily I say unto you, This generation shall not pass away, 31 until all these things be accomplished. Heaven and earth shall 32 pass away: but my words shall not pass away. But of that day or that hour knoweth no one, not even the angels in heaven, 33 neither the Son, but the Father. Take ye heed, watch [2]and 34 pray: for ye know not when the time is. *It is* as *when* a man, sojourning in another country, having left his house, and given authority to his [3]servants, to each one his work, commanded 35 also the porter to watch. Watch therefore: for ye know not when the lord of the house cometh, whether at even, or at 36 midnight, or at cockcrowing, or in the morning; lest coming 37 suddenly he find you sleeping. And what I say unto you I say unto all, Watch.

The Passion and the Resurrection

The last night.

14 Now after two days was *the feast of* the passover and the unleavened bread: and the chief priests and the scribes sought how they might take him with subtilty, and 2 kill him: for they said, Not during the feast, lest haply there shall be a tumult of the people.

3 And while he was in Bethany in the house of Simon the leper, as he sat at meat, there came a woman having [4]an alabaster cruse of ointment of [5]spikenard very costly; *and* she 4 brake the cruse, and poured it over his head. But there were some that had indignation among themselves, *saying*, To what 5 purpose hath this waste of the ointment been made? For this ointment might have been sold for above three hundred pence, 6 and given to the poor. And they murmured against her. But Jesus said, Let her alone; why trouble ye her? she hath wrought 7 a good work on me. For ye have the poor always with you, and whensoever ye will ye can do them good: but me ye have not 8 always. She hath done what she could: she hath anointed my

[1] Or, *it* [2] Some ancient authorities omit *and pray*. [3] Gr. *bond-servants*. [4] Or, *a flask* [5] Gr. *pistic nard*, pistic being perhaps a local name. Others take it to mean *genuine*; others, *liquid*.

9 body aforehand for the burying. And verily I say unto you, Wheresoever the gospel shall be preached throughout the whole world, that also which this woman hath done shall be spoken of for a memorial of her.

10 And Judas Iscariot, [1]he that was one of the twelve, went away unto the chief priests, that he might deliver him unto 11 them. And they, when they heard it, were glad, and promised to give him money. And he sought how he might conveniently deliver him *unto them.*

12 And on the first day of unleavened bread, when they sacrificed the passover, his disciples say unto him, Where wilt thou that we go and make ready that thou mayest eat the passover? 13 And he sendeth two of his disciples, and saith unto them, Go into the city, and there shall meet you a man bearing a pitcher 14 of water: follow him; and wheresoever he shall enter in, say to the goodman of the house, The [2]Master saith, Where is my guest-chamber, where I shall eat the passover with my dis- 15 ciples? And he will himself shew you a large upper room fur- 16 nished *and* ready: and there make ready for us. And the disciples went forth, and came into the city, and found as he had said unto them: and they made ready the passover.

17 And when it was evening he cometh with the twelve. 18 And as they [3]sat and were eating, Jesus said, Verily I say unto you, One of you shall betray me, *even* he that eateth with me. 19 They began to be sorrowful, and to say unto him one by one, Is 20 it I? And he said unto them, *It is* one of the twelve, he that 21 dippeth with me in the dish. For the Son of man goeth, even as it is written of him: but woe unto that man through whom the Son of man is betrayed! good were it [4]for that man if he had not been born.

22 And as they were eating, he took [5]bread, and when he had blessed, he brake it, and gave to them, and said, Take ye: this 23 is my body. And he took a cup, and when he had given thanks, 24 he gave to them: and they all drank of it. And he said unto them, This is my blood of [6]the [7]covenant, which is shed for 25 many. Verily I say unto you, I will no more drink of the fruit of the vine, until that day when I drink it new in the kingdom of God.

[1] Gr. *the one of the twelve.* [2] Or, *Teacher* [3] Gr. *reclined.* [4] Gr. *for him if that man.* [5] Or, *a loaf* [6] Or, *the testament* [7] Some ancient authorities insert *new.*

26 And when they had sung a hymn, they went out unto the mount of Olives.

27 And Jesus saith unto them, All ye shall be [1]offended: for it is written, I will smite the shepherd, and the sheep shall be 28 scattered abroad. Howbeit, after I am raised up, I will go 29 before you into Galilee. But Peter said unto him, Although all

'I will smite the shepherd and the sheep shall be scattered abroad.' Shepherds with their flocks of sheep and goats passing one of Solomon's Pools near Jerusalem. The shepherds are armed

30 shall be [1]offended, yet will not I. And Jesus saith unto him, Verily I say unto thee, that thou to-day, *even* this night, before 31 the cock crow twice, shalt deny me thrice. But he spake exceeding vehemently, If I must die with thee, I will not deny thee. And in like manner also said they all.

32 And they come unto [2]a place which was named Gethsemane: 33 and he saith unto his disciples, Sit ye here, while I pray. And he taketh with him Peter and James and John, and began to 34 be greatly amazed, and sore troubled. And he said unto them,

[1] Gr. *caused to stumble.*
[2] Gr. *an enclosed piece of ground.*

My soul is exceeding sorrowful even unto death: abide ye here,
35 and watch. And he went forward a little, and fell on the ground, and prayed that, if it were possible, the hour might pass away
36 from him. And he said, Abba, Father, all things are possible unto thee; remove this cup from me: howbeit not what I will,
37 but what thou wilt. And he cometh, and findeth them sleeping, and saith unto Peter, Simon, sleepest thou? couldest thou not
38 watch one hour? [1]Watch and pray, that ye enter not into temptation: the spirit indeed is willing, but the flesh is weak.
39 And again he went away, and prayed, saying the same words.
40 And again he came, and found them sleeping, for their eyes were very heavy; and they wist not what to answer him.
41 And he cometh the third time, and saith unto them, Sleep on now, and take your rest: it is enough; the hour is come; behold, the Son of man is betrayed into the hands of sinners.
42 Arise, let us be going: behold, he that betrayeth me is at hand.

43 And straightway, while he yet spake, cometh Judas, one of the twelve, and with him a multitude with swords and staves,
44 from the chief priests and the scribes and the elders. Now he that betrayed him had given them a token, saying, Whomsoever I shall kiss, that is he; take him, and lead him away safely.
45 And when he was come, straightway he came to him, and saith,
46 Rabbi; and [2]kissed him. And they laid hands on him, and took
47 him. But a certain one of them that stood by drew his sword, and smote the [3]servant of the high priest, and struck off his ear.
48 And Jesus answered and said unto them, Are ye come out, as
49 against a robber, with swords and staves to seize me? I was daily with you in the temple teaching, and ye took me not:
50 but *this is done* that the scriptures might be fulfilled. And they all left him, and fled.

51 And a certain young man followed with him, having a linen cloth cast about him, over *his* naked *body*: and they lay hold on
52 him; but he left the linen cloth, and fled naked.

53 And they led Jesus away to the high priest: and there come together with him all the chief priests and the elders and the
54 scribes. And Peter had followed him afar off, even within, into the court of the high priest; and he was sitting with the officers,
55 and warming himself in the light *of the fire*. Now the chief priests and the whole council sought witness against Jesus to

[1] Or, *Watch ye, and pray that ye enter not* [2] Gr. *kissed him much*.
[3] Gr. *bondservant*.

56 put him to death; and found it not. For many bare false witness against him, and their witness agreed not together.
57 And there stood up certain, and bare false witness against him,
58 saying, We heard him say, I will destroy this [1]temple that is made with hands, and in three days I will build another made
59 without hands. And not even so did their witness agree to-
60 gether. And the high priest stood up in the midst, and asked Jesus, saying, Answerest thou nothing? what is it which these
61 witness against thee? But he held his peace, and answered nothing. Again the high priest asked him, and saith unto
62 him, Art thou the Christ, the Son of the Blessed? And Jesus said, I am: and ye shall see the Son of man sitting at the right
63 hand of power, and coming with the clouds of heaven. And the high priest rent his clothes, and saith, What further need
64 have we of witnesses? Ye have heard the blasphemy: what think ye? And they all condemned him to be [2]worthy of death.
65 And some began to spit on him, and to cover his face, and to buffet him, and to say unto him, Prophesy: and the officers received him with [3]blows of their hands.

66 And as Peter was beneath in the court, there cometh one
67 of the maids of the high priest; and seeing Peter warming himself, she looked upon him, and saith, Thou also wast with the
68 Nazarene, *even* Jesus. But he denied, saying, [4]I neither know, nor understand what thou sayest: and he went out into the
69 [5]porch; [6]and the cock crew. And the maid saw him, and began
70 again to say to them that stood by, This is *one* of them. But he again denied it. And after a little while again they that stood by said to Peter, Of a truth thou art *one* of them; for
71 thou art a Galilæan. But he began to curse, and to swear, I
72 know not this man of whom ye speak. And straightway the second time the cock crew. And Peter called to mind the word, how that Jesus said unto him, Before the cock crow twice, thou shalt deny me thrice. [7]And when he thought thereon, he wept.

The Crucifixion.

15 And straightway in the morning the chief priests with the elders and scribes, and the whole council, held a

[1] Or, *sanctuary* [2] Gr. *liable to.* [3] Or, *strokes of rods* [4] Or, *I neither know, nor understand: thou, what sayest thou?* [5] Gr. *forecourt.* [6] Many ancient authorities omit *and the cock crew.* [7] Or, *And he began to weep.*

consultation, and bound Jesus, and carried him away, and
2 delivered him up to Pilate. And Pilate asked him, Art thou
the King of the Jews? And he answering saith unto him, Thou
3 sayest. And the chief priests accused him of many things.
4 And Pilate again asked him, saying, Answerest thou nothing?
5 behold how many things they accuse thee of. But Jesus no
more answered anything; insomuch that Pilate marvelled.

6 Now at [1]the feast he used to release unto them one prisoner,
7 whom they asked of him. And there was one called Barabbas,
lying bound with them that had made insurrection, men who
8 in the insurrection had committed murder. And the multitude
went up and began to ask him *to do* as he was wont to do unto
9 them. And Pilate answered them, saying, Will ye that I release
10 unto you the King of the Jews? For he perceived that for envy
11 the chief priests had delivered him up. But the chief priests
stirred up the multitude, that he should rather release Barabbas
12 unto them. And Pilate again answered and said unto them,
What then shall I do unto him whom ye call the King of the
13 Jews? And they cried out again, Crucify him. And Pilate said
14 unto them, Why, what evil hath he done? But they cried out
15 exceedingly, Crucify him. And Pilate, wishing to content the
multitude, released unto them Barabbas, and delivered Jesus,
when he had scourged him, to be crucified.

16 And the soldiers led him away within the court, which is the
17 [2]Prætorium; and they call together the whole [3]band. And they
clothe him with purple, and plaiting a crown of thorns, they
18 put it on him; and they began to salute him, Hail, King of the
19 Jews! And they smote his head with a reed, and did spit upon
20 him, and bowing their knees worshipped him. And when they
had mocked him, they took off from him the purple, and put
on him his garments. And they lead him out to crucify him.

21 And they [4]compel one passing by, Simon of Cyrene, coming
from the country, the father of Alexander and Rufus, to go
22 *with them*, that he might bear his cross. And they bring him
unto the place Golgotha, which is, being interpreted, The place
23 of a skull. And they offered him wine mingled with myrrh: but
24 he received it not. And they crucify him, and part his garments
among them, casting lots upon them, what each should take.
25 And it was the third hour, and they crucified him. And the
26 superscription of his accusation was written over, THE KING OF

[1] Or, *a feast* [2] Or, *palace* [3] Or, *cohort* [4] Gr. *impress*.

Courtyard of the Church of the Holy Sepulchre. The traditional site of Golgotha is included in this church

27 THE JEWS. And with him they crucify two robbers; one on his 29 right hand, and one on his left.[1] And they that passed by railed on him, wagging their heads, and saying, Ha! thou that 30 destroyest the [2]temple, and buildest it in three days, save 31 thyself, and come down from the cross. In like manner also the chief priests mocking *him* among themselves with the scribes 32 said, He saved others; [3]himself he cannot save. Let the Christ, the King of Israel, now come down from the cross, that we may see and believe. And they that were crucified with him reproached him.

33 And when the sixth hour was come, there was darkness over 34 the whole [4]land until the ninth hour. And at the ninth hour Jesus cried with a loud voice, Eloi, Eloi, lama sabachthani? which is, being interpreted, My God, my God, [5]why hast thou 35 forsaken me? And some of them that stood by, when they 36 heard it, said, Behold, he calleth Elijah. And one ran, and filling a sponge full of vinegar, put it on a reed, and gave him to drink, saying, Let be; let us see whether Elijah cometh to 37 take him down. And Jesus uttered a loud voice, and gave up 38 the ghost. And the veil of the [2]temple was rent in twain from 39 the top to the bottom. And when the centurion, which stood by over against him, saw that he [6]so gave up the ghost, he said, 40 Truly this man was [7]the Son of God. And there were also women beholding from afar: among whom *were* both Mary Magdalene, and Mary the mother of James the [8]less and of 41 Joses, and Salome; who, when he was in Galilee, followed him, and ministered unto him; and many other women which came up with him unto Jerusalem.

The Burial and the empty tomb.

42 And when even was now come, because it was the Prepara- 43 tion, that is, the day before the sabbath, there came Joseph of Arimathæa, a councillor of honourable estate, who also himself was looking for the kingdom of God; and he boldly went in 44 unto Pilate, and asked for the body of Jesus. And Pilate marvelled if he were already dead: and calling unto him the centurion, he asked him whether he [9]had been any while dead.

[1] Many ancient authorities insert ver. 28. *And the scripture was fulfilled, which saith, And he was reckoned with transgressors.* [2] Or, *sanctuary* [3] Or, *can he not save himself?* [4] Or, *earth* [5] Or, *why didst thou forsake me?* [6] Many ancient authorities read *so cried out, and gave up the ghost.* [7] Or, *a son of God* [8] Gr. *little.* [9] Many ancient authorities read *were already dead.*

45 And when he learned it of the centurion, he granted the corpse 46 to Joseph. And he bought a linen cloth, and taking him down, wound him in the linen cloth, and laid him in a tomb which had been hewn out of a rock; and he rolled a stone against the door

Tomb with rolling stone door at Michmash, north of Jerusalem

47 of the tomb. And Mary Magdalene and Mary the *mother* of Joses beheld where he was laid.

16 And when the sabbath was past, Mary Magdalene, and Mary, the *mother* of James, and Salome, bought 2 spices, that they might come and anoint him. And very early on the first day of the week, they come to the tomb when the 3 sun was risen. And they were saying among themselves, Who 4 shall roll us away the stone from the door of the tomb? and looking up, they see that the stone is rolled back: for it was 5 exceeding great. And entering into the tomb, they saw a young

man sitting on the right side, arrayed in a white robe; and they
6 were amazed. And he saith unto them, Be not amazed: ye seek
Jesus, the Nazarene, which hath been crucified: he is risen; he
7 is not here: behold, the place where they laid him! But go,
tell his disciples and Peter, He goeth before you into Galilee:
8 there shall ye see him, as he said unto you. And they went out,
and fled from the tomb; for trembling and astonishment had
come upon them: and they said nothing to any one; for they
were afraid.

EPILOGUE

9 [1]Now when he was risen early on the first day of the week, he
appeared first to Mary Magdalene, from whom he had cast out
10 seven [2]devils. She went and told them that had been with him,
11 as they mourned and wept. And they, when they heard that
he was alive, and had been seen by her, disbelieved.

12 And after these things he was manifested in another form
unto two of them, as they walked, on their way into the
13 country. And they went away and told it unto the rest:
neither believed they them.

14 And afterward he was manifested unto the eleven themselves
as they sat at meat; and he upbraided them with their unbelief
and hardness of heart, because they believed not them which
15 had seen him after he was risen. And he said unto them, Go
ye into all the world, and preach the gospel to the whole
16 creation. He that believeth and is baptized shall be saved; but
17 he that disbelieveth shall be condemned. And these signs shall
follow them that believe: in my name shall they cast out
18 [2]devils; they shall speak with [3]new tongues; they shall take
up serpents, and if they drink any deadly thing, it shall in no
wise hurt them; they shall lay hands on the sick, and they shall
recover.

19 So then the Lord Jesus, after he had spoken unto them, was
received up into heaven, and sat down at the right hand of
20 God. And they went forth, and preached everywhere, the Lord
working with them, and confirming the word by the signs that
followed. Amen.

[1] The two oldest Greek manuscripts, and some other authorities, omit from ver. 9 to the end. Some other authorities have a different ending to the Gospel. [2] Gr. *demons*. [3] Some ancient authorities omit *new*.

COMMENTARY

I. 1–13. INTRODUCTION

The Notes in this Commentary are of two kinds: those in larger type deal mainly with the more important points concerned with the subject-matter and the history of the book; those in smaller type are concerned with minor points of translation, reading, interpretation, and allusion.

I. 1–8. *John the Baptist.*

I. 1–3. The construction of these verses is ambiguous.

(*a*) Is verse 1 a kind of title? (Of course the gospel was originally produced with no title at the head, like all ancient books.) Then 'John came' is the apodosis to 'as it is written'. So read, the verses suggest that this book records only 'the beginning of the gospel', implying perhaps that the work of the Church was a continuance of the same gospel. This idea is certainly suggested in Acts 1^1.

(*b*) Or is the quotation parenthetical? Then 'the beginning' and 'John came' are in apposition. The coming of John was the beginning of the Gospel; and this is certainly in accord with Mark's view of John, which regards the Baptist as merely Christ's herald.

gospel. The word in this form (εὐαγγέλιον) is found two or three times in the LXX, where, however, the form εὐαγγελία is more common; the verb εὐαγγελίζειν is also used in the LXX. There is then no reason for doubting that the word was used of their message by the Apostles, and was probably used by Our Lord Himself. It is ascribed to Him five times in Mark, in 1^{15}, 8^{35}, 10^{29}, 13^{10}, 14^9 (also proleptically in 1^{14}, as well as in the unauthentic conclusion of the gospel 16^{15}). In Our Lord's mouth the word no doubt meant 'the good news of the Kingdom of God', which He proclaimed. Jesus did not proclaim Himself. But Mark on the other hand must mean by the word 'the good news about Jesus Christ Himself'. By Mark's time 'the gospel' was that of which Christ was the subject.

Note that 'gospel' still means 'spoken good news'. It has not yet come to be applied to written records.

Christ, at first a title = the Messiah. In Paul it becomes virtually a name, used by itself or together with 'Jesus'. The same is the usage here.

the Son of God (υἱοῦ θεοῦ). These words are not in the great MS. Aleph nor in the quotations of this verse in some of the Fathers. But they have strong MS. authority.

Mark certainly thought of Our Lord as Son of God. To him it meant the ascription to Jesus of Messianic status, i.e. of a unique relation to God. Whether Mark went farther and could enter into the Christological views of Paul as set forth e.g. in Phil. 2^6, we cannot say. No trace of a metaphysical idea of Christ's pre-existence appears in the gospel.

2, 3. The first half of the quotation is not from Isaiah but from Mal. 3^1; the second half is from Isa. 40^3. (Hence some copies of the gospel read ' the prophets ' in verse 2.) In both quotations slight but significant changes of the pronouns have been made; '*thy* face' and '*thy* way' instead of 'before *me*', '*his* paths' instead of '*for our God*'. These changes imply that Christ is equated with God or is regarded as fulfilling that which was originally spoken of God.

The Malachi quotation occurs in Mt. 11^{10}, Lk. 7^{27} with reference to John the Baptist, but not in the context of his appearance, as here. It is thus a part of Q, but we need not infer that Mark derived it from Q and placed it here. It was probably a very common quotation in Christian circles.

The error by which quotations from Malachi and Isaiah are introduced as from Isaiah might be explained by saying that the two passages were combined in a Christian collection of ' Proof-texts ' or 'Testimonies' (cf. Introd. A. i). But no such trace of the use of Testimonies is found elsewhere in Mark. Indeed this is the only place where Mark quotes the O.T. for himself. Moreover, the quotation from Malachi follows the Hebrew version, while that from Isaiah, in accordance with the usual custom of the O.T. citations in this gospel, follows the LXX. Hence many scholars believe the Malachi quotation to be the insertion of a later scribe; and the Isaiah quotation may be so too.

4. *The wilderness* is the desert land rising from the lower Jordan and the Dead Sea to the central ridge which forms the spinal column of Palestine.

5. The stir caused by John is described in exaggerated terms, but no doubt his appearance produced a public sensation. It would seem to bode a revival of prophecy; and for 200 years the Jews had been accustomed to think that prophecy had ceased.

6. The description of John recalls that of Elijah in 2 K. 1^8. A hairy mantle is spoken of as the professional habit of a prophet in Zech. 13^4. John's food is typical desert-fare.

7. *he that is mightier than I*; (ὁ ἰσχυρότερός μου). A definite Messiah, but he knows not who.

8. *baptized* (ἐβάπτισα). Is a past tense used because John's work is regarded as ended by Christ's advent, or is this idea far-fetched? The aorist here may be used according to Aramaic idiom, and may be practically a present.

with the Holy Ghost (πνεύματι ἁγίῳ). The Greek has no article. Thus the meaning might be merely 'in holy spirit', i.e. in spiritual power. It is usually hard to know in the N.T. whether a personal divine Agent is in mind or not, when this term occurs. Even the presence or absence of the article is no safe indication.

In John the Baptist's mouth the term would look back to the O.T. view of the Spirit of God as the vital energy of the divine nature; and in the later Jewish literature this energy is often spoken of in such a way that it seems to be trembling on the verge of personification (cf. Wisd. 7^{27}; the divine 'Wisdom' was often identified with 'the Spirit').

It is less certain what Mark would have understood by the term. The early Church undoubtedly believed that the living activity of Jesus was at work in them, and they called this energy 'holy spirit'; it was an operation of Jesus Christ. Paul's use of the term is often similar to this; but at other times he comes much nearer to speaking of the Spirit as a distinct Personality; and this latter conception is certainly found in the fourth Gospel. Mark probably got no farther than the Pauline view, if indeed he got so far. His gospel gives us no clear indication of the extent to which he had absorbed the Pauline doctrine.

This section is purely introductory. Mark's interest in John the Baptist is only in him as the fore-runner of Our Lord. Mark is not writing a biography; he is simply giving the story of the proclamation of Jesus Christ, and his purpose is to show why Christ is held to be 'Son of God', in the sense in which the Roman Christians used the term. Thus he seems in a hurry to arrive at Jesus' ministry, and the preliminaries are given in the barest outline. He records only such of John's teaching as has reference to Jesus and to the difference between the two baptisms; he shows no acquaintance with John's ethical teaching or with his preaching of judgement, except by implication when he describes his baptism as being 'of repentance unto remission of sins'. That Mark actually knew no more about John than he here tells us is unlikely. In

Matthew and Luke a much fuller record of the Baptist's preaching is provided, and that record must come from Q. If, as is likely (cf. Introd. C. iv), Mark was acquainted with Q in some version, and was even perhaps writing to supplement it, we may consider that his account here is an intentional abridgement of the familiar story, and that his purpose led him to eschew any more detailed reference to the forerunner. It is not in fact very likely that Peter could tell nothing more about the Baptist than the meagre sketch here presented.

Baptism was not unknown among the Jews as a ceremony of purification from Levitical defilement, and it was used at the admission of proselytes to Judaism. The peculiarity of John's baptism was that he baptized Jews as well as gentiles. His purpose apparently was to use the act as a symbol of purification, whereby those receiving it declared their renunciation of sin and their intention to live righteously, and so put themselves in a condition to receive that forgiveness of sins which was the promised blessing of the Messianic Kingdom which John was proclaiming to be at hand.

Mark's description was doubtless intended to show candidates for Christian baptism that the Christian rite had had its anticipation in the ministry of Christ's forerunner. The difference between John's baptism and Christian baptism lies for Mark in the fact that in John's baptism the Holy Ghost was not given (cf. Acts 19^{1-6}).

In Mt. 3^{11}, Lk. 3^{16} John is described as saying that the Messiah will baptize 'with the Holy Ghost and with fire'. Some suggest that his actual message was 'I baptize you in water; if you do not repent, he will baptize you with fire', i.e. the fire of judgement; that this reference was translated by the Christians into a reference to the Holy Ghost, of Whom fire was a symbol (e.g. at Pentecost); that we find it so in Mark, whilst in Matthew and Luke the two ideas are both given. This is a neat conjecture, and may be right. But it may be too neat; John need not have used but one phrase to express his message. But Rawlinson (note *ad loc.*) remarks with justice on the existence of 'a progressive tendency in the Christian tradition to draw the Baptist, as it were, more fully within the circle of the Christian movement, and to represent him, more and more exclusively, as having been consciously a fore-runner and herald of Jesus Christ'.

The suggestion has also been made, on the strength of Mk. 1^{8},

Acts 1^5, that the contrast is between a baptism in water and a baptism in spirit, and that 'baptism' in Christian usage was at first a mere metaphor for spiritual illumination, the use of water being introduced into the Church later. This is an unconvincing theory. The use of water on admission into the Church was a practice so natural in itself, and for which so much precedent existed, that it would be strange if the Christians had not adopted it. The records in Acts certainly say that they did; and Jn. 1^{25} seems to imply that the Messiah was expected to baptize, when he came.

But it is less certain that Christ Himself baptized. Jn. 3^{22} compared with Jn. 4^2 leaves the point doubtful. Perhaps He did not. But Jn. 4^2 distinctly says that His disciples did, even during His life on earth; and the tradition of Mt. 28^{19} shows that the Church believed baptism to be a rite ordained by Our Lord. A definite ceremony of initiation into a society is something which is likely to have been in use from the foundation of the society; and seeing that the first Christian preaching was Messianic, it is not unlikely that John's use of baptism as a preparation for the Messianic Kingdom was a precedent which the Christian Church would be ready to follow, and that Our Lord Himself would sanction the use of the rite by His followers.

I. 9–13. *The Baptism and Temptation of Jesus.*

9. *Nazareth of Galilee.* Galilee was a fertile district, and thickly populated. Its population was predominantly, but not exclusively, Jewish. It comprised a strong gentile element. Lying farther from the capital, it was less anti-foreign and less rigidly legalistic than the population of Judaea; yet the fanatical movement called zealotism later arose in Galilee. It probably contained many quiet and pious families who kept aloof from politics; in such a circle Jesus seems to have been born and brought up. But there is little ground for Bacon's suggestion that the people of Galilee included any large number that were opposed to the observance of the Law and were despised and 'unchurched' by the Rabbis (see Introd. D. ii). The synagogue system was strongly established in Galilee, and the people were orthodox, though their devotion to the Temple was no doubt mitigated by their distance from Jerusalem.

Nazareth is not mentioned in the Old Testament, nor referred to in Josephus or the Talmud. It was not big or important and may for some reason have been despised. It lies in a basin of the hills above the plain of Esdraelon. But 'the moment you climb to the edge of this basin, which is everywhere within the limit of the village boys' playground . . . you see thirty miles in three directions. It is a map of Old Testament history'. The main roads for pilgrims, caravans, and armies passed underneath within sight. And the strong gentile element in the Galilean population would make the customs of gentile living and thinking very familiar to Galilean Jews. 'He who wandered among the hills and valley of Galilee was never far from some great and populous city. It was not as a rustic preaching to rustics that Our Lord went about. He went forth in a part (of the Roman Empire) full of Roman civilization, busy and populous, where at every turn He would meet with something to mark the empire to which He belonged.' [1]

Mark gives no reason for Our Lord coming to John's baptism. It was soon felt to be a doctrinal difficulty that He, of whom Christians said that He was 'without sin', should have undergone a baptism of repentance for the remission of sins. Mt. $3^{14,15}$ shows an attempt at explanation of the difficulty. We should realize that the description given of John's baptism is probably affected by the Church description of Christian baptism.

But, even though John called men to repent, he did not exact a confession of sin from those whom he baptized. A good man might come to John and consecrate his good resolves, without thereby declaring himself a sinner. On general grounds we may say that Our Lord might see a fitness in thus identifying Himself with His countrymen in the expression of the new religious aspiration which John was quickening.

10. *straightway* (εὐθὺς) is used 41 times by Mark, and loses any sense of immediate sequence. It becomes a mere connecting link, like the 'and so' which an unskilled narrator will use to connect the stages in his story.

the Spirit, here with the article (τὸ πνεῦμα); it is certainly a personification of the Spirit of God as also in verse 12. In Philo we find the dove taken as a type of the divine Wisdom. Cf. Swete, *Holy Spirit in the New Testament*, Add. Note A.

[1] From Besant's lecture in *The City and the Land*, 114f., quoted in Adam Smith's *Historical Geography of the Holy Land*, p. 432, from which the preceding quotation was taken. Adam Smith's description of the site of Nazareth is worth reading in full.

upon Him. The Greek is εἰς and may mean 'into' Him. In any case it is conceived that Jesus is henceforth full of the Spirit.

he saw. The subject is grammatically Jesus, not John; and the tense is probably to mark this out as a moment of spiritual illumination or consecration to Our Lord.

11. Properly 'thou art my Son, the Beloved'. These were technical epithets of the Messiah. The words are reminiscent of Isa. 42[1], Ps. 2[7] and recall also Gen. 22[2]. In the LXX the word 'Beloved' used here (ἀγαπητός) appears as μονογενής; it expresses not merely divine affection but a unique relation to God, and means 'the Chosen'.

12. *driveth.* Gr. ἐκβάλλει.

the wilderness. This is not John's wilderness, but which it is is not specified.

Mark's account of the Temptation is very brief, as compared with the Q story recorded in Mt. 4, Lk. 4. But it has two peculiarities which those gospels do not record: (1) the reference to the animals, which may be a graphic touch put in to emphasize the solitude; or the picture may be Messianic, and the intention may be to symbolize Our Lord's mastery over the animal creation; (In Ps. 91[11-13] the ministry of angels and mastery over the brutes are combined, and the passage may have been treated as Messianic); or the addition of this feature may have been suggested by the arena at Rome, where the Christian martyrs had to face wild beasts in very reality. (2) Mark does not say that Our Lord fasted, but that the angels ministered to Him; he seems to conceive that Our Lord was maintained by supernatural supplies, like Elijah.

(1) Mark's account, like that of John's preaching, is very short as compared with the Q story preserved in Matthew and Luke; the question again arises whether Mark knew Q and abridged its record or whether he knew no more than he gives us. The temptation as a time of spiritual struggle is only hinted at in the words 'tempted of Satan'. It is clear at any rate that Mark regarded John's preaching, the Baptism, and the Temptation as the traditional preliminaries of Our Lord's Ministry.

(2) The story of the Voice from heaven at the Baptism need not be taken literally here, any more than in the parallel story of the Transfiguration (Mk. 9[2-8]). It is a piece of what the Rabbis

called *midrash,* wherein by poetic convention legendary details were inserted into stories in order to bring out the spirit of the text. This was part of a synagogue method of teaching called *haggadah.* The Rabbis spoke of a *Bath qol* (=‘daughter of the voice’), which they sometimes identified with the Spirit of God, symbolizing both by a dove, as being a way by which the purpose of God was declared on certain occasions. A famous instance is recorded in Josephus (*Ant.* XIII. x. 3), where Hyrcanus the high-priest is said to have heard a voice telling him that his sons had just then overcome Antiochus Cyzicenus, and Josephus identifies this as the voice of God. Whether Mark took his story here in a literal way we cannot say. But obviously the story grew up in an atmosphere where the synagogue method was familiar; and we may take the detail as merely expressing the sense of divine assurance and authority which henceforth came on Jesus.

It is more important to note that this *midrash* on Isa. 42^{1-4} implies a view of Jesus as God's Servant, full of God's Spirit, destined to be the agent of the revealing and redeeming Wisdom of God. This is the only place in Mark where such a Christological view is put forth; it is a view which occurs in Paul.

(3) The story of Jesus' Baptism is no doubt put in for the purpose of impressing Christian catechumens in preparation for their own baptism. But the story is full of controversial difficulty. Thus (*a*) is Mark's position ‘Adoptionist’ or not? He nowhere refers to Christ's conception or birth, or treats Him as Messiah from His birth. Does he consider that God adopted Jesus as Messiah at His Baptism? Does ‘I am well pleased’ (εὐδόκησα) imply pre-existence or merely fore-ordination? It is known that Gnostic heretics, like Cerinthus, who taught that ‘Jesus was the son of Joseph and Mary according to the ordinary course of human generation’, but that ‘after his baptism, Christ descended upon him in the form of a dove from the Supreme Ruler . . . but at last Christ departed from Jesus, and that then Jesus suffered . . while Christ remained impassible inasmuch as he was a spiritual being’, used the gospel of Mark as their basis (Iren. *Her.* I. xxvi 1; III. xi. 7) These heretics were called Docêtists, inasmuch as they held that Christ was a mere appearance (dokêsis), temporarily embodied in the man Jesus. Does Mark's gospel justify this view? It certainly seems to place the Baptism as the moment when Jesus becomes Messiah. On the other hand it is argued with some force that Mark avoids the version of Ps. 2^7 which says ‘this

day have I begotten thee' (which is actually the reading of the western text in Lk. 3[22]), and that this avoidance is due to the fact that the phrase would definitely have implied the Adoptionist standpoint. It is not possible for us to pass a verdict on these contending arguments. The Adoptionist view is certainly not held by Paul; and it is probably safer for us to think that Mark's view is that the *realization* of His Messianic status came on Jesus at His Baptism, while we leave it an open question whether Mark held Jesus to have *been* already the Messiah or not.

(*b*) It is useless to discuss whether Mark is right or not in this view of his, whether Jesus did or did not already regard Himself as the destined Messiah. The gospels are not psychological studies, and they give us little information to enable us to trace the development, if there was one, in the Messianic self-consciousness of Jesus. But, allowing that Jesus did believe, or did come to believe, that He was the Messiah, we may ask what sort of Messiah did He think Himself to be?

The popular Jewish idea of the Messiah was still the old national one of a son of David to be born at Bethlehem. But in some circles (perhaps only small ones) Messianism had become apocalyptic. A supernatural Being was to come from heaven to usher in the day of God's Kingdom. But, whether regarded as son of David or as mysterious man from heaven, the Messiah was expected to be the deliverer of his people. Doubtless this hope was conceived by some in a vulgar fashion; the day of God's Kingdom was to be marked by the material prosperity of God's chosen people. But many would have more spiritual ideas than that, and would look to something more like a moral and spiritual regeneration of mankind under God's sway.

That Jesus could take up this apocalyptic aspiration is entirely probable. It was the highest religious aspiration of His nation. He must have been familiar with the Messianic idea. What more likely than that He should conceive the belief that it was to be fulfilled in Him? But that, taking it up, He should spiritualize it, is even more certain. Being what He was, how could He fail to do so? His teaching is singularly free from national limitations or concern for national interests. He sits as loosely to national ambitions, even legitimate ambitions, as to care for temporal advantages. His keynote is righteousness, and in this He places self-sacrifice and service in the forefront. This emphasis may have developed in His mind into the idea of His own death, especially as He advocated non-resistance to violence and non-violen activity.

(*c*) It is a further question whether His conceptions of Hi mission were directly influenced by the picture of the Sufferin Servant of Jehovah in Isa. 42 and 53. That picture was no congenial either to the apocalyptic ideas of the Messiah or to thos ideas which looked for a Messiah who would owe his rights to hi Davidic lineage. The Suffering Servant, we may say, was no an element in the Jewish Messianic hope. But it played a ver large part in the early Christian interpretation of the Messiani work of Jesus; and we may feel it to be probable that it had it share in moulding the conceptions of Jesus Himself. After all those chapters were in the Jewish Bible, and their main idea o the redemptive value of suffering was not absent from some of th Psalms (e.g. Ps. 22). We can see for ourselves that this idea i the highest and noblest to which Old Testament thought eve reached. Even if, without dogmatic prepossessions, we conced to Jesus only that He was the supreme spiritual genius of Hi race, it is hard to think that such an One would not have been abl and likely to recognize and to make His own the supreme spiritua truth to which the greatest of His predecessors had attained (se Introd. D. iii. Montefiore's discussion of this subject is extra ordinarily sane and helpful, *op. cit.*, p. 46f.).

I. 14–VIII. 26. SCENES IN GALILEE.

I. 14–III. 6. The Beginning of the Ministry.

I. 14–20. *First message and call of first disciples.*

14. The implication is that Jesus comes forward at first as th Baptist's successor, preaching a similar message. The fate o John is not described till 6[17f.]; here it is assumed that the stor is familiar.

came into Galilee, on his return from His Baptism and Tempta tion. We are given no indication as to the length of the interva or as to how Jesus proceeded during the time. The story is a mer synopsis, and the detailed narrative does not begin till verse 16 Mt. 4[12,13] says that Jesus withdrew into Galilee (ἀνεχώρησεν); h does not say what He was withdrawing from, and his narrativ might be taken to imply that Jesus was in danger of sharin John's fate; but to go to Galilee would not be a good way of avoid ing Antipas, as Galilee was his tetrarchy. The word 'withdrew in Matthew may therefore only mean 'returned'; or Matthew's word may hint some knowledge of a ministry in Jerusalem which excited Pharisaic jealousy. This latter is the account given in Jn. 4[1]. Matthew goes on to say that Jesus left Nazareth and came to live at Capernaum. Lk. 4[16f.] has the same account as Matthew, but adds the story of Jesus' unsuccessful preaching at Nazareth.

the gospel of God may mean 'good news about God' or 'good news from God'. The nature of the preaching is defined in the next verse. Mark probably understands the term in the full Christian sense. But if Our Lord Himself used it, as may well be the case (cf. Note on I. 1–3), He would most likely at present simply mean 'the good news that God's Kingdom is at hand'.

15. This is Mark's own summary. A simpler and perhaps more original form of the message is given in Mt. 4[17]. But we are not to think that Jesus' preaching consisted in the mere repetition of a formula. It was, at least in public, always occasional and unsystematic. Mark's summary however suggests that this preaching contained at least two elements (1) the eschatological announcement of the Kingdom of God at hand, (2) the moral call to repent.

16. Here the anecdotes begin, and verses 14, 15 might be taken (as Wellhausen takes them) with verses 1–13 as part of the general introduction to the gospel narrative. Nothing is said of the general effect of Jesus' first preaching, except what is implied in the readiness of the four disciples to follow Him.

The public reputation of Jesus, when it is noted, rests on the grounds of His cures and exorcisms.

by the Sea of Galilee, at or near Capernaum. We are not told of Jesus entering Capernaum till verse 21, and yet He is at once obeyed when He calls Capernaum residents. Mark, it is clear, was only interested in the call and its effects; to him it was the Messiah's imperative, such as many Christians of his own day might hear, involving an immediate renunciation of other ties. To the four who first followed it must have appeared merely as a call to attach themselves to a teacher or prophet. It may be that we should infer that this was not the first time that the four had heard or met or heard of Jesus; and Jn. 1[35] states that Simon and Andrew had been disciples of the Baptist, and were first drawn to Jesus by his testimony. This may be true; but the sudden following of a previously unknown 'holy man' is a phenomenon not unfamiliar in the East, e.g. among Indian *gurus*; it is illustrated in the beginning of Kipling's *Kim*.

The narrative here is lifelike and graphic; e.g. the details as to the 'mending' of the nets, and the presence of Zebedee and of hired servants.

casting. The Greek word here used (ἀμφιβάλλοντας) is rare. But the noun ἀμφίβληστρον is common. Mt. 4^{18} has *βάλλοντας ἀμφίβληστρον*. Lk. 5^{2-12} connects the call with a public preaching and the miraculous draught of fish.

17. They were to become disciples so as to become fishers of men. As 'fishers of men' they would have to gather in men to the Messianic Kingdom, or to a state of preparation for it. The phrase in this place has every mark of authenticity. But Mark probably understood it more ecclesiastically of gathering men into the Church. The parable of the drag-net in Mt. 13^{47} gives the same idea.

The prophets of the Old Testament had disciples; but no call of a disciple by a prophet is recorded save that of Elisha by Elijah (1 K. $19^{19f.}$).

18. Zebedee is mentioned by name, but not the father of Simon and Andrew, either because Zebedee was present at the call, or because he was well known in the Church, or because James and John were such common names that the two brothers were distinguished by their patronymic.

19. *mending*; Gr. καταρτίζοντας. This may perhaps include the general preparation of their gear.

According to Jewish expectation, God by the agency of His Messiah would establish the theocracy on earth. This idea was variously interpreted by various men according to their spiritual depth or shallowness.

That Jesus spiritualized and sublimated the notion is clear. His teaching is, much of it, detachable from eschatological conceptions. The imperiousness of His moral demands gave an ethical flavour to the qualifications for the new era. And there are other strains in some of His uses of the term which enlarge its connotation; in some places it seems to be almost equivalent to 'heaven', in others it is treated as an invisible spiritual principle working in men's hearts, in others again it seems to imply a visible and organized society of which the Church is the matrix or nucleus. In Mark the eschatological view is almost wholly dominant.

Similarly, some of Jesus' teaching represents the Kingdom as a future event which will come suddenly, while in other places He speaks as if it were already present and growing slowly. However we deal with the dilemma of these two presentations, it is at least fairly certain (1) that Our Lord spoke of a crisis or severance between good and evil as near, and called men to repent in preparation for its coming; (2) that He laid His emphasis on the announcement of this event as a good news. In John's preaching the emphasis had been on the idea of wrath to come. Thus though Our Lord may have taken up John's message, He changed the proportion of emphasis between its parts in such a way that what had been a warning of doom became a message of cheer.

Some commentators deny that Our Lord can have uttered both the call to repent and the declaration of a good news. If the coming of the Kingdom was good news, how could He logically invite men to repent in preparation for it? On the other hand, if the Kingdom, as in John's message, was to come with judgement, how could He call tidings of its advent good news? This is palpably pedantic logic. The prophets of the Old Testament give enough precedent for the combination of the summons to repentance and the promise of grace. It was good news that the Kingdom was near. But if men were to escape its terrors and to enjoy its blessings they must get ready for the day by a moral change of mind and heart.

We cannot say whether Our Lord had already reached His full idea of the nature of the Kingdom or not; the gospels, as has been said, do not provide us with a sketch of His mental development. So too we cannot say whether He had yet learnt to think of Himself as the Messiah or not; He certainly does not call Himself so, but that is all that we can affirm. It may be that He started His Ministry with no fixed programme before Him at all; that He was content to speak God's words and to do God's business, as opportunities offered, and that any formula which might express His conception of His mission only shaped itself gradually in His mind. That He deliberately embarked on a campaign to restore the lost sheep and redeem the status of the 'unchurched' seems a most unconvincing hypothesis (see Introd. D. ii), almost as unconvincing as the allied supposition that this also was John the Baptist's programme and that Jesus took it on from him.

Finally let us note that Jesus' message of the Kingdom had

direct reference only to the Jews. All Messianism treated the Jews as the chosen children of the Kingdom. In Mark no sign is given of any development in Our Lord's teaching which would widen the reference. In the other gospels there are passages where such a widening is plainly contemplated; this is so especially in Luke. The story of the way in which this enlargement of the scope of salvation gradually lodged itself in the early Church's mind and practice may be read in the Acts and the Pauline epistles.

I. 21–45. *Preaching and signs and their effect.*

This section narrates a series of incidents, told rather breathlessly with no artistic connexion (*καί* in every case is the copulative), but giving an impression of consecutiveness such as we do not often get in the first half of this gospel. It may be the story of the initial day after Peter's call, or, perhaps more probably, of a typical day in the Galilean ministry (but see note on verse 37). The unifying purpose of the section is to record the impression which Our Lord produced from the outset, as witnessed by the wonder of the people and the confessions of the demons.

We may note that Mark, like Luke, shows a great interest in Our Lord's healings and especially in His exorcisms. This was not due to a merely crass hankering after prodigies. The world in the time of the Evangelists was convinced of the reality and power of demoniac agencies; and Our Lord's power over the 'possessed' (which there is no reason to doubt) would appear both to the writers and to their readers as a strong illustration of the force of God's Spirit to triumph over the evil spirits; it would be a sure testimony that in Jesus the Kingdom of God was 'come upon' men(cf. Mk. 3^{26}, Mt. 12^{28}, Lk. 11^{20}). It is a striking fact that neither in Paul's epistles nor in the fourth gospel is there any reference to or notice of Our Lord's exorcisms; and moral and spiritual fruits are directly exalted by Paul more than once over the power of working signs. But in both sets of writings there is abundant evidence of demonological ideas and of the conviction that Christ was manifested to destroy the works of the devil (cf. Rom. 8^{38}, 1 Cor. $2^{6,8}$, 7^{5}, $10^{10,20}$, Eph. 6^{12}, Col. 2^{15}, Jn. 8^{44}, 12^{31}, 14^{30}, 16^{11}, 1 Jn. 3^{8}, 5^{18}).

The question of Our Lord's views on demoniacal possession need not exercise us much. Even if He knew the current beliefs to be false, it would be out of His purpose, and probably out of

His power, to introduce a new philosophy of evil to take their place. We may also ask whether Jesus, in His human character, was not bound to share the pre-suppositions of His contemporaries as to cosmic influences. Finally we may ask whether it is so certain, as many assume it to be, that the idea of demoniacal possession is false. The experience of workers in the mission-field, and in the home-field too, would often be found to suggest very strongly that diabolical agency is a great supernatural reality. Whatever our views on this point, however, we shall at least agree with Allen that, to a man who, in a world believing unanimously in demoniacal possession, is thought and thinks himself to be so possessed, the mere 'belief is demon enough' to call for even divine treatment; and how else could he be successfully treated except by one who would assent to the fact of his possession, and persuade him to believe it ended?

21. *Capernaum* is not mentioned in the O.T. That it was a big city in Our Lord's time is certain, but its site is not certainly identified. The alternatives are Tell Hûm, on the North-western border of the Lake, where are the remains of a large synagogue, and Khan Minyeh, a little farther West.

on the sabbath day. Gr. plural, τοῖς σάββασιν. This may be an Aramaic quasi-plural, unless it is meant that Jesus taught on more than one sabbath.

The synagogues were meeting-houses for the purposes of common prayer and religious teaching and preaching. A school for children was often held there too. The building was under the control of local elders; but the office of teaching was not restricted to them; any layman was allowed to preach if invited. It was in this way that the Christian preachers of the Church's early days had their opportunity of addressing Jews and (in gentile cities) the 'god-fearing' gentiles who attended the synagogue services.

22. *the scribes* were the professional interpreters of the Law of Moses, and were a very influential profession in Palestine at this time. The Law had gradually become the supreme religious force in Jewish minds; ever since the return from Exile in 536 B.C. and the reform of Ezra in 445 (?) its power had been increasing. The scribal expositors had become much more influential than the priests. Though the priests held the reins of office, the Temple was a single place, and many Jews only visited it very occasion-

ally; the Law on the other hand was everywhere, taught in every school, and expounded in every synagogue. The synagogue was far more the religious home of the people than the Temple.

The teaching of the scribes was a matter of precedents and the balance of authoritative opinions of great Rabbis; as such it is contrasted with Our Lord's teaching which has a personal and direct authority of its own, such as is illustrated in the Sermon on the Mount ('it is said . . . but I say').

23. Would then a demoniac be admitted into the synagogue?

a man with an unclean spirit (Gr. ἐν πνεύματι ἀκαθάρτῳ an Aramaic idiom). The phrase 'unclean spirit' is found only once in the LXX (in Zech. 13^2), and is almost unknown in Greek outside the N.T. Mark has it eleven times, Matthew and Luke only once except in passages derived from Mark. The phrase may mean 'causing ceremonial uncleanness', unless it is used of moral impurity, perhaps of a sexual kind.

24. *the Holy One of God* (ὁ ἅγιος τοῦ θεοῦ) a Messianic title, quoted as such in Acts 2^{27} from Ps. 16^{10}; cf. also Jn. 6^{69}, Acts 4^{27}. We do not know that this title in the Psalm was applied in Judaism to the Messiah.

Note that Mark is plainly convinced that the demons recognized and acknowledged Jesus' Messiahship, whilst men did not perceive it, partly through blindness, and partly because Jesus sought to veil it. This is a theory of Mark's (1^{34}), and it lands his account in perplexities and contradictions. If the demons publicly proclaim Jesus as Messiah, of what use is it for Him to forbid it to be published? Jesus never seems to have refused to heal; how could He hope for the news of His powers to be silenced?

We may suppose that the cry of the demons was quite inarticulate and unmeaning to the people, and that the interpretation of it as an acknowledgement of Jesus as the Christ is Mark's own, or more probably the Church's own, interpretation. Our Lord's cures we may take as the natural expression of His pity; they would of course provoke wonder and surmise, but would not of themselves at once awaken the idea that He was Messiah. He can hardly have expected that they would not be talked about.

We feel that the account has been confused by the reading back into the incidents of Mark's theory of the demonic recognition. But we may surmise that at least Our Lord shrank from the publicity, and the kind of publicity, which His miracles attracted to Him; that it caused Him no elation, and that He must often have been torn between the contending claims of His compassion on the one side and His desire to avoid the reputation of a wizard on the other.

25. *hold thy peace* Gr. φιμώθητι = be muzzled. The word is found in good late Greek literature.

27. They had found authority (ἐξουσία) in His teaching, and now they find it also in His acts. But it is an attractive suggestion to alter the punctuation so as to read 'A new teaching with authority! and he gives orders to the unclean spirits' (διδαχὴ καινὴ κατ' ἐξουσίαν· καὶ κ.τ.λ.). So Wellhausen.

31. His gesture is noted, as in verse 41.

32. A characteristic redundancy of expression; notice also the accumulation of adverbs in verse 35, πρωὶ ἔννυχα λίαν.

34. *healed.* The Greek word (ἐθεράπευσεν) is regularly used of medical treatment. In Matthew and Mark it is nearly always used for Christ's cures.

36. *followed.* The Greek word (κατεδίωξεν) is not found elsewhere in the N.T., but is frequent in the LXX, usually with a hostile sense.

37. The story is very curt. Jesus puts foot in Capernaum, immediately leaves it, and 'all men' seek Him. More than this probably must have happened, even if the disciples' message is treated as excusable exaggeration.

38. *towns* Gr. κωμοπολεῖς, only found here in the N.T., means country towns of the large village type, such as were numerous in Galilee.

came I forth (ἐξῆλθον). This might mean 'I came forth (from the Father)', as in Jn. 16^{28}, or more simply 'I came out (from Capernaum)'.

The account tells us merely that Jesus came forth to pray, and that when asked to return to Capernaum, He expressed a desire to go elsewhere as well. It may be reading too much between the lines to suggest that the stir caused by His cures and exorcisms drove Him to go out to meditate on His future course, and that He decided to withdraw from Capernaum; for He exorcises as well as preaches elsewhere too (v. 39) and later on He sends the twelve to do the same two things ($3^{14,15}$). But we may at least feel that He regarded the preaching as the really important work, and sought to check a popularity based on wonders.

40. Many forms of skin disease came under the head of 'leprosy'; all were 'unclean', but some were curable.

41. The act of touching was a striking contravention of the ritual law.

being moved with compassion. The Gr. (σπλαγχνισθεὶς) is not found anywhere before Mark; it occurs in Mt. 18[27] and in Luke three times (besides passages drawn from Mark). Allen infers that it was a vernacular word of the first two centuries A.D. The 'western' reading here is 'being angry' (ὀργισθεὶς) which is so difficult to understand that one wonders how it could ever have got into any text if it were not original.

43. *strictly charged him* (ἐμβριμησάμενος αὐτῷ) *and sent him away* (ἐξέβαλεν αὐτόν). Strong words. The latter is the same as occurs in Mk. 1[12]. The first is used in classical Greek of 'snorting' and in the LXX is expressive of strong anger; it has that sense also in Mk. 14[5]. In Mt. 9[30], Jn. 11[33,38] it is less definite, and expresses only vehemence. We do not see any reason why Our Lord should here be angry; various suggestions have been offered, e.g. (i) that the man had come into the house (we are not told that they were in a house) and had so committed a ritual offence; (ii) that Jesus was vexed at the stir His works were causing; or (iii) at the man's flattery of the physician; or (iv) that the man was already cured, and only needed to be declared cured, and tried to get the prophet to do this, and so to dispense him from the legal necessity of offering his sacrifice. All these theories seem very thin. Unless we are to take the Greek word in the sense given to it in the R.V., we must confess the reference to anger to be a puzzle, as puzzling, if not quite so difficult, as the western reading in verse 41.

44. The ritual prescribed in the Law for the case is given in Lev. 14.

for a testimony unto them, of what? That he is cleansed? or that there is a wonder-working prophet in Israel? or that Jesus respects the Law? The last seems the most likely, and probably gives the purpose for which the story was related at first; Matthew's version of the story (Mt. 8[2-4]) is far simpler than Mark's. Luke's version (Lk. 5[12-14]) is largely coincident with Matthew's. Both of them omit the points of difficulty in Mark, perhaps because they too were puzzled by them as they found them in Mark or in Mark's source (this narrative may be from another source than the Petrine tradition). Mark, however, uses the story as a further illustration of the great impression produced by Jesus' mighty works. The tale must have been preserved in circles which cared much to show that Jesus was not a breaker of the Law; this view of Him is, however, probably authentic, nor would it be entirely alien to Mark's way of thinking; though he was writing for gentile Christians, he was a Jew; and even Paul does not in his practice go so wholly against the Law as his theory in Galatians would logically imply. (Cf. Acts *passim* and Rom. $11^{13f.}$ and Essay B in Galatians or Essay D in Acts in this series.)

45. *he went out.* If this means the leper, this is one more instance of the impossibility of suppressing the report of Jesus' works. The stir which they cause is proving an obstacle to His work of preaching. That this is a general implication of this whole section has already been stated. But Allen makes the attractive suggestion that this verse means 'he (i.e. Jesus), went out and began to preach much and to make public the word' (as in 2^2), with the result that His preaching attracted multitudes to Him, and He had to avoid cities and keep in the open, where the crowd could have easy access to Him. This certainly fits the grammar better; the harshness of the change of subject is obscured in the English by putting 'Jesus' where the Greek has merely 'he' (*αὐτόν*). This harshness is no great obstacle, in Marcan Greek, to the other interpretation. But Allen's suggestion is quite possible, and has the merit of introducing a further reference to the preaching, of which otherwise so little notice has been taken.

II. 1–III. 6. *Opposition.*

The general purpose of this section is to give characteristic instances of the way in which opposition to Our Lord arose; an apparent climax is reached in 3^6 in a rupture with the Pharisees, and the beginning of their plots to make away with Jesus. There is, therefore, a logical sequence in the succession of incidents. But we need not think that they are chronologically arranged; still less is it to be thought that we have here more than a selection of typical scenes. No indication is given as to the length of time occupied by this stage of the Ministry. All that we may infer is that Our Lord was engaged in a work of itinerant evangelization of the Lake-side district, with Capernaum as His centre.

The selection of incidents and the nature of the teaching which they occasion is obviously influenced by the desire to support the Church's case against the Jewish Synagogue. This in no way shows that it is un-Petrine. Peter might quite well have been the authority for the bulk of the material here collected. But the Evangelist, in assembling the material, is guided by the wish to provide an answer to the question why the Church's observances differ from those of the Jews and why Christians are indifferent to the regulations of the Mosaic Law with regard to e.g. fasting, the sabbath, and association with those whom the Law condemns as 'sinners'. The cure of the palsied man is also made the opportunity for a justification of the Church's claim to declare the forgiveness of sins through Jesus Christ.

II. 1. *the house.* Whose? Peter's, or one that Jesus Himself occupied in Capernaum? Mark is similarly vague in 3^{20}, and indeed his notes of place are often quite indefinite.

2. *the word.* No doubt in a technical sense. The Greek is τὸν λόγον.

4. It is very difficult to imagine what happened. The house would be one-storied and flat-roofed, possibly with an external staircase. Mark says they uncovered the roof (ἀπεστέγασαν) and then broke or digged it up (ἐξορύξαντες). They could not do both. Luke says they removed the tiles (ἀναβάντες ἐπι τὸ δῶμα διὰ τῶν κεράμων καθῆκαν αὐτόν Lk. 5^{19}). Matthew leaves the detail out altogether (Mt. 9^{2-8}). Wellhausen thinks 'uncovered' may be a mistranslation of an Aramaic word meaning 'they brought him to the roof'; and there is good textual authority for omitting 'when they had dug it up'.

5. *their faith,* not of the paralytic himself; but it is implied. 'Faith' in such cases only means trust in Jesus' ability and willingness to effect the cure. But Mark may have thought it meant 'religious faith'; at any rate he would mean to suggest the value of such faith to his readers.

7. That God could forgive a penitent sinner was certainly a Jewish belief. Jesus' claim to be able to forgive sins would sound like a blasphemy to the Rabbis.

8. *in his spirit,* Gr. τῷ πνεύματι. Only elsewhere used of Christ in Mk. 8^{12}, Mt. 27^{50}.

9. It is easier to *say* 'thy sins are forgiven', for the result cannot be tested, but it is a harder and higher thing to absolve the soul than to cure the body.

10. *Son of man,* here used for the first time in this gospel; it recurs in Mk. 2^{28}, but not again till after Peter's confession in 8^{31}, after which its use is common. It certainly looks as if Mark

meant his story to suggest that Jesus veiled the Messiahship which the title implied (at least in Mark's mind), in the earlier part of His Ministry. Are these two instances then inconsistencies due to carelessness on Mark's part? Or is this theory of Jesus' veiling of His Messianic status something which modern students have read too fancifully into this gospel? It may be so; yet the theory does fit the general impression which the gospel makes.

The further question, whether Our Lord here made public claim to a Messianic title, calls for more detailed consideration (*vid. infr.*).

11. *bed* (κράβαττον as in verse 4). The bed of the poor. It was a pallet and could easily be carried. The Greek word is vernacular; in Latin it becomes *grabatus*.

This paragraph 1–12 is decidedly difficult. Can we believe that Our Lord so early not only called Himself Son of Man, but also publicly claimed the divine right of absolution to be His? Is it easy to believe that, as verse 10 suggests, He wrought a miracle only in order to justify His spiritual claim? And does not His whole speech in this scene suggest that He is endorsing the common and commonplace view that disease always implies sin?

As to this last point, Montefiore (*ad loc.*) maintains that Our Lord never combats the doctrine that disease implies sin. He admits, but makes little of, the contrary evidence in Lk. 13$^{1-5}$ and Jn. 9^{2}, as also of Our Lord's general view that God's action in nature shows no moral favouritism. But this evidence is stronger than Montefiore seems ready to allow. And it is hard to credit that Jesus was helpless before a doctrine which had aroused questionings in Jewish minds for centuries, which had been strongly combated in the book of Job, and which is certainly transcended by the author of the fourth gospel.

The difficulties noted in this paragraph give force to the suggestion that the incident was originally a simple miracle of healing; that the story went 'Jesus seeing their faith saith to the sick of the palsy (v. 5), I say unto thee, Arise', &c. (v. 11); and that Mark himself, or some one else, interpolated a detail intended to justify Christian absolution in the Church by pointing to Christ's power over bodily ills as evidence of His power over spiritual ills. This may seem too convenient a theory to be probable. Yet the exceedingly clumsy resumption from verse 5 in verse 10 'he saith to the sick of the palsy' does give some colour of probability to the conjecture that a process of compilation has here been at work.

The title 'Son of Man' is never put except in Christ's mouth in the gospels, and is used by nobody else and nowhere else in the N.T. except in Acts 7^{56}. Its disuse in Church literature is no doubt due to its vagueness and non-Greek quality. These facts very strongly suggest that its use was actually a characteristic of Our Lord's speech. Some scholars doubt if He actually used it; but their view is more surprising than convincing. The title is never explained in the gospels, whether by Jesus or by the evangelists, nor is it ever hinted that it was a riddle to the disciples.

By Mark the name is unquestionably used in a Messianic significance. Its Messianic use is found in embryo in Daniel 7^{13}, where, however, the picture is not individualized; the coming ruler is 'like unto a son of man'. But in the apocryphal book of Enoch (1 Enoch 37–71) the Messiah is styled individually 'the Son of Man'. We do not know, however, if this had become a specifically Messianic title in common Jewish usage. Jn. 12^{34} suggests that in Judaea at least the ordinary Jew would not understand this term in a Messianic sense. As a Messianic title it may only have been known to limited circles, probably in Galilee. The common and familiar conception of the Messiah was nationalistic; as Son of David, the Messiah would be the ideal King who should rule as an earthly monarch and restore justice and righteousness. The Enochian 'Son of Man' was certainly not the commonly accepted idea in Judaea of what the Messiah would be.

We have further to recollect that the Aramaic form of the title, which Christ presumably must have used, is *barnasha*, which means simply 'man', as e.g. in Ps. 8^{4}. Thus Our Lord, in using it, might be taken by his hearers to have none but this ordinary meaning in mind. Whether in His use of it He never had any but a Messianic idea in His own mind is a question which we cannot answer. Whether He adopted it as an enigmatic phrase, into which He gradually imported, to Himself as well as to others, a more and more Messianic connotation, is a problem bound up with the more general problem of the growth of His Messianic self-consciousness, about which we have already had to confess our inability to pronounce.

The use of the title in the two passages of this chapter rouses more definite and manageable questions. Thus, firstly, is it used in a Messianic sense in 2^{10} and in 2^{28}, or is it there purely equivalent to 'man'? As to 2^{28} we believe that it is there fully Messianic, and is a Christian comment on Our Lord's dictum in verse 27 (see note *ad loc.*). The case of the use in 2^{10} is more difficult. Could Our Lord mean that 'man' has the power to forgive sins? The parallel passage in Mt. 9^{1-8} ends with the comment that God had given such power 'unto men'; but the reference there seems to be to the miracle and not to the absolution. We must probably conclude that Our Lord, if He used the phrase in Mk. 2^{10}, meant it of Himself. In that case He may mean it in a Messianic sense, but we can feel no certainty that his hearers would so understand it. Of course it is possible (i) to suppose that Mark, by a piece of carelessness, had read the use of the title back into a time earlier than that in which Our Lord began to use it more publicly (reading it back e.g. from Mk. 13^{26}), or else (ii) to interpret Our Lord's meaning to be merely 'I will prove to you that I, a man, can forgive sins', the Messianic implication being veiled by the use of an enigmatic and ambiguous phrase. But the crux of the difficulty is not the use of the title, but the fact that, whether Our Lord used the title or not, the claim that He could forgive sins was in itself a claim to be more than man, and would merit the charge of blasphemy, which He apparently was not at present willing to provoke. Thus the conjecture of an editorial interpolation seems to be the most promising way of escape from the difficulty.

With our conclusion on this point will follow a conclusion as to the second question, how came Mark to read the use of the phrase back into this scene, when its use (which to him is frankly and always Messianic) is inconsistent with his apparent view of the progress of Our Lord's self-revelation? Either the passage is an interpolation, or the writing is careless and Mark has distorted the original significance of the scene in the interests of the teaching which he wishes to convey. Either of these explanations is possible, and either seems preferable to a theory which would reveal Our Lord in a position which, so far as we can make out, He was not at present prepared to adopt.

14. *the place of toll* (τελώνιον). Capernaum was on the main road from Damascus to the coast of Jerusalem; and *octroi* duties would be levied on caravans. Or, possibly Levi's office was at the Lake-edge for ship-borne trade. Levi would be an officer of Antipas' service, not of the Emperor's. Nor must we suppose that the 'publicans' of the next verse are anything like the great

tax-farmers (*publicani*) of whom we hear in Roman history. Levi and his friends would only be the small toll-collectors of the local revenue service. The reputation of such men for venality and 'graft' was notorious. Among the Jews their occupation was the more unpopular, because it involved unrestricted intercourse with gentiles. The 'sinners' of verse 15 probably means nothing more than gentiles; 'sinners of the gentiles' as a strict Jew would call them (Gal. 2^{15}). Others think that they were Jews who were lax in observance of the Mosaic Law and so were ceremonially 'unclean'; or were they men of morally unsatisfactory life? We are given no precise indication. But that they were gentiles and such Jews as consorted with gentiles is a probable supposition.

Levi the son of Alphaeus. The western text has 'James' for 'Levi'. In Mt. 9^9 the incident occurs with 'Matthew' for 'Levi'. Had the man a double name, or was he re-named by Christ after his call? In Mk. 3^{18} the name 'Matthew' occurs in the list of the Twelve without any notice to explain who he is, and the name 'Levi' does not appear.

15. *there were many*; many disciples? or many publicans and sinners? or more generally, many people of all sorts? Jesus no doubt had other followers besides the five whose call has been recorded, or the Twelve whose names are known. But the sentence here reads like a gloss put in to explain the presence of the scribes.

We do not know whose house is here referred to. Was it Levi's or Jesus'? If the feast came at once after the call, it should be Jesus', for Levi followed Jesus. But such immediacy of sequence need not be assumed.

16. *scribes of the Pharisees*, a phrase found only here. Not all scribes need have been Pharisees. But the Pharisees were the party who practised exact and entire obedience to the Law and the traditional scribal interpretations of it. Thus scribes and Pharisees are usually found acting together in the gospels. We never hear of 'scribes of the Sadducees', for the Sadducees (the priestly families), while obeying the Law, were less observant of the 'tradition'. Most of the Jews were neither Sadducees nor Pharisees. But the Pharisees were held in popular respect as the ultra-Jews.

17. *the righteous* here means the Pharisees; we need not go beyond the immediate reference of the irony, and be so stupid as to ask if Jesus has no call for good people.

Jewish ideas admitted a place of penitence for sinners, but tended to leave their conversion to God, and did not encourage the seeking of them. Herein Jesus' practice was revolutionary in Jewish notions. Bacon sees in this phrase an announcement of Jesus' programme to call the 'unchurched' masses. This has already been considered in Introd. D. ii. The theory reads a great deal into the words used here, which are, like so much of Jesus' teaching, addressed directly to the occasion alone, though they suggest principles of permanent and universal value and beauty.

18. Another incident, obviously unconnected with the preceding feast, but giving another subject of dispute between Jesus and the Jews. Rawlinson suggests with great probability that the reference here is not to an ordinary fast, but to a special fast that John's disciples were keeping after their master's death (or possibly during his imprisonment) and that the incident is therefore chronologically misplaced. This certainly gives some help on the perplexing question whether Our Lord would have been likely to foretell publicly His own death (verse 20) at such an early date. In Mark it is not till 8^{31} that He definitely anticipates it, and it is then a surprise to His disciples. But if this incident took place later, at or about the time of John's death, He might see in that an omen of His own possible fate. Rawlinson further suggests that the references to the Pharisees in this paragraph have been inserted by Mark, and that originally the question was merely of a difference between the behaviour of the two sets of disciples on a particular occasion.

Mark doubtless meant the paragraph to justify the difference between Christian and Jewish customs of fasting. It is possible that the words 'in that day' (*ἐν ἐκείνῃ τῇ ἡμέρᾳ*), i.e. the day on which the Bridegroom was taken away, are used by Mark with a definite reference to a Christian fast on Friday. By A.D. 100 the Christian fasting-days were Wednesday and Friday.

Our Lord's answer merely replies to the point actually raised and does not deal with the spirit of fasting; but it implies that Christians need not fast till they have a reason to do so. The answer is then connected (by Mark or his source) with two bits of more general teaching, which do not bear directly on the point raised before and need not be thought to have been given at the same time. These two verses 21 and 22 are concerned with the incompatibility of the new religious principles of Christ with the old Judaism. This incompatibility had been proved in the experience of gentile churches. That Our Lord may have spoken in this strain is scarcely to be doubted.

19. *sons of the bride-chamber*, Gr. υἱοὶ τοῦ νυμφῶνος, an Aramaic idiom for the more normal Greek νυμφευταί. They were practically 'groomsmen'. Jewish marriage celebrations often lasted several days.

21. *undressed.* Gr. ἀγνάφου, properly 'unbleached', here means 'new', and is found in this meaning in papyri. ἐπιράπτει, and πλήρωμα meaning 'patch', are unusual Greek. The latter word recurs in Mk. 6^{4} meaning the 'fillings' of the baskets. The Greek of the sentence here is rough, and is modified in Mt. (9^{16}), and still more in Lk. (5^{36}), who for instance, changes πλήρωμα to the normal ἐπίβλημα.

23. A dispute on sabbath observance.

If the corn was ripe, the time must be April or early May. *as they went.* Gr. ὁδὸν ποιεῖν might be taken as to 'make a road', but the normal sense 'to walk' is more likely.

24. The Law allowed such an action as that of the disciples, provided that no sickle was used; cf. Dt. 23^{25} and Lev. $19^{9,10}$. The objection was apparently that by rubbing and eating the corn, they were doing a kind of threshing. Luke makes this point clear (6^{1}).

26. The reference is to 1 Sam. 21^{1-8}. But we are not there told that David actually entered the shrine; this detail may have been a traditional addition. The law of the shew bread is given in Exod. 25^{30}, Lev 24^{5-9}. That law is probably of later date than David's time; but Jewish opinion accepted the whole Pentateuch as Mosaic, and Christ's argument challenged the Rabbis on their own presuppositions.

In 1 Samuel the priest's name is Ahimelech, not Abiathar.

27. Some of the more liberal Rabbis might have agreed with Jesus' principle; but the legalistic outlook was more general in Palestinian Judaism.

28. This verse may have formed part of Our Lord's own words, in that case, He would almost certainly have been understood by His hearers to mean that 'man' is lord of the sabbath; a doctrine shocking to orthodox Judaism, and going farther than the words in verse 27 properly allow, which only state that service to man was the purpose of the institution. But verse 28 is probably best understood as a Christian comment on the paragraph; 'so, then, Christ (the Son of Man) is lord even of the sabbath'.

III. 1. We are not told where the synagogue was.

2. The Rabbis allowed medical relief to be given on the sabbath,

if life was in danger. Our Lord's action asserts the general right to abrogate the sabbath for a work of mercy, even though the need be not immediate.

The penalty for breaking the sabbath was death (Exod. 31^{14}), but permission from the civil authorities would be required before it could be inflicted.

4. Not to do good is 'to do harm', not to save is in effect 'to kill'. It is far-fetched to see in the words a hinted meaning that the Jews who were seeking to injure Jesus were breaking the sabbath more really than He was.

5. *hardening* (Gr. πωρώσει). Mark is obviously much impressed throughout his gospel with the thought of the Jews as having their heart hardened. See Introd. D. iii for the supposition that he owed this point of view to Paul's ideas.

There is in this verse a reference, as so often in the gospel, to Jesus' glance and to His emotions.

6. The 'Herodians', as an apparently distinct political party, are not known to have existed before the accession of Herod Agrippa I in A.D. 41. But there must have been, before then, a section of Jews who favoured and supported the Herodian dynasty, whether because of its patronage of Hellenistic culture, or because they saw in it the best chance of any national prosperity under Rome. These may already have been called Herodians, or Mark may be using the later party-name for them.

Ordinarily the whole dynasty and its supporters would be anathema to the Pharisees. But if they wished to prosecute Jesus for sabbath-breaking, they might need sanction from the civil authority; or if they wished Jesus to be interfered with, they might think it worth while to make interest with the officials of Herod's court and service to further their wish. In fact they 'complain to the police', as Burkitt puts it.

We may doubt whether the intention to 'destroy' Jesus would have shaped itself so early as this. Mark is probably summing the whole process of gathering hostility into the climax to which it came.

This combination of Pharisees with the civil power is seen again in Mk. 12^{13}, whence it comes also into Mt. 22^{16} (it is alluded to in Mk. 8^{15}). These three are the only passages where the name 'Herodian' occurs in the gospels.

There is much probability in Burkitt's view that this scene represents the open rupture between Christ and the Pharisees, and that henceforth, though He had committed no civil offence which could justify His arrest by Herod's orders, His movements seem to be determined by the recognition that Antipas' dominions are not safe for Him. Thus in verse 7 He is described as 'withdrawing to the Lake' (ἀνεχώρησεν); His journeys to the other side of the lake become frequent and sometimes seem hurried; and He is never said to enter a synagogue again, except on the one occasion in 'his own country' (6^{1}), and then His preaching was a failure. Such a theory as this is quite probable in itself, and provides some sort of clue by which to understand the story of the next few chapters.

III. 7–VI. 13. THE TWELVE.

III. 7–35. *The separation of the Twelve.*

In the following sections the sense of any, even if only vague, chronological sequence vanishes. Notice how entirely indefinite are the phrases of connexion in, for instance, $3^{7,13,19}$; 'he withdrew to the sea', 'he goeth up into the mountain', 'he cometh into a house'; and this vagueness continues in 4^{1}, 5^{21}, $6^{1,6}$. Nor is the logical connexion so clear as in cap. 2. The main interest seems, however, to be concerned with the setting-apart of a chosen band of closer disciples. Thus in 3^{7-35} the Twelve are chosen and Our Lord's family ties are renounced. 4^{1-34} draws attention to the special education of the Twelve, who are sent on their mission in 6^{7-13}, their return from it being related in 6^{30-32}. The logical connexion of these episodes is, however, broken by 4^{35}–5^{43}, which records various miracles, and by 6^{1-6} which is entirely indefinite in time, though its purpose may be (as in 3^{31-35}) to show how Our Lord gave up His natural social relations in order to constitute the new spiritual relation within the society of His disciples. The narrative of John the Baptist's fate in 6^{14-29} is interposed at the moment when the mission of the Twelve has drawn official attention to Jesus.

We cannot make any really consecutive story out of this miscellany of anecdotes. But Mark's general purpose may perhaps be conjectured. After (1) narrating the opening of Jesus' Ministry, and the stir and opposition which it caused, he (2) now proceeds to a section where Jesus specializes His work among His nearest disciples; (3) after 6^{13} the thought seems to be mostly of the process by which Our Lord is led to withdraw from

Galilee altogether, and to contemplate His adventure to Jerusalem. Thus this division of the gospel (3^7–6^{13}) may be entitled 'the Twelve', as they are the chief centre of the evangelist's interest.

7. *withdrew* (Gr. ἀνεχώρησεν). Mark probably uses the word in reference to the plot of the Pharisees and Herodians. As we have suggested, their opposition can scarcely have become really dangerous at once, but it may have been threatening enough to cause inconvenience to Jesus and His disciples.

The 'great multitude' comes from wherever Jews lived, from Galilee and Judaea, from Idumaea south of the Dead Sea, from Peraea 'beyond Jordan', and from the country north of Galilee which stretched from the coast to Damascus. The obvious implication is that Jesus' work had been going on long enough for His fame to spread far and wide throughout the land. Idumaea had been compelled to become Jewish by John Hyrcanus (the Hasmonaean King) in 128 B.C. Notice that Jesus' reputation is regarded as being due to His miracles, rather than to His teaching.

9. *should wait.* The Greek προσκαρτερῇ literally means 'to stick to,' 'to persevere'.

10. *plagues* Gr. μάστιγας = scourges.

pressed upon him Gr. ἐπιπίπτειν.

11. *the Son of God,* a Messianic title. There was among some Jews at this time the idea that the Messiah to come would be a supernatural being, who was pre-existent in heaven until the time for his appearance on earth had come. We notice here once more Mark's idea that the demons recognized Jesus for what He was and were forbidden to divulge it. Cf. note on 1^{24}.

13. *the mountain.* We are not told which mountain is intended. Perhaps the central plateau of the country.

An inner ring of disciples is now marked out from the bigger crowd of those who followed Jesus. Their number is twelve, corresponding to the twelve tribes of Israel. Their position as leaders in the early Church is clearly seen in Acts.

14. *twelve, whom also He named apostles.* So R.V. margin and most of our MSS.; but the 'western text' omits the last words, which some think to be an intrusion here from Lk. 6^{13}. The mission of the Twelve does not begin till 6^{12}; meanwhile they are 'to be with him'. It has been doubted whether Our Lord Himself

used the title 'apostles'. It assumed a quasi-official significance in the early Church; but in itself the word means nothing but 'delegate' or 'messenger'.

16. Some MSS. insert again here 'and he appointed the twelve' (καὶ ἐποίησεν τοὺς δώδεκα); but the words seem to be a mere repetition from verse 14 (καὶ ἐποίησεν δώδεκα).

The Greek here is very awkward; it runs 'and he appointed the twelve . . . and gave the name Peter (accusative) to Simon, and James (accusative) &c.' Gr. *καὶ ἐπέθηκεν ὄνομα τῷ Σίμωνι Πέτρον, καὶ Ἰάκωβον κ.τ.λ.* Westcott and Hort read the words 'and gave the name to Simon' as a parenthesis, thus making 'Peter' the object of 'appointed', like the rest of the names.

It is not here implied that Simon received his new name at present.

Peter, James, and John are put together as the pillar-apostles in Gal. 2^{9}, and seem to have been privileged to special intimacy with Jesus on certain occasions such as the Transfiguration and the Agony in Gethsemane.

17. *Boanerges.* The name as originally given had probably a mythical meaning, 'Dioscuri' (=sons of Zeus 'the heavenly twins'). As given in Aramaic it was understood to mean 'sons of thunder', and was then misread and transcribed into Greek as Boanerges. The incident in Lk. 9^{54} is conjectured to be the explanation of the applicability of the title. In the form *Bene Baraq* (=children of the lightning) it survives in the name of a site near Jaffa which probably was an ancient sanctuary.

18. *Cananaean* is a transliteration of an Aramaic word meaning 'zealous' or 'zealot', and so Lk. (6^{15}) rightly explains it. The zealots were the fanatically patriotic party at the time of the last siege of Jerusalem in A.D. 66. We do not hear of this party before that date; so we may suppose that Simon belonged to it later, or else that the word as applied to him means only 'the zealous one'.

19. *Iscariot.* For this word there is no parallel. It is supposed to mean 'man of Kerioth', which appears as a place in Moab in Jer. $48^{24, 41}$. Another suggestion is that it is a transliteration of an Aramaized form of the Latin *sicarius* = assassin. The 'Assassins' are referred to in Acts 21^{38} and in Josephus, who describes them as a sort of secret society formed to assassinate obnoxious Romans or philo-Roman Jews. Other suggestions connect the name with the tribal name Issachar, or with an Aramaic word *shkr* = betray.

In the list here given of the Twelve, we may note (1) that Simon is a hellenized form of Symeon, while Andrew and Philip are Greek names (all three came from Bethsaida, where Hellenism was strong), (2) that Levi is missing, unless he is to be identified with Matthew, (3) that the list does not exactly correspond with the other lists in the gospels. Thus Lk. (6^{14}) has another Judas in place of Thaddaeus, as also in Acts 1^{13}. These may be two names of the same man. Jn. 1^{45} mentions a Nathanael, who has been very precariously identified with Bartholomew. It seems as if Church tradition was uncertain as to some of the names of the Twelve; nor is this surprising; for they formed no official Board of Control, and some of them may have figured very little in Church affairs.

a house. The topography is quite vague, as previously also in verse 13.

21. *his friends* (Gr. οἱ παρ' αὐτοῦ). His kindred no doubt, for this incident seems to be continued in verse 31. The Beelzebub controversy is interpolated rather clumsily; but the connexion is obvious. Our Lord's foes are men of his own country and men of his own kin. Mark seems to be fond of inserting one incident into the story of another, as here; he does it again at 5^{25}, 6^{14}, and less obviously at 11^{15} (between 11^{14} and 11^{20}) and 14^{3} (between 14^{2} and 14^{10}).

22. We are not told how these scribes came to be present.

Beelzebub means 'lord of flies' and seems to have been a by-name for Satan. But the right reading here is 'Beelzebul'. This is a word unknown outside the gospels, and may mean 'lord of the dwelling' or 'lord of dung'; perhaps it is used by word-play to cast contempt on the Greek *Zeus Ouranios* ('Zeus of the sky').

by the prince Gr. ἐν τῷ ἄρχοντι. It may be worth while to note that the scribes were ready with this explanation of Our Lord's miracles, and that they seemed little impressed by them.

23. *parables.* The first occurrence of the word in this gospel. But here it means not a story, but a metaphor. The purpose of Our Lord's answer is clear. He accepts the current conception of a united Kingdom of Satan and shows the absurdity of supposing it divided against itself. The only reasonable inference from His beneficent works is that a 'spirit' is present which is able to

conquer the demonic spirit. The power and value of this belief, in the demon-haunted world of the time, is a point to which notice has already been drawn (note at 1^{21}). We can imagine such a verse as 27 being the text of much encouragement. Jesus was strong enough to bind the strong man (i.e. Satan), and His Church was spoiling his house.

The Beelzebub controversy occurs also in Mt. 12^{25-29} and Lk. 11^{17-22}; the two narratives there are practically identical, and contain features in common which are not to be found in Mark. It is probable therefore that Matthew and Luke are reproducing the story from Q and not from Mark; Mark may here be reproducing the Q account from memory, and his omissions may be unintentional; or else they are due to the fact that the version of Q which he knew was different from that used by the other two Synoptists.

28. *Verily;* the word is 'Amen'. Its constant appearance in introducing strong asseverations by Our Lord may be taken to be a genuine reminiscence of a characteristic in His way of speech.

the sons of men Gr. τοῖς υἱοῖς τῶν ἀνθρώπων; an Aramaism, only found here. Mt. $12^{31f.}$, Lk. $12^{10f.}$ agree in omitting this phrase and in adding a clause drawing a distinction between blasphemy against the 'Son of Man' and blasphemy against the Holy Spirit. We may therefore again suppose them to be drawing from Q. Some suggest that the phrase 'sons of men' here in Mark may be an inaccurate recollection of the reference to the 'Son of Man' in Q.

29. *the Holy Spirit.* Here obviously in the personal sense. The phrase translated 'is guilty of an eternal sin' is somewhat obscure. The Greek is ἔνοχός ἐστιν αἰωνίου ἁμαρτήματος, which may mean 'is in the grasp of eternal (aeonian) sin', or (by an Aramaism) 'is liable to an eternal punishment for sin'. The difference between the two senses is not so important as it may at first seem. Blasphemy against the Spirit is not, any more than any other sin, a mere matter of a single act. It becomes 'aeonian' or 'perpetual', only when it has become a fixed part of the character; and, when a man is fixed in a condition of blasphemy against the Holy Spirit, he is self-excluded from forgiveness; not because God ceases to offer it, but because he has lost the power to accept it; for the forgiveness of God is not a judge's declaration of a formal verdict, but a father's offer of a living relation, which can only take effect when it is accepted.

We cannot and need not try to define too closely wherein 'blasphemy against the Holy Spirit' consists. It is, as has been said, not a single act, but a condition to which single acts render a man 'liable'. In the case here cited the act is one of calling evil that which is plainly good. The extent to which prejudice or vanity or wilful ignorance may cause such acts is a commonplace of experience. They are often sins of ignorance; but they may be actual sins against the light; or a man's light may be darkness through his own fault. The final state to which such a tendency leads is that wherein Evil becomes a man's Good. Whether any man here or hereafter becomes *finally* fixed in this condition we are unable and have no right to be positive about. But, speaking relatively, history knows of some men, if only a few, who seem to have come to delight in evil because it is evil; and the minor forms of delight in evil or of refusal to acknowledge good are so common that men are only too fatally disinclined to see their full dangerousness. 'Blasphemy against the Holy Spirit' is in fact not one act of sin, nor even one species of sin; it is the generic condition of Sin itself when made complete and final. Our Lord's words here are therefore identical in meaning with the phrase in Jas. 1^{15}, 'the sin, when it is full-grown, bringeth forth death'. Every several sin helps the growth of the Sin-power; the complete Sin-state is the final maturity of that process.

30. This, of course, is the evangelist's own comment.

31. This passage and that in 6^{1-6} are the only places in this gospel where Jesus' kindred are mentioned; in both passages their unbelief is the only characteristic which is noted. Whether Mark knew more about them or not we cannot say; if he did, it was not to his purpose to relate it; and stories of the Lord's family would not be specially in place in catechetical anecdotes.

It seems reasonable to infer that Our Lord had not been long at His public work when this incident occurred; we have already drawn attention to the chronological uncertainty of Mark's narrative.

The fact that Jesus' mother is mentioned, and not her husband, is held by some to suggest that Joseph was by now dead. On the question who were Jesus' 'brethren' see 6^3 note.

35. Jesus' work left Him no room for the usual offices due to family ties and worldly connexions. We need not suppose Him to have renounced His family absolutely; indeed the gospels make it plain that He did not. But the great saying in this verse

enlarges the conception of family affection and duty to embrace all God's true children. It is the ideal of the Church which is here proclaimed, or rather the ideal of the redeemed human race, of which the Church is intended to be the nucleus. Implicitly, though not explicitly, Jesus here transcends the bounds of Judaism, and lays down the principle of the new Israel. We may feel sure that this verse was one of the great texts of any gentile Church in the first century, until the controversy with Judaism had ceased to agitate the Church.

IV. 1–34. *The teaching of the Twelve.*

We have here a series of parables, strung together in the loosest possible way; the word of connexion is simply 'and he said' (καὶ ἔλεγεν) in each case; see verses 2, 21, 24, 26, 30. That these parables were all spoken in this order and at the same time is patently incredible. It is probable that collections of Our Lord's parables had soon begun to be made, and that Mark is here drawing on such a collection.

The principle upon which Mark has selected and brought together these parables is fairly clear. Of course each parable has its own particular significance; but in general they all seem in one way or another to arise from the problem of the Jewish rejection of the Gospel message, or, more widely, of the merely partial success attending Christian preaching. The parable of the sower finds the explanation of this in the varieties of receptiveness shown by various hearers. The Gospel cannot expect to win a universal success at once, for some like the Jews are hardened or are insincere. But some success is won, and this makes the work of preaching worth while. Success is in God's hands and so is sure; and when it comes, it will be very great (so the parables of the husbandman and the mustard-seed). With this promise is coupled the missionary command to go on propagating the truth, which may be the point of the parable of the lamp.

The intention of the section is further to represent the message of the Gospel as a mysterious secret, not understood by the multitude, but explained to the Twelve and in the possession of the Church. It is veiled in parabolic form from the generality of hearers; and this also explains the rejection of the message by so many. They do not understand it, because they have not tried to, or because they have not yet had it explained.

This theory as to the veiling of the message is analogous to the theory as to the veiling of the Messianic secret, and is indeed only another version of it. It leads Mark into various inconsistencies in this section, which will be noticed as they occur. As we shall see, it is possible to doubt whether Our Lord intended His parables as enigmatic riddles; it may be that such a representation of His intention is due to the after-thoughts of the Church, which in some respects found the parables difficult to explain and thought this difficulty had always been inherent in them and had been intended to veil the Gospel message from the understanding of those who were too careless to study it or too hardened to discern it.

The general subject of the section may be described as 'the teaching of the Twelve'; for though the parables are spoken in public, the exposition of their meaning is definitely stated to be reserved for private colloquies with the circle of disciples (v. 34).

1. The place is as indefinite as the relation of the section to what precedes; but the picture is graphic. The 'boat' may possibly be a reference back to 3^9.

again (πάλιν) is of very frequent occurrence in Mark's style.

8. *growing up and increasing*; these are neuter plural participles, agreeing not with 'fruit' but with 'others' (ἄλλα).

The reading at the end of the verse is doubtful. Westcott and Hort have εἰς τριάκοντα καὶ ἐν ἑξήκοντα καὶ ἐν ἑκατόν. But such a combination of prepositions is intolerable. We have ἐν three times repeated in verse 20, and should probably have it here also; it is a question whether ἕν in each case would not be preferable.

9. A 'Note well' attached to the parable, to call attention to its importance.

10. *alone*, Gr. κατὰ μόνας a phrase which occurs in the LXX.

Note that here Jesus is alone with the Twelve and others; but in v. 26 He seems to be back with the crowd, as is implied in v. 33, and in v. 36 He is in the boat as at the beginning of the chapter. The connexion of the parables is thus seen to be artificial. We are to read this chapter as a series of pieces of teaching, and not as a consecutive discourse.

asked the parables, i.e. the meaning of them (as in Lk. 8^9), and not, as in Mt. 13^{10}, His reason for speaking in parables. The answer to the request comes therefore in v. 13f., and vv. 11 and 12 are an intrusion into the story (no doubt due to Mark himself), to explain why the parabolic form is used. This intrusion with its general purpose probably explains the use of the plural 'parables' in v. 10, when only one parable has been uttered.

11. *Unto you is given the mystery of the kingdom of God,* a phrase practically equivalent to initiation into a secret. The word 'mystery' is not found in the N.T. beyond this passage and its parallels in Matthew and Luke, except in Paul's Epistles and in the Apocalypse. But we need not call it a Pauline word. It was in common use in the meaning of 'secret', especially bearing an apocalyptic idea. To gentile readers it would bear the added meaning drawn from familiarity with the cults and their mysteries, and would imply a secret mystical knowledge shared only by the members of the Christian society. Whether we can take this phrase to have been used by Our Lord we shall consider in a moment. But its meaning to Mark and his readers would be that of the Kingdom of God as containing a set of spiritual truths, and especially the truth of Jesus' own position, which they knew and others did not.

all things are done in parables i.e. the story is not understood, and their whole relation to the Gospel is befogged.

12. The reference is to Isa. 6^9, where the prophet complains that his message falls on unheeding ears. To the Hebrew mind the difference between what God willed and what God permitted scarcely existed. Thus Pharaoh's heart is 'hardened'; and yet this does not exempt him from responsibility for his obstinacy. This theory of the hardening of Israel against the Gospel is the theme of Rom. 9–11 (cf. especially $11^{25f.}$). But to call it 'Pauline' is an exaggeration. It was probably a current explanation in the Church of the Jewish rejection of Christ (see Introd. D. iii).

It is doubtful whether Mark's explanation of the use of the parabolic method by Jesus is true to Our Lord's original intention. In considering this question we must note (1) that the use of parables was no new method in Jewish teaching. Parables were frequently employed by the Rabbis. A Semitic 'parable' is anything from a metaphor to an allegory. The explanation here given of the parable of the sower makes it a quasi-allegory. More often, however, the Semitic parable is intended to illustrate only one special point and must not be pressed into a complete allegory.

(2) Though Jesus undoubtedly appealed to the spiritual discernment of His hearers, and wanted to make them think, it is hard to believe that He intended to befog any of them. Esoteric teaching is quite foreign to His usual spirit.

(3) The point of a parable is to illustrate and not to be mysterious. Jesus' parables were probably clear enough in their original context, though we unfortunately do not as a rule possess this.

(4) To the later Church the parables had become less clear, since their context was lost, and it was then easy to think that Jesus had never intended them to be clear. This is Mark's theory, but it seems to be the view of the later Church rather than the intention of Jesus Himself.

(5) It is quite likely that the explanation of one or two of the parables was authoritatively provided by the Church; but such explanations do not seem to be those of Jesus Himself. He may, perhaps He must, have reflected on His failure to win the Jews, and He may have used Isa. 6^9 to explain that failure. But the interpretation here given of the parable of the sower seems too general to be His; it appears to reflect the success and failure of Christian preaching in general. Thus the sower is any preacher. The first two cases of failure are due to carelessness in the hearers, to a lack of spiritual sincerity on their part. The third case is that of those who for worldly reasons forget their first enthusiasm and apostatize under pressure of affliction or persecution, such as came on the Church. We may therefore conclude that Mark's theory was the one current in the Church at a time when the parables had come to be regarded as enigmas applicable to the Church's circumstances, and that the interpretation here given sees in this parable an explanation (1) of the causes why the Gospel so often failed to win or keep disciples; the direct contrast in view is no doubt that between the responsive gentiles and the unresponsive Jews, but the parable has a wider application than to this special case; (2) of the backslidings within the Church itself. It is because hostile circumstances are at work to counteract the effects of Christian preaching. The same is the purport of the explanation of the parable of the tares in Mt. 13.

13. Notice *all the parables*; it seems a reference to a known collection.

14. *the word* Gr. τὸν λόγον = the Gospel.

16. There is a lack of precision in the interpretation, which however does not obscure the general meaning. Thus in verse 15 there are 'men by the way-side where the word is sown', whilst in verses 17 and 18 the men themselves are spoken of as 'sown upon rocky places' or 'among thorns'. The distinction need not be pressed. The

general point is clear enough; the word is sown, but men's hearts ar
variable soils for its reception.

17. *endure for a while.* Gr. *πρόσκαιροί εἰσιν*. A late Greek wor
meaning 'short lived'. *σκανδαλίζονται* is a technical term for back
sliding; it and its analogues are common in the LXX, meaning eithe
'a snare', 'to ensnare', or 'a stumbling-block', 'to make to stumble'

19. *lusts of other things* (*αἱ περὶ τὰ λοιπὰ ἐπιθυμίαι*) means sensua
lity.

21. Verses 21–5 are found scattered in different contexts i
Matthew and Luke,

21 in Mt. 5^{15}	Lk. 11^{33}
22 in Mt. 10^{26}	Lk. 12^{2}
24 in Mt. 7^{2}	Lk. 6^{38}
25 in Mt. 13^{12}, 25^{29}	Lk. 19^{26}.

It seems therefore likely that Matthew and Luke derived then
from Q. Mark may have done so too and assembled them her
by his own choice. But they may have been short sayings recorded by general Christian tradition. Their connexion here wit
one another is often very difficult to trace, and we cannot fee
confident that they are placed in their original context.

21. The implication of this verse is that of revealing a secret
This means probably the Christian duty of preaching the word
All may not bear fruit, but all must receive the seed, all must b
shown the light. The word has been given to them in secret, bu
only that it may be revealed to others. We may notice the suggestion that the policy of secrecy is only temporary and 'economic'. This idea is not consistent with that in vv. 11 and 12
which implies that the secrecy is in order that some shall no
understand.

24. The meaning seems to be 'Listen carefully, so that yo
may be able to hand on properly what you hear'. The connexio
of the next phrase with this is, however, very obscure. It wa
probably a current maxim of the time. As applied here it ma
mean 'the more attention you give to the word, the more yo
will profit by it', or perhaps 'the more diligently you teac
others, the greater will be your reward'. In v. 25, which seem
independent of 24 and is more in place in connexion with th
parable of the talents, as in Mt. 25^{29}, Lk. 19^{26}, the direct contrast
is between Christians and Jews; the former have and receive
more; the latter lose even what they have. A connexion with the

preceding verse can only be established by a serious straining of the sense.

26. This parable occurs only in Mark. It may be a doublet of the parable of the sower. But, as it stands, it emphasizes the idea of the unseen forces that promote growth. The Kingdom of God is sown and is growing to harvest; but God is overseeing the process. Man must not try to hurry it or repine if it be slow. No doubt the parable may have been aimed originally at those who wished to force the coming of the Kingdom. To Mark and his readers it would provide an answer to the question why the Church progressed so slowly and the Parousia delayed.

ὡς ἄνθρωπος βάλῃ is not Greek. There is little doubt that we should read *ὡς ἐὰν ἀ. β.*, the *ἐὰν* having fallen out by similarity with the first syllable of *ἄνθρωπος*.

29. *παραδοῖ* may mean 'presents itself' or 'permits'. The emendation of *καιρός* (= season) for *καρπός* is strongly recommended.

The last words are a reminiscence of Joel 3^{13}.

30. The opening of this parable is put in the form of Semitic poetry.

31. 'Small as a mustard seed' was a Jewish phrase. The point of this parable is not, as is so often said, that of slow growth. For (1) the mustard-seed grows very rapidly, and its flower often reaches quickly to 6 feet or more in Palestine; (2) as a matter of fact, the early Christians always thought that the advent of the Kingdom was near at hand. The parable here must be intended to contrast the small beginnings of the Kingdom with the growth to which it is (rapidly) to attain, sufficient to shadow the world. It is worth noting that this is the only parable in Mark where 'the Kingdom' seems to be regarded not so much eschatologically but rather as coming in the growing Church.

The Greek in v. 31 is anomalous. *ὅς . . . μικρότερον ὄν.*

The final words are an exaggeration. The mustard-plant does not grow big enough for birds to nest in it. But the phrase is probably a reminiscence of Dan. $4^{12,21}$ or Ezek. 17^{23}.

33. *The word* (*τὸν λόγον*) as in 2^{2}.

The passage implies (1) that Jesus' normal teaching was in parables, (2) that Mark knew of other parables; further (3) that Jesus so spoke, in order to meet the capacity of His hearers, i.e. the parables were meant to be illustrative and not enigmatic. This then is again an inconsistency with the view in vv. 11 and 12;

to which, however, v. 34 reverts, once more singling out the disciples as the recipients of special explanations.

IV. 35–V. 43. *Various miracles.*

This section is unconnected with the main subject of interest, which since 3^{7} has been the Twelve, whose mission is recorded in cap. 6. Thus it breaks the sequence, such as it is, of the narrative.

The first, third, and fourth of these miracles are alike in exhibiting the power of Faith. The second is a story of exorcism.

35. *on that day.* This seems to refer back to 4^{1}, where Jesus was teaching in a boat at the Lake-side. The intervening parables are treated as if they had all formed part of His teaching on that occasion.

36. *other boats.* A detail given by Mark alone. The whole story is life-like and seems the product of direct reminiscence.

37. The Sea of Galilee is remarkable for sudden storms, which abate as quickly as they arise.

38. *the cushion* (τὸ προσκεφάλαιον). Such boats as these often had a sort of platform in the stern, where distinguished passengers would sit. This detail is found only in Mark.

Master (διδάσκαλε = Rabbi). The tone of irritation in the question is avoided in the versions of Mt. (8^{25}) and Lk. (8^{24}).

39. *Peace, be still* (σιώπα πεφίμωσο). The second word is that used (φιμώθητι) to the unclean spirit in 1^{25}. Mark perhaps thought of the storm as the work of demons.

40. This is the first place in this gospel where the disciples are censured for lack of faith or of understanding.

V. 1. *the Gerasenes.* Some MSS. have Gergesenes = Girgashites, a reading probably due to a conjecture of Origen's. But there is a real geographical puzzle here, which Origen perhaps felt. Gerasa was in Gilead, 30 miles from the Lake; this is too far off, since v. 14 implies the presence of a city near by. Did Mark not know how far Gerasa was from the Lake? Or was there another Gerasa? There is now a Khersa near the middle of the eastern shore of the Lake, which some identify with the scene of this story; but there is no steep place nor city near it. Mt. 8^{28} has 'Gadarenes'; Gadara is six miles south-east of the Lake, which also seems rather too far off to fit this story. Stanton suggests that a copyist may have substituted 'Gerasa' for some less well-known name in the text.

2. *tombs.* These would be rock-caves. Demons were supposed to haunt burial places.

3. The Greek sentence here is very badly constructed.

7. *Most High God.* Cf. Acts 16^{17}. It was apparently a heathen title; perhaps this man was a heathen. Gerasa was a half-heathen country; and none but heathen or very lax Jews would either own or herd swine, which are unclean animals to orthodox Jews.

torment me not (βασανίσῃς). Matthew and Luke understand this as referring to the final punishment reserved for demons; thus Mt. (8^{29}) has 'before the time' i.e. the last judgement, and Lk. (8^{31}) records the demons' entreaty not to be sent 'into the abyss'. It may, however, refer to the paroxysm which might accompany the expulsion of the demon. Of course in these cases of possession the man and the demon are temporarily identified, and we cannot distinguish between what the man says and what the demon in the man says.

8. Note how inconsecutively the story is told.

9. Popular superstition held that to exorcise a demon, a knowledge of its name was needed. Here the demon gives not his name but his number.

Legion. λεγιών; a Roman word transliterated into Greek.

10. Demons haunted particular localities and would presumably be loth to leave them.

17. The demand is due to superstition or to resentment at the loss of so much property, or to both.

18. The man has become a convert; he is now to be a missionary. The command here is in contrast to the usual injunction of secrecy (cf. 5^{43}). Perhaps Jesus wished the man to speak of Him, since He Himself could not remain in the district. But the contrast with His usual way of acting is surprising.

the Lord (ὁ κύριος). Mark's readers, and probably Mark himself, would understand this title to refer to Jesus; and so the man proclaims his cure as the act of Jesus (v. 20). Our Lord, if He used the word here, probably meant God. Lk. (8^{39}) in fact substitutes 'God' in this place. We find the word used for God in Mk. 13^{20}. Jesus perhaps uses it of Himself in Mk. 11^{3}. It became of course the regular title for Jesus in Christian mouths.

20. *Decapolis,* a federation of cities east of Jordan.

This is a strange and unsatisfactory story, and is awkwardly told. We may if we like speculate on the exact incidents which gave rise to it, and so try to explain it, or at least to explain away its unsatisfactory features. But we had better regard it as a story which has passed from mouth to mouth and acquired the characteristics of a popular tale. Perhaps it reached Mark from Gerasa itself, and was not a part of the Petrine narrative.

To Mark the story recorded another instance of Jesus' power over the forces of Evil.

21. The stories of the raising of Jairus's daughter and of the cure of the woman with an issue of blood are fitted into one another. We saw on 3^{21} that this is an occasional feature of Mark's method of narrative. The whole account here is graphic and life-like.

22. *One of the rulers of the synagogue.* A big synagogue had more than one 'ruler'. We are not told if this was a synagogue at Capernaum or not. The phrase, however, may here mean only 'one of the class of synagogue-rulers'. These 'rulers' had administrative charge of the affairs of the synagogue, and did not necessarily take part in the services. As a class, they would be opposed to Jesus, but the man's need drove him to resort to the Healer.

Jairus (Ἰάειρος) is the Hebrew Jair, as in Num. 32^{41}, Judges 10^{3}, Esther 2^{5}.

23. Notice the elliptical Greek *τὸ θυγάτριόν μου ἐσχάτως ἔχει, ἵνα ἐλθὼν ἐπιθῇς.*

25. Notice *οὖσα ἐν ῥύσει αἵματος* and the seven consecutive participles.

The woman's complaint was probably one that made her ceremonially unclean. The slighting reference to physicians is toned down in Lk. 8^{43}, whilst it is omitted altogether in Mt. 9^{20}. Lagrange (quoted by Rawlinson *ad loc.*) tells us that even to-day in the East it is common to employ many doctors whose diagnoses and prescriptions, frequently conflicting, result only in the expenditure of money to no purpose.

29. *plague.* Gr. *μάστιγος* as in 3^{10}. So also in v. 34 here.

30. Gr. *ἐπιγνοὺς ἐν ἑαυτῷ τὴν ἐξ αὐτοῦ δύναμιν ἐξελθοῦσαν.*

Our Lord seems here to ask a question for information.

31. Lk. 8^{45} puts the question in Peter's mouth.

33. The woman is afraid because she is made the centre of attention, or because she fears that the cure may be reversed.

34. It is perhaps too modern a view that Jesus wishes to make
ıer realize that it is a faith-cure. For Mark speaks definitely of
.he 'power proceeding from Jesus'. But the commendation of the
voman's faith is equally definite.

35. *troublest.* Gr. σκύλλεις = 'flay', and had been weakened by
ıow into the meaning 'annoy'. It is clear that the power of
aising the dead was not yet attributed to Jesus.

36. *not heeding.* Gr. παρακούσας, better 'overhearing', as in R.V.
narg.

37. These three disciples are selected on other occasions for closer
ntimacy with Our Lord.

38. These are not the funeral rites as in Mt. 9^{23}, for there had been
ıo time to collect the funeral *cortège*. The 'many' in R.V. text repre-
ents no word in the Greek. Only the household was yet present.

39. The doubt arises, as in the narrative of Acts 20^{10}, whether
his was an actual case of death or only of temporary syncope.
)id Our Lord mean what He said literally, or did He only mean
hat her death is not the end of the story, or even that death is
ıot final? He is here represented as speaking before He sees the
hild. In Lk. 8^{51-52} he sees the child first, but Luke (v. 53) makes
t clear that all the bystanders thought her to be dead.

41. *Talitha cumi.* One of the cases where an Aramaic phrase is
reserved and translated.

43. Mark is faithful to his usual idea that Our Lord did not
vish His miraculous cures to become known. In this case we may
vell ask how the incident could possibly be concealed. Cf. note
n 1^{24}.

The command to give the girl something to eat seems a genuine
eminiscence. It is an instance of Our Lord's courteous sympathy,
ut might also be intended by Him to mitigate the impression of
narvel; the parents are to treat the restoration of their daughter
ıs an ordinary recovery.

/I. 1–13. *The mission of the Twelve.*

We revert once more to the Twelve. In verses 1–6 we are told
f Our Lord's failure in an effort to convert His home and town;
ınd then in verses 7–13 the dispatch of the Twelve (in 6 pairs) on
vangelizing tours is recorded.

The failure at Nazareth follows on the comparative failure at
Gerasa. Our Lord perhaps is beginning to envisage the need for

something more than evangelistic preaching. Opposition an difficulties are increasing. But before He gives up Galilee, H will try to spread His message by the mouth of His disciples.

1. *his own country* (πατρίδα). This must be Nazareth, wher He had lived as a child. Lk. 4^{16-30} gives a detailed account of Hi preaching on this visit, which he places at the beginning of th Ministry.

Jesus comes as a Rabbi with His disciples; it is not a privat visit but an effort at public work.

2. *mighty works.* They had heard of these by rumour; so fa He had only preached in Nazareth itself. In v. 5 He works som cures, and possibly this took place before the synagogue-scene.

3 The comments are very true to human nature. Jesus is on of themselves, so they are unwilling to believe in His greatness

the carpenter (ὁ τέκτων). Mt. 13^{55} has 'the carpenter's son, Lk. 4^{22} has 'Joseph's son'; but both these gospels contained th story of the Virgin Birth. Some scholars think that Mark's tex originally read 'the son of the carpenter Joseph and Mary', an that Christian copyists altered it in the interests of the doctrin of the Virgin Birth. But it is as probable that the original 'th carpenter' was altered in Matthew to 'the carpenter's son', out of mistaken feeling that it was an indignity for Our Lord to hav been a working-man.

Son of Mary. Why not 'of Joseph'? Joseph may have been b now dead, but Jewish usage gave the father's name, whether h were alive or dead. The case of Jephthah (Judges 11^{1}) suggests tha to call a man the son of his mother was a covert insult, reflectin doubt on his alleged paternity. If this is the purpose of the phras here, then Mark knew of Jewish insults to the Virgin, and there fore probably also knew of the Virgin Birth.

Our Lord's brethren subsequently became believers (1 Cor. 9^{5}) and held a leading position in the church of Jerusalem. Tha there are only two references to them in this gospel (here and i $3^{20,21,31-35}$) suggests that Roman Christians were not muc interested in them. The 'sisters' are not mentioned elsewhere nor are their names known. The question whether these brethre are younger sons of Joseph and Mary (so Tertullian), or are sons o Joseph by a former marriage (so Origen), or are Our Lord's cousin (so Jerome), was of great ecclesiastical interest, when the theor of the perpetual virginity of Our Lady had arisen in the Church A full discussion of it may be found in Lightfoot's *Galatians*.

5. *could not.* The conditions of unbelief made His power ineffective. His power was not 'magical' but 'spiritual'. Mt. 13^{58} modifies the phrase to 'he did not', and does not record His 'wonder', no doubt because these phrases seemed to imply human limitations in Our Lord. The second half of v. 5 is regarded by some scholars as a 'rectifying gloss'.

The significance of the story is (1) that it gives an instance of Jewish rejection of Christ; and (2) more widely, that it provides a comforting precedent for the failures of Christian missionaries in their work. Their Master Himself had known failure.

7. This is one of the passages where Mark's use of Q, or of a version of it, seems obvious. The instructions to the Twelve in Mt. $10^{1, 5-15}$ and in Lk. 9^{1-5}, 10^{4-12} (Luke, however, divides up the instructions between the Twelve and the Seventy) are much more extensive. It is the easiest inference that Mark has abridged Q or used a version of Q.

by two and two (δύο δύο). Like Jewish collectors of alms. But they are not to go as beggars, though they are to live on the hospitality of their hearers. So they are not to take a 'wallet' (πήραν) = a beggar's collecting-bag.

The itinerant preacher or philosopher was a familiar figure in the Hellenistic age. The Church copied the custom, with her wandering prophets and missionaries. This explains Mark's and his readers' interest in these instructions. We find that in the early second century these evangelists sometimes abused their position. Thus the *Didaché* prescribes that an itinerant 'apostle' is to be well-received 'as the Lord'; but if he remains more than two days, he is a false prophet.

The Church fully believed that Our Lord had given to her not only the command to preach, but also power over unclean spirits.

8. The 'staff' is here allowed, in Mt. 10^{10} and Lk. 9^{3} it is forbidden too. So too in Mt. and Lk. (10^{4}) they are ordered to be bare-footed. These divergences may be accidental.

9. The Greek is very harsh; *ἵνα μηδὲν αἴρωσιν . . . ἀλλὰ ὑποδεδεμένους σανδάλια, καὶ μὴ ἐνδύσασθαι* (v.l. *ἐνδύσησθε*) *δύο χιτῶνας*. Allen thinks the *ἀλλά* may be a mistranslation of an Aramaic 'and not.'

They are not to wear 'two coats' at once, i. e. a second tunic under their mantle. Mt. 10^{10} and Lk. 9^{3} seem to say they are not to have a change of tunic with them.

it should be noted that, as Montefiore and Abrahams admit, Apostolic poverty was a new thing in Judaism.

11. *Shake off the dust* (Gr. *χοῦν,* so used too in the LXX). Cf. Acts 13^{51}, 18^{6}.

12. The message is given very briefly, as the readers would know what it was. Matthew expands here 10^{5-7}.

13. The only other reference to unction in the Church is in James 5^{14} where we see that it was used in cases of sickness. Oil was of course in regular use in the East for sores and wounds. But the connexion of unction with exorcism here seems to suggest that it was used by the disciples religiously rather than medically.

The return of the Twelve from their mission is recorded in 6^{30}.

Wellhausen doubts whether the record of this mission in Our Lord's lifetime is historical, and points out that, successful as it is said to have been, the disciples are yet as slow and stupid after it as they were before it. That may be so. But the fact that the mission instructions are recorded in Q as well as in Mark gives strong reason for accepting them as authentic; and they ring true and primitive in themselves. Nor can we see any reason why Our Lord should not have enlarged the reach of His work in this way. While He himself was preaching in the Galilean villages, He might well send out His disciples in various directions to carry the preaching to districts which He Himself could not touch. It may even be thought that this widening of activity was responsible for exciting the attention of Herod, and that Our Lord's difficulties in Galilee were thus so much increased that He eventually withdrew from Herod's territory ($7^{24, 31}$, 8^{27}).

VI. 14–VIII. 26. LEAVING GALILEE.

The contents of these sections are miscellaneous; and the relation of the several incidents to one another is uncertainly indicated. Thus the feeding of the 5,000 occurs in 'a desert place'. Our Lord and His followers then take ship to Bethsaida, but arrive at Gennesaret. No special incident happens there, and we are not told where the controversy on ritual which follows took place. The scene then changes to Phenicia, where the Syro-Phenician's daughter is cured. There follows a journey from Tyre through Sidon and through Decapolis to the Sea of Galilee, where the dumb man is healed. The scene of the feeding of the 4,000 is left quite indeterminate. The little company then go to Dalmanutha, the site of which is unknown. We are then told of the Pharisees' request for a sign, but are not told where this occurred. The lake is again crossed and this time Bethsaida is reached, where a blind man is given his sight.

It looks as if Mark had simply grouped a series of single incidents together as best he could, and as if each is best taken as a single episode by itself. But some method in the grouping may be inferred, if we note (1) that the series begins with the notice that Herod's attention had been excited by the report of Jesus' works. We are not told of any action against Jesus being taken by Herod; the story of John the Baptist's fate is interposed, and when the narrative is resumed in 6^{30} we hear no more of Herod. But we had already heard in 3^6 of the Pharisees' conspiracy with the Herodians, and the fact of their joint hostility is suggested in 8^{15}. (2) Most of the incidents take place outside Herod's dominions, and the series ends with a journey right away to Caesarea Philippi, after which Our Lord makes no further public appearance in Galilee; in 9^{30} He seems to wish His presence in Galilee to be unknown. (3) In Lk. 13^{31} we hear that Our Lord was warned of Herod's designs against Him. It is therefore a very possible inference that Our Lord's movements were now influenced by the fear of Herod's intentions, and that the fate of John the Baptist gave Him a warning which He was not slow to read. It may even have given to Him the first clear premonition of His own prospects; for it is at Caesarea Philippi that He first overtly foretells His Crucifixion (cf. note on 2^{18} however). We therefore shall probably be doing justice to Mark's purpose if we read the main interest of this division as being Our Lord's gradual withdrawal from Galilee, which ends in His resolution to challenge His destiny in Jerusalem.

VI. 14–29. *Herod and John the Baptist.*

14. This story is dovetailed in between the record of the sending-out of the Twelve and the notice of their return. Cf. note on 3^{21}.

King Herod. Antipas was not 'king', but 'tetrarch' of Galilee. Possibly the title 'king' was given to him by popular courtesy. Lk. 9^7, Mt. 14^1 have the correct title, though in 14^9 Mt. calls him 'king'.

he said. The reading ἔλεγον for ἔλεγεν is translated in R.V. marg. 'they said', and this is better sense. Herod's own statement is given in v. 16.

15. The expectation of a prophet ('as one of the prophets' i.e. one of the great succession) was perhaps based on Deut. 18^{18}.

16. Loisy comments that Herod's meaning may have been no more than 'this is a case of John the Baptist over again'.

17. We had heard of John's arrest in 1^{14}. We are given no date for his execution, but it must have been about A.D. 29–30.

The story here given must be set side by side with the narrative of Josephus, *Ant.* xviii. 5. According to Josephus, Herodias was first married to Herod, who lived at Rome. Antipas, who was married to the daughter of Aretas, the Nabataean King of Petra, fell in love with Herodias, and offered to repudiate his wife and marry her. His wife discovered his intentions and fled to her father, who went to war with Antipas to avenge the insult to his daughter. Antipas' army was severely defeated (in A.D. 36), and this defeat was regarded by some Jews as God's punishment for Herod's murder of John the Baptist. For Antipas, fearing that John's preaching might result in a popular disturbance (Messianic?), had him imprisoned at Machaerus, a castle overlooking the Dead Sea, and had him put to death there.

We note (1) that the name of Herodias' first husband is there given not as Philip, but as Herod. Philip, who was tetrarch of Ituraea till he died in A.D. 34, was another of Antipas' brothers, and married Salome, the dancer of Mark's story. Of course two of Herod the Great's sons may have been called Philip; but it is possible that Mark has confused Herodias' son-in-law with her first husband. (2) Josephus places John's murder at Machaerus, Mark seems (v. 21 'the chief men of Galilee') to think that it took place in Galilee, perhaps at Tiberias. There was, however, a palace as well as a prison at Machaerus, and the court may have been there at the time. Mark's story is quite vague as to the locality, and the phrase in v. 21 need not be taken to imply more than it says. (3) Josephus says nothing of Herod's personal ground of dislike for John. This, however, is of no importance. Josephus was concerned with political matters, and had no special interest in the minor scandals of the Herodian family. (4) Josephus does not mention the banqueting-scene, and it is said that it would be outrageous for a royal lady to dance an Oriental solo dance before an assembly of men; and further that Herod's promise in v. 23 was beyond his rights, as his tetrarchy was under Roman control. But we cannot be sure that any indecency would have been considered too outrageous for the

Herodian court, and Herod's promise need surely not be taken literally.

Mark's story therefore, though it is told with a popular colouring and with no exactness of circumstances, may be true even in detail. We may admit, however, that in its colouring it seems to be reminiscent of the stories of Elijah's confrontation of Ahab and Jezebel, and of Esther's appearance before Ahasuerus. It was no doubt a tale frequently told among the people after John's death, and the feelings of the Jewish people with regard to the character of the Herodian Court, and their hate for Herodias would make the tale lose nothing in the telling. Mark would not be interested in the exact circumstances of the execution; he recorded the story as it was generally current, because it suited his homiletic purpose. We cannot say, however, whether the story in this form comes from Peter or not. Peter, we should suppose, would have known the true facts; but we cannot be sure even of this. There was no public agency for the dissemination of public news, and Eastern countries are even now the home of stray rumour. How far correct information of the doings of royal personages got about is a point on which we can have little certainty.

It seems that the later Evangelists themselves felt uncertainty as to the details of the story. Luke omits it altogether except for a guarded reference in 3^{19-20}. Mt. (14^{1-12}) abridges it; he retains the mention of Philip, but omits any mention of Galilee or of the King's promise of half his kingdom. He says that Herod wanted to execute John but feared the people, though he adds that he was grieved at being constrained by his oath to comply with Herodias' request.

Herodias was a grand-daughter of Herod the Great, and so was niece to her two husbands, who were half-brothers of one another.

18. Jewish law might even compel a man to marry his deceased brother's wife, if she was childless. But Herodias' first husband was still alive, and so Antipas' action came under the prohibitions of Lev. 18^{16}, 20^{21}. Herodias either deserted her husband or repudiated him by some process of Roman law; Jewish law did not allow a wife the right of divorce.

19. *set herself against him.* Gr. ἐνεῖχεν αὐτῷ.

20. *kept him safe,* i.e. protected him (Gr. συνετήρει).

was much perplexed. πολλὰ ἠπόρει v.l. ἐποίει (R.V. marg. 'did many things'). Notice the character of Herod here depicted. The picture corresponds with that in Lk. 23^{8}.

21. *convenient.* Gr. εὐκαίρου perhaps = 'empty' and so 'festival'.

on his birthday. Gr. τοῖς γενεσίοις.

lords. Gr. μεγιστᾶσιν.

high captains. Gr. χιλιάρχοις. This was the title of the Roman military tribunes, but here it would mean officials of Herod, perhaps not military at all.

22. *the daughter of Herodias herself.* There is strong MSS. support for the reading 'his daughter Herodias' (τῆς θυγατρὸς αὐτοῦ Ἡρωδιάδος) but this is a mistake. She (her name was Salome) was grand-niece and step-daughter of Antipas. But the other reading would seem to give the meaning 'her daughter Herodias' (τῆς θ. αὐτῆς τῆς Ἡρ.). It may be best to omit αὐτῆς.

damsel. Gr. κορασίῳ a diminutive of κόρη = 'maiden'. Salome was perhaps about 20 years old or more. But diminutives are a feature of Mark's style.

23. Cf. Esth. $5^{3,6}$, 7^{2}.

25. *in a charger* (ἐπὶ πίνακι), a detail perhaps read back into the request from v. 28.

26. *reject.* Gr. ἀθετῆσαι. Better 'break faith with'.

27. *soldier.* Gr. σπεκουλάτορα a Latin word, used of a scout or spy, and then of an officer who carried messages and so would sometimes have to act as an executioner.

29. *corpse.* Gr. πτῶμα as in Mk. 15^{45}. The tomb was probably some rock-tomb near by.

VI. 30–56. *The feeding of the Five Thousand and other miracles.*

30. The return of the Twelve from their mission (6^{7-13}) is barely recorded, and is used merely as an introduction to the miracle of the feeding. No effect of their mission is reported. On the word 'apostles' cf. note on 3^{14}.

32. We are not told where Jesus was at the time of the apostles' return, nor where the desert place was (Lk. 9^{10} says Bethsaida); but this last must have been near the Lake-side. That it was not sandy wilderness is shown by the mention of 'green grass' in v. 39. It was apparently (v. 33) within walking distance of some cities, probably of Capernaum.

33. If the wind was light, the people on foot might easily have got round a short distance more quickly than the boat would go. But the topography is left quite indefinite. Neither Mt. (14^{13}) nor Lk. (9^{10}) records that the multitude 'outwent' those in the boat. Jn. 6^{22-23} says that the multitude went in search of Jesus to Capernaum, and states that there were other boats at hand.

34. *he came forth* (ἐξελθών); from the boat. Hort suggests 'from some sequestered nook in the desert', but this seems unnecessary.

The zeal of the crowd excites His compassion, as He thinks of the inadequacy of their official leaders.

37. *two hundred pennyworth.* The 'penny' was a *denarius,* worth about 9½*d*; it was the daily wage of a labourer. The figure here may be a minimum estimate of the sum that would be required; it may have been more than Jesus' party had in its common purse (cf. Jn. 6⁷).

38. *go and see*; presumably to their boat, to see how much they had brought; or they were to inquire whether there was any food in the wallets of any of the crowd (Jn. 6⁹).

39. *by companies.* Gr. *συμπόσια συμπόσια.* So in the next verse 'in ranks' *πρασιαὶ πρασιαί.* The idiom is un-Greek, and is the same as that in 6⁷ δύο δύο = 'two and two'. The word translated 'ranks' means literally 'garden plots'. The crowd was arranged in regular companies. It is probably fanciful to see here any reference to the colouring of their clothing marked off against the green grass. The vividness of the description is, however, unmistakable.

41. Jesus acts as the Jewish house-father; but what would more interest Mark's readers is that He also acts as did the Christian presbyter at the Eucharistic meal.

This miracle is recorded in all the four gospels. Those who will not accept the possibility of any miracle would read the story as a symbolical legend, based on or influenced by the tale in 2 Kings 4[42-44]; or else they try to rationalize the account, as e.g. by suggesting that the number has been exaggerated, or that the eaters were not physically satisfied, but took a mere morsel as a symbolical act of brotherhood. But the story here is very simply told, and its symbolism is not even hinted at. On the general possibility of miracles each must decide for himself (cf. Introd. C. ii). But that in some striking way Jesus once made a multitude His guests is the least that we can admit, if we have any respect at all for our authorities. That He could not marvellously multiply the food is something that we may only assert, if we know what were the limits of His power over Nature.

It is of course obvious that the incident was capable of more than one symbolical application. Thus John (cap. 6) connects it with the teaching about the Bread of Life; and we can well suppose that the details of the story would have a very direct Eucharistic reference for the early Christians, at whose sacramental meals the deacons, like the apostles here, carried the sacred elements round to the assembled worshippers. Again, the story, as teaching Our Lord's care for bodily need, would have an obvious interest for a Church which from the first began to care for the poor and the distressed. There may also be some force in Pfleiderer's suggestion that the example given in the story of a sharing without reserve would go home to Christian minds at a time when the local churches had each its common purse, and the local community of Christians gathered at times for a common social meal (the *Agapé* or love-feast) to which all who could contributed.

But it is one thing to admit that symbolical applications were read out of the story; it is another to treat the story as a fiction concocted to suggest symbolical lessons. It does not read like that, and the attempts to rationalize the miraculous element out of the story are not very convincing.

43. *basketfuls.* The 'basket' here mentioned was in regular use by the Jews. The word is κόφινος. In 8[8, 20], we have a different word σφυρίς. Allen quotes a note by Hort to the effect that the former was the agricultural basket, the latter the basket of the fisherman.

45. We are given no reason why Jesus got rid of His disciples so quickly, or why He did not go with them. Jn. 6[15] says that He saw signs that the crowd wished to make him king. If so, the immediate dismissal of His company was the first precaution against such a danger; and we can understand that this evidence of the unreasoning enthusiasm of the mob would prompt Him to a desire for a special time of prayer.

Bethsaida was in the north, not far from Capernaum, at the point where the Jordan enters the Lake; but it was in the domains of Philip, not of Antipas.

46. *taken leave.* Gr. ἀποταξάμενος = 'bid farewell to'.

the mountain; presumably the hills behind Tiberias, or simply a hilly rise near the shore.

47. *in the midst of the sea.* This means no more than 'well out to sea'. If it was the season of the Paschal moon (the mention of 'green grass' suggests that it was early spring), the boat would be visible from the land.

48. *the fourth watch* would be about 3 a.m. The statement that 'he would have passed by them' (Gr. ἤθελεν παρελθεῖν αὐτούς =he wished to pass by them) is strange, and only Mark gives it. It is equally hard to explain, whether we read the narrative

literally or symbolically. No satisfactory comment on it has been offered by anybody. That He 'looked as if He were going to pass by them' would of course be simple; but the Greek seems to say more than this.

49. *apparition*. Gr. φάντασμα.

51. Cf. 4^{39}. Some suggest that the story here is a 'doublet' of the story of the stilling of the storm.

In relation to this story, we are once more asked to believe that it is a piece of mythological symbolism; and once more we may admit that the symbolic application of the incident would be obvious to a Church which was tossing on the sea of persecution. Matthew's version ($14^{22\text{-}33}$) heightens the symbolic significance by adding the incidents of Peter's walking on the water, of his doubt and his sinking, of his rescue by Our Lord, and of the disciples' homage to Jesus.

52. *they understood not*, i.e. the truth about Jesus which was implied in these evidences of His power. The 'hardening' of their heart (ἦν πεπωρωμένη) is constantly noted by Mark, with regard both to the slowness of the disciples and to the opposition of the Jews. It is Paul's explanation of Israel's disbelief in Rom. $11^{25f.}$. It was probably the standard Christian explanation of the slowness of the Gospel's progress.

53. They had started for Bethsaida, but they reach Gennesaret, a fertile plain on the north-western shore, south of Capernaum, and in Antipas' dominions. Was this because the storm diverted their course? Or is Allen right in following the western text 'they came thence (i.e. from Bethsaida) to Gennesaret'? Or was Mark himself vague as to the exact relation of these places to one another? Mark was a Jerusalemite and not a Galilaean.

55. κραβάττοις. The same word as in $2^{4,11}$.

56. *the border* or 'tassel'. The word 'market-places' is loosely used here of any open space. Strictly speaking, none but a town would have an *agora*; and we are told here that he went not only into cities, but also into villages and 'into the country' (εἰς ἀγρούς) = 'to scattered farms or hamlets'.

The account of Jesus' sojourn in Gennesaret seems as if it were leading up to some special incident. But nothing follows. The ritual controversy in $7^{1\text{-}23}$ is unrelated to what precedes, and we are not told that it took place in Gennesaret at all; of course it might have done so; but if the suggestion is well founded, that

Jesus was at present refraining from public activity in Antipas' tetrarchy, it is surprising to find Him not only the centre of general attention (that perhaps could not be helped, if the storm had brought Him to Gennesaret), but also involved in a public controversy with Pharisees and scribes. It is not necessary, however, to suppose that the dispute of 7^{1-23} took place in Gennesaret, nor even that it took place at this particular moment in Our Lord's career. We have already noticed how uncertain is at times the chronological sequence of the incidents in the Marcan story. It is, however, probable that Mark intended to point the contrast between the enthusiasm of the crowds and the opposition of the official classes.

Luke's 'great omission' begins with Mk. 6^{45}. He makes no use of any Marcan material between that verse and Mk. 8^{27}. The bearing of this fact on theories of the composition of this gospel is considered in Introd. C. iv.

VII. 1–23. *Teaching about cleanness.*

This narrative reads like a compilation of separate pieces of traditional teaching. Notice the frequency of introductory phrases in vv. 6, 9, 14, 17, 20; vv. 8 and 9 are duplicates; an editorial note is clumsily interpolated in vv. 3 and 4; and the connexion of thought is not quite clear and logical, as we shall see below.

To Mark's readers this section had a very direct interest. The great battle within the early Church had raged round the question whether Jewish Christians might eat with Gentile Christians (cf. Acts 15). By the time that Mark wrote, this battle had ended, and the Pauline point of view was triumphant. But echoes of the controversy no doubt still survived. Furthermore the controversy with Jews was still hot, and the Jews would both feel and express contempt for the disregard of the Mosaic food-laws by the Christians. Thus any teaching of Our Lord's which seemed to abrogate those laws would be carefully preserved and gladly listened to.

1. This may refer to the scribes mentioned in 3^{22}, or perhaps to a new contingent of scribes who had been called in from Jerusalem to help against the new teacher.

2. *ate their bread* (τοὺς ἄρτους) a Semitic idiom for eating in general. *defiled.* The Gr. κοιναῖς (*lit.* 'common'; cf. Acts 10^{14}) means secular as opposed to sacred. A secular thing was not necessarily unclean in itself, but it became unclean where consecration was demanded.

No question whether of hygiene or of cleanliness is at stake in the controversy here. Ceremonial lustrations are often, so far as cleanliness is concerned, a mere pretence; and some Jewish ordinances (e.g. that of slaughter) may be pre-eminently hygienic or humane. Nor is the debate concerned with the point whether Jewish observances should be continued as a distinctive national badge. Nor does it question the advisability or even the rightness of certain voluntary abstinences for purposes of discipline (e.g. it cannot be applied to condemn fasting as a means of spiritual discipline). All these may be debatable points. But the debate here deals simply and solely with ceremonial uncleanness as defined by Jewish rules; and the question raised is whether there is such a thing as religious impurity in a material sense, whether *things* are unclean or only *persons*, and whether persons can be spiritually defiled by things or only by themselves.

The view of ceremonial pollution which Our Lord attacks goes back to primitive taboos based on animistic superstition; things were unclean because they were for some reason supposed to contain a dangerous spiritual potency in themselves. Such superstition was no longer alive in Judaism; but the principle of ritual uncleanness was maintained and even elaborated by the Rabbis, on the ground that the law enacted it.

The great principle which Our Lord proclaims in v. 15 lays the whole emphasis on moral and inner uncleanness as the only religious uncleanness. It is a destructive utterance, enfranchising men from that burden of external scrupulosity which hung so heavy on Judaism, as on all ancient religion.

There is an anacoluthon in the grammar of vv. 1, 2, 5, due to the interposition of the parenthesis in vv. 3 and 4. *συνάγονταί τινες ἐλθόντες . . . καὶ ἰδόντες . . . καὶ ἐπερωτῶσιν.* The omission of either one or the other *καὶ* would regularize the construction; but the harshness is quite Marcan.

3. vv. 3 and 4 are a note added by the author for the benefit of non-Jewish readers, as are also the notes in vv. 2 and 11. Jewish scholars accuse the statement in these verses of exaggeration; they deny that 'all the Jews' accepted the tradition which successive scribes had added to the Mosaic Law, and assert that the chief burden of ceremonial strictness lay on the priest, and to a very much less extent on the layman. But some competent scholars doubt the validity of these criticisms. In any case, as

Mark only uses the term *οἱ Ἰουδαῖοι* here (except in the phrase 'King of the Jews' in c. 15) and couples 'Jews' with 'Pharisees', he may mean by it only the more strictly orthodox as distinct from the crowd. It is certain that Judaism was identified to the Gentile world with ceremonial carefulness; the tone of contempt for Jewish observance which the language here conveys reflects the irritation which this Jewish trait excited in Gentile minds.

diligently. Gr. *πυγμῇ* = 'with the fist'. The meaning is unknown, and probably the text is corrupt. Some MSS. have *πυκνά* = 'frequently'.

4. *wash.* Gr. *βαπτίσωνται.* v.l. *ῥαντίσωνται* = 'sprinkle'.

pots. Gr. *ξεστῶν* a Latin word *sextarius* meaning a vessel holding a certain measure; and so used of a small pitcher. The Western text adds 'and beds' i.e. 'eating-couches' (*καὶ κλινῶν*).

6. The quotation is very nearly the LXX version of Isa. 29[13]. The Hebrew text is different, and would not give the point needed here. It seems probable that Our Lord would not have quoted the LXX, and that this quotation therefore was one current in the Church.

7. '*in vain*', because their obedience is external.

8. It is probably perfectly true that Our Lord did set Himself in opposition to the increasing power of the oral tradition.

9. *reject.* Gr. *ἀθετεῖτε* the same word as in 6[26]. The tradition, which was meant to be a fence for the Law, often overrode it; where the two collided, the tradition was preferred.

10. Our Lord here gives an instance of the overriding of the Law by the tradition. The exact case in point is not easy to decide, but the old Syriac version, which is nearest to the original dialect, has *qurbān dᵉ thethhannē men*(*i*)='I swear that thou shalt have no benefit at all from me'. The word translated 'benefit' ='things brought near', 'offered in sacrifice', but in New Testament times also 'gift' to a king or other honoured person. The Marcan Greek gloss is artificial and betrays ignorance of the Semitic idiom, whereas the Syriac is live speech with meaning and obviously preserves the original. It is unnecessary therefore to discuss the various alternative explanations of this passage that have been offered, since they are but artificial attempts to make sense of what is, to begin with, an artificial gloss.

But Our Lord's instance need not be taken as expressing the

general teaching of all Rabbis, or of the tradition as a whole. The tradition in fact (or some Rabbis at least) did allow the cancelling of vows where parents suffered, whilst the Law nowhere permitted the infringement of a vow. Thus the tradition to some extent mitigated the absoluteness of vows. But Our Lord's point is that the vow in itself is contrary to the spirit of the Law, and that to allow evasion of the vow in certain cases is not the way to deal with the circumstances of such a vow. Probably He has some notorious case in mind, in which one school of Rabbis had stuck out for the sanctity of oaths in all cases. It is certain that the Christian Church learnt to treat humanity as a prime element in man's duty to God.

10. The quotations are from Ex. 20^{12}, Deut. 5^{16}, Exod. 21^{17}.

11. *Corban,* an Aramaic word, = 'consecrated gift'. Note the anacoluthon of λέγετε ἀφίετε.

14. *again* i.e. as in similar situations. We had not heard of the presence of the crowd before.

15. Jesus now turns from the question of the ceremonial uncleanness of persons to that of the general distinction between clean and unclean meats. The connexion is that meats touched with 'unclean' hands became unclean. But His dictum logically suggests a wider application, which is explicitly drawn in v. 19. This application, the entire denial of any distinction of meats, was not fully understood by the Twelve till long after (Acts 10), and so the rebuke of v. 18 here for slowness of understanding would be seen to have a special pungency by Gentile Christians, who remembered how long and furiously controversy had raged in the Church round this very point.

Here Our Lord goes farther than to set the Law in opposition to the tradition, and undermines the Law itself, subordinating its ceremonial to its moral requirements. Montefiore draws attention to the logical inconsistency of Our Lord in first appealing to the Law against the tradition and then contravening the Law itself. The inconsistency may be admitted. But Our Lord is concerned with laying down a great new principle, and does not care for exact logical coherence in setting it forth.

17. *parable.* Here merely a proverbial saying.

We had not heard of any house before. It may be suggested that the explanation which follows is that which the Church provided. Cf. 4^{10} note, 10^{10}.

19. *draught.* Gr. ἀφεδρῶνα a rare word, and its meaning here is doubtful. It should properly mean 'latrine', but Wellhausen would take it to mean 'bowel', a sense given by the reading here of D ὀχετόν.

making clean. Gr. καθαρίζων, a masculine nominative participle. Grammatically the rendering of R.V. is alone correct; and the phrase looks like an addition by the author or an editor. It may not be too harsh for Marcan style to take the participle either with 'it' or with 'draught'. But the R.V. certainly gives the best sense.

20. *he said* ἔλεγεν. It may mean that this was a frequent saying of Our Lord's. The expansion in vv. 21–3 looks like the work of the evangelist.

21. The plurals mean 'acts' or 'purposes' of the several evil things. 'Evil thoughts' or 'deliberations' οἱ διαλογισμοὶ οἱ κακοί; πλεονεξίαι are 'coveting' or 'self-seeking'; 'wickedness' (πονηρίαι) are acts of 'deliberate malice'; 'deceit' (δόλος) or 'guile'; 'lasciviousness' is 'open immorality' (ἀσέλγεια). 'An evil eye' (ὀφθαλμὸς πονηρός) means 'grudging jealousy' (*Lat. invidia*). 'Railing' is βλασφημία, 'slander' or 'detraction'. 'Pride' is ὑπερηφανία 'self-approbation'. 'Foolishness' is ἀφροσύνη, the quality of 'moral wrongheadedness', whereby we are unable to know God.

Allen quotes an interesting Buddhist parallel from *Sacred Books of the East*, x. 2, p. 40. 'Destroying life, killing, cutting, binding, stealing, speaking lies, fraud and deceptions, worthless reading, intercourse with another's wife—this is defilement, but not the eating of flesh.'

VII. 24–VIII. 26. *Miracles outside Galilee.*

24. *thence.* The last locality named was Gennesaret. But we do not know if 7^{1-23} took place there or not, nor if this incident follows on what precedes.

The borders of Tyre and Sidon (many MSS. omit 'and Sidon') would mean the hinterland of those two towns, which stretched, north of Galilee, almost to Damascus. Jesus probably did not enter either of the two great towns; nor did He necessarily go far into the country. But He is out of Galilee and in a purely heathen neighbourhood. The last section with its teaching that all meats are clean may have been intended by Mark as a preliminary to justify this move into entirely non-Jewish land.

26. A 'Greek' i.e. a non-Jew by religion. A 'Syro-Phenician' (as distinguished from a Carthaginian Phenician) by nationality.

27. *be filled.* χορτασθῆναι. As in 6^{42}.

dogs κυναρίοις, a diminutive: it means the small house-dogs. The gentiles were often called 'dogs' by the Jews. But nothing here compels us to believe that Our Lord endorsed the contempt; such an attitude would be very unlike Him. His phrase here is gently whimsical, we may suppose, and more than half humorous.

Whether Our Lord had yet conceived of His work as applicable to more than Jews we cannot say. The version of His answer in Mt. 15^{24} would imply that He had not. Some commentators suggest that the woman's phrase enlarged His own point of view and struck Him as an intimation of God's will. This seems far too precise an inference from the language of the narrative. But that His direct and immediate concern was with His own countrymen seems to have been His general point of view.

It is clearly self-evident to Mark that Jesus came for the Jews; and though the word 'first' in v. 27 may be taken vaguely to foreshadow the extension of the Gospel to the gentiles, v. 29 on the other hand treats the present case as exceptional. Obviously Mark has not recorded this incident under Pauline influence; for though Rom. 1^{16} speaks of the Gospel as being 'to the Jew first, and also to the Greek', Paul's whole energy was bent on maintaining that 'the Greek' was not to be only an exceptional case. Luke, who is pre-eminently the gentile historian, omits this incident altogether, no doubt because it did seem so to treat the offering of grace to the gentiles. (Cf. Introd. C. ii.)

28. The woman's repartee takes up the idea in Our Lord's phrase, and puts the case that even a gentile has a place in God's world. The story here is a brilliantly human narrative, and bears on its face its stamp as a direct reminiscence.

crumbs Gr. ψιχίων, said by Montefiore to mean the pieces of bread on which the eaters wiped their fingers, and which they then threw on the floor. The word occurs in the N.T. only here and in the parallel Mt. 15^{27}.

Lord Gr. Κύριε, in the heathen woman's mouth, would only mean 'Sir', though to Mark of course its higher use as applied to Our Lord would be familiar. The conversation with the woman was quite probably carried on in Greek. Most Galilaeans or even most Jews were to some extent bilingual at this time. For the use of Κύριος in this gospel see note on 5^{18}.

30. It is worth remarking that the only two cures which Our Lord effects 'at a distance' occur in the case of gentiles, namely here and with the centurion's servant in Matthew and Luke.

31. The geography is impossible. Sidon is far north of Tyre. Mark's geography, we have often noted, is very weak. Wellhausen suggests 'Sidon' to be a mistake for 'Saidan' in the Aramaic, which is a form of Bethsaida.

The journey here described must have taken months; Our Lord still keeps out of Antipas' territory.

32. We do not know if this man was a Jew or a gentile. The population of Decapolis was mixed. The story here is told very graphically.

The Greek word here used 'μογιλάλον' means 'speaking with difficulty'. In Isa. 35^{6} LXX it is used to translate the Hebrew 'dumb'. This man may have been a deaf-mute.

33. The man is cured by the use of saliva and the touch, as in the very similar cure 8^{22-26}; both stories occur in Mark alone, perhaps because Matthew and Luke did not like to record such use of external means by Our Lord in His cures. Saliva was often regarded in the ancient world as having curative properties, and the Rabbis discouraged its use as quasi-magical. Vespasian is said to have cured a blind man at Alexandria by the use of saliva (Tac. *Hist.* 4. 81. '*oris excremento*').

34. *Ephphatha,* an Aramaic word. 'The use of the word in a latinized form ('*Effeta*'), accompanied by an application of saliva to the ears and nose of the candidate, came eventually to form part of the ceremonial of Baptism according to the usage of the Western Church (the so-called *aurium apertio*).' (Rawlinson.)

35. *his ears* Gr. αἱ ἀκοαί.

36. The usual Marcan idea of a charge of silence after a miracle. Cf. note on 1^{24}.

37. The words are reminiscent of Isa. 29^{18}, 35^{5}.

VIII. 1. No clear note of time, and no note of place is given. We are not told how the multitude had been gathered or had been 'three days' at hand. There is much to be said for the theory that this story is a 'doublet' of the feeding of the 5,000 (though plainly Mark took the two as separate stories, cf. vv. 19 and 20), as it seems incredible that the circumstances should have reproduced themselves with such substantial similarity, and that the memory of the first feeding of the multitude should have so faded from the disciples' minds that they are equally perplexed here. Indeed the similarity between the two contexts extends further. In both the miracle is followed by the crossing of the

Lake, by a controversy with the Pharisees, and by a cure at Decapolis in the first case, and at Bethsaida in the second.

If the two incidents are separate, we need not, however, believe them to have occurred at so short a distance of time from one another as the narrative suggests. We have already seen that Mark's chronology is vague.

Bacon may be right in suggesting that the two narratives are intended to symbolize the feeding of Jew and gentile by Christ. The first takes place in Galilee, the latter in Decapolis. A further but perhaps a fanciful refinement sees a similar symbolism in the numbers of baskets of fragments, the 12 representing the Twelve apostles, who preached to the Jews, the 7 representing the Seven deacons of Acts 6³, whose work led to the extension of the Gospel to the gentiles. It is, however, possible to overpress the symbolical purpose in Mark's narrative, and Bacon in particular seems to overpress it to an inordinate extent. That symbolical purpose is to some degree present in the gospel may be admitted; but on the whole Mark's story does not bring it out at all emphatically. The element of symbolism seems to be far stronger in Matthew and Luke and above all in John than in this gospel, which appears to aim in general at telling its story simply and directly.

8. *σφυρίδας*. Cf. note on 6⁴³. The variety of word suggests that Mark has two written parallel sources before him.

10. *Dalmanutha*. This place is unknown; we do not even know on which side of the lake it was, but probably on the west, since Our Lord at once comes into controversy with the Pharisees and, crossing the lake again, comes to Bethsaida. Mt. 15³⁹ has 'Magadan', which is also unknown, unless this is another form for Magdala, which was between Capernaum and Tiberias. It has been suggested that the word 'Dalmanutha' has come from an illegible original or from a corruption in an Aramaic text. Cheyne proposes 'Migdal-nunia', a suburb of Tiberias.

11. *a sign*. Cf. 1 Cor. 1²². The miracles might be treated as magical. They want a 'sign from heaven' such as a 'voice out of heaven', as an incontrovertible proof. The second temptation in Mt. 4⁶ would be a temptation to give such a sign.

12. Notice the Greek rendering of a Hebraistic form of strong negation ἀμὴν λέγω εἰ δοθήσεται κ.τ.λ.

Our Lord's answer here seems to imply that the Pharisees, being outside the kingdom (as in 4¹¹,¹²) are to be granted no sign.

The parallel passages in Matthew and Luke have interesting variants, and are based on Q; we cannot tell if Mark in this instance is abridging Q; more probably he is following a different tradition. Mt. 12[38-42] makes Our Lord offer His Resurrection (of which Jonah was a prototype) as a sign. Lk. 11[16,29-32] takes the same illustration of Jonah and makes the sign consist in Our Lord's own Personality (the 'greater than Jonah').

14. Burkitt suggests that the lack of food was because the departure was hurried to avoid a worse clash with the authorities.

15. This verse is no doubt genuine. But without it the narrative would read more straightforwardly. It may be a separate saying which Mark has intruded here. Its original meaning was probably a warning against not only the hostility of the Pharisees and Herod, but also against the tendencies in them which blinded them to Our Lord's character. Thus Mt. 16[12] does not misinterpret by referring it to their teaching (though he reads 'Sadducees' instead of 'Herod'). The combination of these two enemies has been found already in 3[6] and recurs in 12[13].

16. The verse is obscure in meaning, if v. 15 is read as part of the story. Without it the sense is plain 'they were arguing with one another about the fact that (because) they had no bread', διελογίζοντο πρὸς ἀλλήλους ὅτι ἄρτους οὐκ ἔχουσιν.

17. *hardened* πεπωρωμένην. Cf. 3[5], 6[52]. Their lack of understanding seems at first sight to consist in being in fear of material want, after the two miracles of feeding. But it is possible that, as in the similar cases 4[13], 6[52], 7[18], the significance is less superficial, and that Mark means to imply that the miraculous feedings were signs of Our Lord's power in general, and pointed farther. The reference would be to the Eucharist, where Christ gives spiritual food to His followers, and which the Church saw pre-figured in these two miracles. If so, the implication would be that the disciples were yet blind to the inferences of Christ's power to satisfy spiritual need, of which the giving of material food to the multitude was a sign.

18. Cf. Isa. 6[9], Jer. 5[21], Ezk. 12[2]. The words are also used in Mk. 4[11,12].

22. *Bethsaida*. Still out of Antipas' dominions. It is not the blind man's home, but is the place where Jesus is staying. It is strange that it should be called a 'village' (vv. 23, 26), for Philip had enlarged it into a town of some size. Some think that

there was an old village of Bethsaida, which is here in question. Or the use of the word here may be a piece of ignorance or carelessness on the author's part.

The parallelism between this story and that in 7[31-37] has already been noticed. Here, however, the cure is gradual, which is perhaps another reason why Matthew and Luke omit it.

24. Gr. βλέπω τοὺς ἀνθρώπους, ὅτι ὡς δένδρα ὁρῶ περιπατοῦντας. The sense is clear enough: he sees blurred images like moving trees (his blindness cannot then have been congenital). But the Greek has to be rendered 'I see men, because I behold them walking like trees'. Some suggest that 'because' is a mistranslation of an Aramaic 'whom'. But we have already seen reason to doubt whether the case for regarding this gospel as a translation from Aramaic can be accepted. Cf. Introd. F, i. We must then take the expression here as a piece of loose Greek.

25. *clearly*. Gr. τηλαυγῶς.

26. Obviously a suggestion of silence.

VIII. 27–X. 45. THE WAY OF THE CROSS.

The Marcan picture of Our Lord has so far been on the whole singularly dry and meagre. Very little of the mind or heart of Jesus has been exposed to view. We read the gospels so much as a composite story, our picture of Christ is so much a composite picture incorporating traits from each of the gospels, that it requires a real effort on our part to isolate one gospel for examination. But if, trying to do so here, we turn over once more the chapters of Mark up to the point which we have reached, we cannot help noticing that the portrait is very defective in the attractive and gracious features which are so prominent in the general Christian conception of Our Lord's Personality. We see that He makes big claims; He calls disciples, He claims the power to forgive sins and to 'spoil the house' of Satan. His teaching and His religious attitude present a few striking suggestions of novelty; He eats with publicans and sinners, He seems destitute of ceremonial particularity, He is free and unconventional in his views on Jewish sabbatarian rules and food-restrictions. But these suggestions are few, and their bearing is not elaborated. That which is made so emphatic in Matthew and Luke is not more than hinted in Mark. The supernatural powers of Jesus have indeed been frequently illustrated; but the fame which these bring to Him seems to be little to His taste. He appears to regard teaching as His main work, and we are told that His teaching had a new ring of authority. But very little of it has been recorded, nor has anything like a general outline of His 'gospel' been attempted. Mark has given us nothing like Matthew's Sermon on the Mount, nor Luke's Sermon on the Plain; he has given us nothing of the Lukan teaching on prayer and very little of the catholic humanitarianism which Luke brings out so strongly; he has not given us the Lord's Prayer, nor any teaching about the Fatherhood of God, nor more than a very few hints of Our Lord's ideas about the brotherhood of men. And the consequence is that the Galilaean Ministry in Mark seems comparatively aimless. We have had indications of the difficulties and opposition which it provoked; but Our Lord seems to avoid meeting His opponents face to face. No clear objective of His work is suggested; the narrative of the Temptation, which might have supplied this, and which does supply it in Matthew and Luke, is the barest statement.

Now, so far as this apparent 'aimlessness' is concerned, it may be suggested that it was perhaps a fact in the earlier part of Our Lord's public work. The early years of the Franciscan movement show a similar characteristic, at least up to the point when the Primitive Rule was sanctioned by the Pope. It may be that Our Lord at first went about Galilee calling disciples, preaching, and healing, without giving any clear indication of the wider purposes germinating in His mind.

We must also remember that Mark may have written his gospel to supplement the Q record of Our Lord's teaching (cf. Introd. C. iv); he certainly wrote it for readers who had knowledge of what Jesus had taught and were familiar with the portrait of Jesus' Character and Purpose as preserved in the loving reverence of the Church; he was not writing a biography of Jesus for people who knew nothing about Him, he was only aiming to supply stories for catechetical purposes about One whom the Church already knew and believed in. We can thus explain without much difficulty the austerity and comparative colourlessness of the Marcan record of Our Lord's Galilaean Ministry. But we can also see good reason why in process of time the second gospel fell into a position of secondary importance compared with that which the first and third gospels assumed.

But from 8^{27} onwards a change comes over the character of

Mark's record. Purpose and Tragedy both enter into it. The division 8^{27}–10^{45} is marked out by three predictions of disaster (8^{31}, 9^{31}, 10^{33}), which, as J. Weiss puts it, 'ring out like muffled strokes of a bell', and give to the whole section a tense and solemn character. We get the impression that Jesus is about to offer a deliberate challenge. It is His own Will to lay His life down (Jn. 10^{18}), and He sternly rebukes Peter for questioning His determination; He even tells His disciples that the bearing of the Cross is a contingency which any follower of His must be prepared to face.

Whether Jesus went to Jerusalem with the purpose to die or with the purpose of trying a last stroke for victory and only of dying if it failed, who can say? Commentators have argued the point. But is it not exactly analogous to the question about some of the O.T. prophets, whether their announcements of doom were made conditionally or absolutely? On the one hand they predict doom as certain; on the other hand they call to repentance, and they would not do so if they were certain that no repentance could come and that nothing could avert the doom. A reluctance to be too precise in pronouncing as to Our Lord's views on the prospects of His challenge seems to be the only reasonable, as it is the most reverent, course.

But we can at least be sure that His purpose was to challenge His nation at the heart of its life, and that He plainly saw the risk that this would entail. That risk was in fact obvious enough. Up to now He had offended the feelings of the most influential religious party of the Jews (the Pharisees), who had even gone so far as to ask help from the hated Herodian power to suppress the offender. But the Pharisees had no official position. A riot and murder (as happened to Stephen) was one possibility; but Our Lord was popular with the Galilaean mob, and a riot against Him would not be easy to excite in Galilee. A forcible attempt by Herod (such as had ended the career of John the Baptist) was another possibility; but Our Lord had of late been avoiding Galilee, and outside Galilee Antipas had no power. But in Jerusalem Jesus would have to meet the Sadducaean priesthood, who were in a way the official magistrates of Jerusalem, with official powers of arrest and inquiry in certain cases, and with the official right to complain to authorities who had the power of life and death. True, that authority was not a Herod Antipas, but a Roman governor; and Roman justice in the provinces was not at this time corrupt or aggressively cruel as it had often been under the Republic. But the chief ambition of any Roman governor was to keep his province free of public disturbances; and Judaea was notoriously turbulent and restive under Roman rule. If the choice had to be made between the danger of a popular riot, and the surrender to an excited Jewish mob of one of their fellow-provincials (not a Roman citizen; Paul's citizenship probably saved him more than once from a similar fate), who for some reason had become obnoxious to them, it would have to be an exceptionally strong and conscientious governor who in such a case would weigh at all carefully the claims of abstract justice for the individual who was provoking the excitement. Thus Jesus, in going to Jerusalem, was running into a danger to which He could not be blind. He went there and gave His challenge under no illusions as to its probable consequences.

The suggestion of the gospel story is therefore that at this point an actual change, or at least a conscious development, of intention took place in Our Lord's own mind. He had started to proclaim the Kingdom of God in Galilee; He had aroused angry opposition, and had also won much popularity; but the latter had been the result of His healings rather than of His preaching, and caused him little satisfaction. He now resolves to change the *venue* of His Ministry; and when He arrives at Jerusalem we find that, whether of set purpose or through force of circumstances, His method of preaching is also changed. So far He seems to have used little of the language of denunciation (though, it is true, the Marcan record of the Galilaean Ministry is so meagre that we cannot be sure that it did not show this characteristic merely because no trace of it is recorded); He provoked opposition rather by disregard of current religious regulations than by open attack upon them and those who would maintain them. But in Jerusalem His attitude to established usages and leaders is publicly and actively aggressive (Mk. 11^{15}, $12^{12,38}$).

Such an interpretation of the story is at least legitimate. So far as our data go, it accords with them. But critics are often tempted to go farther. Thus, Our Lord certainly accepts Peter's ascription to Him of the Messianic title at Caesarea Philippi; and at Jerusalem He makes or allows a public Messianic entry. In Galilee He seems to have refrained from claiming the position of Messiah (though this inference is made insecure by the Marcan idea of public demonic recognition, cf. note on 1^{24}, and by the language of $2^{10,28}$, cf. note at end of 2^{11}).

We cannot say whether any of the disciples or any one else had in Galilee stumbled on or guessed at the Messianic explanation; Peter's confession is not treated in Mark as a surprise, though it is so treated in Matthew; but at least a desire to veil His Messiahship seems to be indicated. May we then infer that He only now reached for Himself the conviction that He was Messiah? Or had He always (at least since His Baptism) thought of Himself as Messiah? Had He hoped at first for a peaceful triumph of His Gospel by the general repentance of the people, and had He only now decided that the Kingdom of God could only come by His death? Or had an atoning death always been a part of the prospect in His mind, and did it now merely come for Him into the foreground as the climax drew near?

These questions raise interesting speculations; but we have no data by which to answer them. On the one hand Lk. 2^{52} tells us that Jesus 'advanced in wisdom . . . and in favour with God', and this may reasonably be taken to include a growing consciousness of His divine mission and a growing realization of the right way to discharge it; the story of the Temptation by itself implies some mental balancing of alternatives. But on the other hand the gospels are not studies in the psychological history of Our Lord, and give us no groundwork for speculations as to the processes of His mental development. That such curious psychologizings jar on Christians may be due to their religious prepossessions; but even if for a moment one could lay aside such prepossessions, one would still have to say that, the character of our records being what it is, these psychological speculations are and can only be excursions into the fanciful, rather than scientific comment.

The most we can say is that Mark's gospel, regarded as a work of literature, is so written that at 8^{27} it becomes a close-knit story, intimate and purposeful, written in a tone of strong tragedy. True, it still has, as we shall see, its inconsecutive incidents and details. But it produces a deep effect of Purpose working itself out, of a big Personality doing a big Thing, gripping Fate by both hands, and dominating the turmoil of circumstances to carry through an intention on which He is fully determined. Bacon entitles this section 'The Way of the Cross', and the title is so apt that we have borrowed it gratefully. For the story is that of the way in which Our Lord showed His power to lay down His life and to take it again, and its purpose is to make Christians understand what Christian discipleship ultimately means. Indeed Wellhausen is entitled to say, as he does, 'Here for the first time, properly speaking, begins the Gospel as it was proclaimed by the Apostles; we have seen little of it hitherto. The determination to go to Jerusalem . . . brings about a remarkable change. A transfigured Jesus stands before us. . . . He no longer teaches in general terms, He makes predictions about His own Person. He speaks no longer to the people, but addresses Himself to a narrow circle of disciples, and to them He discloses His nature and vocation. He does so, moreover, esoterically; they are to say nothing to any one until the predictions are fulfilled, and until they are fulfilled the disciples do not even themselves understand His teaching. The opportunity to strip off the *incognito* which He has maintained till now is afforded by the acknowledgement of Peter "Thou art the Christ", an acknowledgement which He had Himself elicited and which He accepts, but only with an immediate correction; He is not the Messiah who is to restore the Kingdom to Israel, but quite another Messiah. He goes to Jerusalem not to establish the Kingdom, but to be crucified.[1] Through suffering and death He enters into the glory of the Kingdom, and only by this same path can others enter therein. The Kingdom of God is no Jewish Kingdom; it is destined only for certain chosen individuals, sc. for the disciples. The idea of the possibility of a "repentance" of the Jewish people is abandoned.[1] Instead of the summons to repentance, addressed to everybody, we have the demand "Follow Me", which only few are capable of fulfilling. The idea of discipleship itself loses its proper significance of literal "following", and assumes a higher meaning. . . . It is a question of bearing the Cross after Jesus. For the Kingdom's sake disciples must make an absolute breach with family and nation, must sacrifice all that binds them to life, and life itself. . . . A breach with the world is demanded, which leads to martyrdom. Thus are the situation and mood of the earliest Christian community reflected beforehand in Jesus, as He goes forward to meet His fate. On this depends the lofty pathos in which this introduction to the Passion excels the Passion itself'.

Some critics see in this emphasis on the Cross a sign of Pauline influence on Mark. This point has been already considered in Introd. D. iii, and hardly seems to call here for further notice.

[1] We have already considered whether such absolute statements as this are wholly justifiable or not.

It is very hard to think other than that the emphasis which Paul certainly laid on the Cross was a part of the general Christian interpretation of Our Lord's Personality and Work, and that Our Lord Himself fully understood what He was doing and meant His disciples to understand it too; and the Marcan point of view at once is seen not as the product of Pauline influence, but as a genuine reflection of that which the Church as a whole rightly read as a chief conviction in the Mind of Jesus Himself.

The section forms one continuous story. But for convenience of comment it may be divided into three subsections: (1) 8^{27}–9^{29}. The first prediction of the Cross; teaching on the duty of Cross-bearing, together with an assurance of the Kingdom and of salvation for the disciples, of which assurance the Transfiguration is as it were the overt pledge. This subsection therefore may be entitled 'Cross and Crown'. The cure of the epileptic boy (9^{14-29}) is loosely attached to the story of the Transfiguration. (2) 9^{30}–10^{31}. Second prediction; the moral qualifications in the Kingdom, humility (9^{33-37}, 10^{13-16}), sincerity (9^{38-50}), detachment (10^{17-31}). The teaching on divorce (10^{1-12}) seems intrusive in this section; it may, however, be taken to give the ideal of matrimony for those in the Kingdom. (3) 10^{32-45}. Third prediction. The special question of rank in the Kingdom. The final qualifications are shown to be suffering and service.

VIII. 27–IX. 29. *First Prediction. Cross and Crown.*

27. *The villages,* i.e. the daughter-towns. Caesarea Philippi lay on the southern slopes of mount Hermon, twenty-four miles north of Bethsaida. Formerly named Paneas, it had now been rebuilt and renamed by Herod Philip.

28. Cf. 6^{14-16}. The expectation of Elijah's return depended on Mal. 4^{5}. 'One of the prophets' may mean 'a new prophet', or 'a former prophet returned to life' (Lk. 9^{19} understands it in the latter way). In 2 Esdras 2^{18} the return of Isaiah and Jeremiah is prophesied.

The grammar here is harsh, the two names being in the accusative, whilst the last clause is ὅτι εἷς τῶν προφητῶν.

29. This is the first use of the title 'Christ' in this gospel, as also the first appearance of Peter in a separate role. We may note in comment on this very important passage that (1) Our Lord's question suggests that He had not yet made before His disciples any (or at least any unequivocal) claim to be the Messiah. This

reflects light on the point raised in connexion with the language in $2^{10,28}$ (see notes *ad loc.*). (2) No special significance seems to be attached by Mark to Peter's confession, as is done in Mt. 16^{17}, where he receives special congratulation. Indeed by his theory of the public demonic proclamations of Our Lord's status Mark has estopped himself from treating Peter's acknowledgement as a novelty. We may yet conjecture that it was in some way a climax to the disciples' wonder at their Master. Mark reserves the note of surprise for Our Lord's announcement of the Cross as in store for Him. He accepts the homage offered to Him, but at once declares a new conception of Messiahship. (3) Our Lord's command to keep silence about His Messiahship is of course in accord with Mark's general theory of His veiling of His true status. But here at least we may be fairly sure that the command is historical. Our Lord would not want Himself to be publicly proclaimed until He was ready. Schweitzer suggests with some plausibility that Judas' betrayal consisted not only in suggesting where Jesus could be found apart from the crowd, but also in revealing that He had accepted the Messianic title, a piece of knowledge of which the high priest makes terrible use in 14^{61}.

30. *charged* Gr. ἐπετίμησεν, the same word as is translated 'rebuke' in vv. 32, 33. It would here perhaps mean 'charged under a censure', and expresses strong urgency; scarcely annoyance, since He had Himself elicited the reply.

31. *the Son of man*; here unquestionably Himself as Messiah.

must Gr. δεῖ meaning an inner compulsion or an inevitable prospect, or perhaps that it was in accordance with Scripture, as in 9^{12}.

elders and chief priests and scribes, the clerical and lay aristocracy of Jerusalem, who composed the Sanhedrin or chief Jewish Council.

after three days; reminiscent perhaps of Hos. 6^{2}.

32. *openly* Gr. παρρησίᾳ, perhaps better 'confidently'. It cannot mean, however, that He spoke it to any but the disciples.

We may question whether Our Lord's prediction has not been made more definite and detailed by a Christian reading-back into it of the way in which it was fulfilled. Otherwise it is hard to see why the disciples were so broken by the fulfilment of the first part of the prediction (the Crucifixion). But we cannot be certain on such a point as this. Human courage can play strange tricks in emergencies. But that Our Lord could foresee His death is in no way difficult to credit; nor is there anything impossible in believ-

ng that His faith was equally sure of a divine victory to follow
on His death. (Cf. Introd. D. iii). It is also clear that He at once
changes the idea of the heavenly Messiah, based on Dan. 7[14],
into that of a Messiah who is to suffer and die for God's
Kingdom. To Peter the idea is intolerable (Mt. 16[22]), and he says
so; but Our Lord counters his objection with a tremendous rebuke, which recalls the similar language used in the Temptation
(Mt. 4[8-11]). Peter was in fact only voicing the same idea as had
then presented itself to Our Lord. We may be quite sure that the
rebuke, so stern and so terrific, was preserved in the Petrine
tradition. Nothing else but Peter's own authority would have
sufficed to gain credit for such an address to the great apostle of
the early Church, and of the Roman church especially.

took him. Gr. προσλαβόμενος. Swete says that the word is used of the stronger or wealthier coming to the help of the weaker or poorer, citing Acts 18[26], Rom. 14[1,3], 15[7], and carries here an air of conscious superiority.

33. *seeing his disciples.* The rebuke had to be public and sharp, because the others had heard the remonstrance. Wellhausen thinks that the rebuke (ὕπαγε ὀπίσω μου) should be translated 'Away from me'.

34. The presence of the 'multitude' in this scene is quite incongruous. No hint had been given of their presence, and indeed it was clear that Jesus was alone with His disciples. It is probable therefore that Mark has added on here a piece of Our Lord's teaching originally given in some other context. It is in fact a maxim for all Christians. The variant versions in Matthew and Luke of the subsequent sayings make it probable that they come from Q, to which source Mark perhaps owes it.

deny himself means more than is now conventionally meant by 'self-denial'. It implies the ignoring of self, the refusal to make self the centre of life, and is fully interpreted by Gal. 2[19].

take up his cross. He must be ready to follow Jesus to martyrdom. Criminals were called in Latin *furciferi,* because they had to carry the transverse beam of their cross to the place of execution. This phrase too means very much more than the conventional language about 'bearing one's crosses' implies.

35. *life* Gr. ψυχήν = the whole living man. Neither 'Soul' nor 'Life' quite renders it. 'His Self' would be nearest to the sense. 'Save' = make alive, healthy. The meaning is perhaps primarily

eschatological, but its application as a spiritual principle of active Christian discipleship was very near to hand.

for my sake and the gospel's. The latter word is not in Mt. 16^{25} or Lk. 9^{24}. It makes no difference to the sense. Jesus is the content of the Gospel. The word certainly does not here mean 'the gospel which Jesus preached', but 'the gospel of Jesus' (of which He was the subject).

37. Cf. Ps. 49^{8}.

38. This verse is perhaps a stray sentence added here. Its connexion with what precedes is not clear or logical. In particular it expresses the idea not of a suffering Messiah, but of the Son of Man in glory; it introduces the conception of the Parousia, and may be a piece of Our Lord's more public preaching. But it is not unlikely that at this point Jesus did in some way sound the claim of personal loyalty to Himself.

my words. Cf. 10^{24}, 13^{31}. The phrase hardly means the same as 'gospel' in v. 35, but rather the commands which Jesus gave.

adulterous (= idolatrous). For the meaning cf. Hos. 2^{2}, Ezek. 16^{32}; the words are introduced in a different context in Mt. 12^{39}, Lk. 11^{29}.

his Father. Here only and in 13^{32} does Jesus call God 'His' Father in this gospel.

angels appear at the Parousia in Dan. 7^{10} and in the apocryphal book of Enoch 61^{10}.

IX. 1. This saying, introduced by the vague καὶ ἔλεγεν αὐτοῖς seems to be addressed only to the Twelve; it reads here like an intrusion. Its importance in Christian eschatological hope was very great. It was one of the sayings which excited the early Christian belief that the Parousia was very near; cf. 1 Thess. 4^{17}, Phil. 3^{21}. Our Lord had said that some of those alive then would be left to see its advent. As the Parousia delayed, however, Christian hope changed from eschatology to idealism. We see the change going on in Paul's Epistles; and the fourth gospel shows the process completed. The coming of Christ was seen to have in a sense taken place at Pentecost, or at the fall of Jerusalem, or to be taking place in the growth of the Church and the spread of the Gospel. Thus the prediction was retained, though it had been unfulfilled in the sense previously attached to it. That Our Lord used the phrase, or some such phrase, can hardly be doubted. In what sense He used it we could only settle if we could decide just how far He actually thought in the terms of current Jewish

schatology (which revelled in calculating the date of the Day
f the Lord), and how far He only used it as a vehicle
o express His conviction of God's speedy vindication of His
ervant's work. This question is bound up not only with that of
he extent to which Our Lord spiritualized eschatological ideas
nd language, but also with the more general question of His
uman limitations of knowledge. He confesses ignorance of 'that
lay and that hour' in Mk. 13^{32}. On the general subject see what
s said in Introd. D. iv.

2. The story of the Transfiguration is taken by many critics to
e an obvious legend. At best they hold it to be based on a post-
Resurrection appearance to Peter, on the lines of that recorded in
Acts 10^{1}–11^{18}; though that particular comparison does not strike
ne as very illuminating. At worst they hold it to be a pure
iction, expressing symbolically the faith of the Church as to its
Master.

But, in these days when psychology is investigating recorded
visions' and 'auditions', and finding much evidence for believing
hese to have actually occurred, and even for the occurrence of
uch experiences as those of 'photisms' (appearances of light), it
s hardly scientific to adjudge outright this story to have no
istorical basis whatever, merely on the ground of the nature of
he phenomena; while neither science nor psychology has any
itle to decide how far such experiences may be merely human
allucinations or may be authentic communications from a divine
ource.

That being so, we may take the story as it is given to us, and
rofess a reverent ignorance as to the exact how and what of the
ccurrence. To Mark the purpose of it was to give to Jesus a fore-
aste of the glory to come to Him, and such may in fact have been
God's purpose in vouchsafing it. Its place in this section is equally
appropriate. In a section full of premonitions of the Cross and of
he call to Christians to bear the cross, it stands as the divine
assurance that the shame may be endured for the sake of the
glory to follow after. The note is one of pure encouragement. The
suffering is not for the moment even mentioned, as it is in Lk. 9^{31}
where Christ's 'exodus' is the subject of His conversation with
Moses and Elijah. The story in effect underlines the promise in
8^{35} 'Whosoever shall lose his life shall save it'; it declares that he
who believes shall reign. To a Church in the throes of persecution
it was a story that would speak high encouragement.

after six days. This is the only definite note of time in the gospel before the Passion. Some think it is based on Exod. 24^{16}; this seems fanciful; but we cannot see any purpose in the definiteness with which the date is here given. Six days after what?

mountain. Tradition said Tabor. Hermon would be more likely. But the locality is quite vague as in Mt. 28^{16}.

transfigured. Gr. μετεμορφώθη, a rare word, sometimes used of magical transformations (Lk. 9^{29} changes the phrase). Paul uses it in Rom. 12^{2}, 2 Cor. 3^{18} of spiritual 'transformation'.

4. Moses and Elijah represent Law and Prophets. The biblical tradition of the translation of Elijah, and the extra-biblical tradition of the assumption of Moses, caused these two to be regarded as the chief of those 'who have not tasted death from their birth (2 Esdras 6^{26}).

5. *Rabbi,* untranslated here only and in 11^{21}, 14^{45}; we do not know the reason of these three exceptions.

Not perhaps 'we are glad to be here' but 'it is fortunate that we are here' (for we can act as your servants). Peter's request to build 'booths' (σκηνάς) is probably reminiscent of the feast of booths (the σκηνοπηγία). He desires to prolong the scene.

6. A criticism on Peter's utterance as unsuitable. Earthly tabernacles are not fitting to a celestial Messiah.

7. The cloud is the *Shechinah,* the glory of God. Cf. Exod. 13^{21} 40^{34}. It overshadows 'them', i.e. the three chief figures. A variant is αὐτῷ for αὐτοῖς, i.e. 'him' (Jesus), as at His Baptism.

The 'voice' is a reminiscence of Isa. 42^{1-4}, but with υἱός (son) for παῖς (servant). 'Hear him' recalls Deut. $18^{15,19}$. This detail is comparable with that in 1^{11}, and may again be taken as 'midrashic' in character see notes on 1^{11} and after 1^{12}.

9. For the injunction cf. 9^{30}.

10. *Kept.* Gr. ἐκράτησαν = 'hold fast', 'remember'; or perhaps 'kept silence'. An easier sense would be given by inserting a 'not' 'they understood not the saying'.

The 'rising from the dead' seems here plainly to refer only to the resurrection of Jesus.

11. These three verses 11–13 are very hard.

(1) The Greek is 'they asked Him, saying that the scribes say &c.' This must mean 'they asked Him as to the fact that the scribes say'. In the disciples' mouth at this juncture it might be taken to imply 'Why has Elijah come now, if he is not to come

ill the Parousia?' But it is probably a current scribal objection
hat the Church had to meet, and signifies 'how can the Messiah
have to die, if Elijah is to come first and prepare everything for
him?' It is then a Jewish argument against the Cross, and can
hardly have come to life till after the Christian preaching of the
Cross had begun.

(2) Our Lord's answer is equally difficult to understand. As it
stands, He agrees that Elijah is to come first, and then puts a

Mt. Tabor, the traditional scene of the Transfiguration

counter-question, pointing out that Messiah's suffering is foretold
in Scripture; He thus raises a dilemma, which He solves by saying
that Elijah is come (referring to John the Baptist, as Mt. 17[13]
explicitly states). Wellhausen, however, suggests that v. 12 is
better read as a question 'does Elijah indeed come . . .? How
then &c.?' (The Greek is Ἠλείας μὲν ἐλθὼν πρῶτον ἀποκατιστάνει
πάντα, καὶ πῶς γέγραπται κ.τ.λ.)

Let us notice that this is the only place where Mark definitely
says that Our Lord's sufferings are in accordance with Scripture.
He no doubt has Isa. 53 in mind, which became one of the chief
proof-texts for Christian use. Cf. Introd. D. iii.

(3) The run of the sentence in v. 12 is so strange that, if Well-

hausen's suggestion does not commend itself to us, it may be best to see in 'how is it written . . . &c.' (v. 12b) a marginal gloss on the second part of v. 13, which has then got into the text. Or alternatively we might take 12b from its present place, and attach it to the disciples' question in v. 11.

(4) There is no reference to Elijah's sufferings in canonical Scripture (1 Kings 19^{2-10} hardly meets the reference here). Was there some uncanonical tradition on the point, or do the words 'even as it is written of him' (v. 13c) refer only to Elijah's coming'?

(5) The arrangement of the clauses in Mt. 17^{11-12} makes a logical connexion; 'Elijah cometh, and shall restore . . . but Elijah is come already, and they knew him not, but did unto him whatsoever they listed. Even so shall the Son of Man also suffer of them'. Luke omits the verses altogether, perhaps because he thought the argument too Rabbinical in tone.

(6) Allen says truly that the sequence would be more natural if the clauses were arranged thus; 11, 12b, 12a, 13a, c, 13b; or if we emend καὶ πῶς to καὶ οὕτως we could arrange the verses in the order 11, 12a, 13a, c, 13b, 12b.—To propose this as an emendation seems a desperate course; but at any rate either Matthew had something like this before him, or he himself rearranged the clauses to escape their logical difficulty.

14. The mention of 'scribes' here is incongruous; and they do not reappear in the rest of the incident. (Neither Mt. 17^{14} nor Lk. 9^{37} mentions them.)

15. *amazed*. Why? The language in Mt. 17^{2} and Lk. 9^{29} might suggest that His face still showed signs of heavenly radiance (cf. the case of Moses in Exod. 34^{29}); neither of them, however, mentions the amazement; and Mark does not mention the shining of His face at all. The surprise of the crowd is left unexplained (cf. 10^{32}, but there the reason for the disciples' amazement is easy to conjecture). The story is thus unsatisfactorily attached to the preceding paragraph. But we cannot deny the artistic contrast between the two successive scenes, of which Raphael made so much. And the story in itself is very vivid and seems clearly a product of original witness.

18. The symptoms are those of violent epilepsy.

The words ἀφρίζει and τρίζει occur only here in the N.T. 'Pine away'. perhaps rather 'become rigid'; the Greek is ξηραίνεται = 'dry up'.

19. This is addressed to all, not least to the disciples.

22. Probably not suicidal mania, but accident, which the father ascribes to demonic malignity.

23. The Greek is *Τὸ Εἰ δύνῃ, πάντα δυνατὰ τῷ πιστεύοντι.* Our Lord quotes the father's 'If thou canst', and adds 'all things are possible to him that believeth'; which surely does not mean (though some critics so interpret it), 'I because of my faith can do all things', but 'if you believe, all things are possible to you'. It is, as usually with Our Lord, a proclamation of the power of human faith.

24. The meaning is probably 'help me, though I do not believe enough', rather than 'help me to believe more'.

25. *deaf.* This was not mentioned in 9^{17}.

I command. The 'I' here is emphatic in the Greek; *ἐγὼ ἐπιτάσσω σοι.*

28. If this question was actually asked now, we must suppose that the disciples (who had already exorcised some demons 6^{13}) had acted in this case too self-confidently and without spiritual preparation. But, like other explanations in this gospel (e.g. 4^{10}, 7^{17}) we may better regard this as a later explanation of the Church, to the effect that some demons ('this kind') only yield to the power of special prayer and asceticism. The reading 'by prayer and fasting' (*ἐν προσευχῇ καὶ νηστείᾳ*) has strong MS. support, and may well be right. The full phrase (with 'fasting' mentioned) occurs in some MSS. of the passage in Matthew, and was probably inserted there from here.

IX. 30–X. 31. *Second Prediction. Moral qualifications in the Kingdom.*

30. Since 7^{24} Our Lord and His company had been outside Galilee. The journey to Jerusalem begins here, though its goal is not mentioned till 10^{32}.

Our Lord perhaps wanted to be *incognito* in Galilee because of the danger from Antipas. Mark, however, ascribes the wish to the fact that He was teaching the disciples privately.

31. *is delivered up.* Either this is a prediction of the betrayal, or it means 'is delivered up by the Will of God'.

33. The last mention in this gospel of Capernaum and of a 'house' (perhaps Peter's) in it. Notice that Our Lord asks a question for information.

34. The rival claims to precedence come out again in $10^{35f.}$.

35. *he sat down*; to teach or merely to rest after the journey? *called the twelve*. Does this mean that other followers were present with the company, or merely that he called the Twelve apart from the others in the house?

The sentiment of the greatness of service is repeated and developed in 10^{43-4}. Montefiore comments: 'Kindness and charity are familiar enough in the Rabbinical literature. But I do not think I am wrong in supposing that this touch of eager personal service, especially towards the sinner and the outcast, was a special characteristic of the religion of Jesus, and a new thing when he preached it.'

36. *taking him in his arms* Gr. ἐναγκαλισάμενος. A vivid touch peculiar to Mark, as also in 10^{16}.

37. *in my name* explained in v. 41 as 'because ye are Christ's'. To Mark's readers it would carry the idea of brotherhood specially due to the baptized.

The idea here is that man should 'receive' (='serve' or perhaps 'receive into brotherhood') not merely children nor even those of childlike disposition, but the humble and insignificant. Loisy's idea, that this reflects the views of a section of Church opinion which wanted to claim equality for Paul *vis-à-vis* the Twelve, that Paul therefore is the 'child', is surely fantastic and far-fetched.

Our Lord's words do not make a claim to equality with, or to a unique relation to, God. They simply declare that brotherliness is pleasing to God. But the dynamic effect of the saying in making service to the humble a service to Christ and so to God has been incalculable.

The connexion of v. 37 with v. 35 is imperfect. The child here is not used as an example of humility (as it is in 10^{15}) but as an example of a fitting object for brotherly treatment. But the general idea of service continues. 'Ministry' must regard no brother as too humble to be served.

38. This is the only remark specifically attributed to John in the Synoptists.

39. One who uses Christ's Name is not to be forbidden; he is to be let alone. The most favourable construction is to be put on his conduct. This sentence preaches tolerance for the 'unorthodox' and even suggests the possibility of 'unconscious Christianity'. The converse saying in Mt. 12^{30} deals with the inner relation to Christ

Both sayings may quite well be historical. They do not contradict one another.

The connexion of this paragraph vv. 38–40 with what precedes is made simply by the use of the word 'name'. It is thus verbal and artificial.

Exorcism by non-Christians in Christ's Name was certainly a question that the Church had to consider. Cf. Acts 19[13]. But there is no difficulty in supposing that such cases arose even in Our Lord's lifetime. Exorcism was common among both Jews and Gentiles in this period, and an exorcist, knowing Our Lord's fame, might easily think His Name a strong one to conjure with. Even in heathen magical papyri the Name of Jesus sometimes occurs. Reitzenstein (*Poimandres*, p. 14n. quoted by Rawlinson) cites from a papyrus 'I adjure thee by Jesus the God of the Hebrews'.

Loisy again sees an allusion to Paul in the reference to the exorcist who did not follow the Twelve.

41. The connexion is again merely verbal, in the word 'name'. This verse connects better with v. 37 than with v. 40.

because ye are Christ's Gr. *ἐν ὀνόματι ὅτι Χριστοῦ ἐστε*, *lit.* 'in the name that ye are Christ's'. This is the only place in the Synoptists where Our Lord uses 'Christ' without an article. The phrase 'I am of Christ' is found in 1 Cor. 1[12], and may be a gloss here, to explain 'in the Name'. Mt. 10[42] has 'in the name of a disciple'.

42. *on me* is omitted by many MSS.; but the use of 'believe' absolutely is characteristic of the Church language of a later time.

The reference here is probably to 'simple' Christians, children in faith. But the phrase may possibly include the thought of actual children. The practice of infant Baptism arose probably in quite early apostolic days, on the analogy of circumcision; though it was not till much later that it became the usual custom.

great millstone Gr. *μύλος ὀνικός*. The vehemence of Our Lord's phraseology in these verses is noticeable.

43. The sayings in vv. 43–48 are connected with v. 42 merely through the word *σκανδαλίζειν* ('to make to stumble'). The thought changes to that of 'sincerity'. It is better to be partially incomplete than to enjoy all one's powers, if among them is one which ruins the whole moral and spiritual nature. It is the 'ascetic' principle, and any wise living must have its ascetic element. That

in some cases and in some times a morbid or perverse asceticism has been commended by Christian teachers or Christian saints does not matter to the principle. Human nature being both imperfect and limited, the refusal of some enjoyments because of their dangerous possibilities (the danger will come from different directions in the case of different individuals) is the wisest method by which a man may keep himself 'fit' to concentrate on the things that make most for spiritual health. To the martyr church of Mark's time the principle would be a very clear call; the 'world' was so dangerous to Christian profession that a very stern discipline was needful to the Christians in their relation to it.

hell. The Greek word is *Gehenna,* which occurs here only in Mark. This was the Jewish name for the ravine (the valley of Hinnom) outside Jerusalem, where once sacrifices to Moloch had been offered (cf. Jer. 7^{31}), and which in later times had become the place for the destruction of the city refuse. The name was then transferred as a metaphorical description of the place where the wicked were punished (cf. 2 Esdras 7^{36}). This is to be carefully distinguished from *Hades* (the 'Hell' of the Apostles' Creed) which was the place of waiting between death and final judgement.

48. Some MSS. repeat this phrase in vv. 44 and 46. The phrase itself comes from Isa. 66^{24}. Our Lord uses it simply as a picture of the extreme horror of doom for the finally impenitent. The verse does not imply a doctrine of divine retribution such as has figured too largely in much Christian teaching under the title of 'eternal damnation'.

Life in vv. 43 and 45 is interpreted as 'the Kingdom of God' in v. 47. It means the Messianic Kingdom.

49. The word 'fire' connects this stray saying with what precedes. But here the fire is not destructive but cleansing. Some MSS. make this point clear by adding 'and every sacrifice shall be salted with salt' from Lev. 2^{13}.

50. The idea of savourless salt is derived from the saline deposits of the Dead Sea which preserve the appearance of salt, but out of which the salt is washed by rain. The point here is that the disciple who loses the true spirit of Christ ceases to have any preservative effect on the world. In Mt. 5^{13} it occurs in connexion with the saying 'Ye are the salt of the earth'. Notice that the metaphor of salt is here rather different from that in v. 49. There fire was to salt (cleanse) the disciples, here the disciples are themselves 'salt'. In the second half of v. 50 we recur once more to the

idea of salt in the disciples; and the last clause 'be at peace one with another' brings us back to the original dispute of v. 34.

The sayings in vv. 33–50 occur in Matthew and Luke in different order and sometimes in different contexts from those in which they appear in Mark. The following table shows the extent of the divergence:

Mark	Matthew	Luke
9. 33–34	18. 1.	9. 46
35	23. 11–12	9. 48. 22. 26
36–37	18. 5.10	9. 47–48
38–40		9. 49–50
41	10.42	
42	18. 6	17. 2
43–48	18. 8–9. 5. 29–30	
49		
50a	5^{13}	
50b		
10^{15}	18. 2–4	18. 17.

It may be that Matthew and Luke derived some or most of the sayings from Q. In Mark they are put together generally with merely verbal connexions, such as illustrate how Our Lord's sayings were preserved in oral memory. Mark may also be drawing them from Q, but it seems as likely that he is arranging them himself from memory of the kind of way in which they were orally transmitted.

X. 1. The text and meaning of this verse are both uncertain. Should we omit the 'and', and read 'the borders of Judaea beyond Jordan', which is Peraea? Or are we to think that Our Lord carried on a roving ministry partly in Judaea and partly in Peraea? On either of these views we are surprised to find Our Lord teaching publicly in Peraea, which was part of Antipas' tetrarchy, if we are right in supposing that He had previously been for some time avoiding public work in Antipas' jurisdiction.

Or does it mean that he resumed public work when he reached the boundary between Peraea ('beyond Jordan') and Judaea, because in Judaea Antipas' writ did not run? But can the Greek (τὰ ὅρια) mean anything but 'the territories of Judaea and Peraea'?

Burkitt (*Gospel History*, pp. 96 and 97) suggests that Our Lord, James, and John (cf. Lk. 9^{51-56}) travelled by the route through

Samaria; that Peter and the rest went through Peraea and rejoined Our Lord where their route crosses the Jordan into Judaea; and that the geographical phrase here comes from Petrine recollection, and means the Judaean border on the other side (the Western side, Peter coming from the east) of Jordan. This is a very conjectural interpretation. Mark's geographical indications are in general so vague that we can hardly feel safe in making such elaborate deductions from this phrase. We must simply confess the difficulty.

Our Lord is famous in Judaea, no less than in Galilee. The 'multitudes' would consist not only of Galilaean pilgrims going up to the feast. According to the fourth gospel, this was by no means Our Lord's first visit to Jerusalem; and He had probably visited it more than once for festivals, though Mark tells us nothing of such visits.

2. *Pharisees.* The word is omitted by many MSS.; if we follow them, the sense is 'they came to him', i.e. an undefined set of inquirers.

tempting him; perhaps in hope that He would pronounce against the law and so give a handle against Himself; but it may mean only 'to test His powers' in dealing with a knotty point. Possibly Our Lord's views on divorce were already known to be non-Mosaic like those in Mal. 2^{14-16}.

4. The reference is to Deut. 24^{1-4}, which is intended to provide safeguards of a sort against indiscriminate repudiation. The passage there permits the giving of a bill of divorcement, because a husband 'hath found some unseemly thing' in his wife. It was a point of dispute among Jewish Rabbis what conditions were sufficient to constitute an 'unseemly thing', in the sense of the Law. Shammai, an older contemporary of Jesus, said unchastity alone. Hillel, another famous Rabbi, said many other things as well. This then was probably the point of the question. Did Jesus agree with Shammai or with Hillel?

It is true that the law of Deut. 22^{22} enacted death as the punishment for unchastity. But it is agreed by Jewish scholars that this law was probably obsolete by Our Lord's time, and that the unchaste wife was only divorced. The question here therefore does not exclude the case of unchastity, but asks whether Jesus allows other justifications for divorce.

5. The Mosaic law on the point was an accommodation to

human weakness. Here Our Lord goes near to openly denying the perfection and permanent validity of the Law, or at any rate of one of its regulations.

6. Some commentators take, perhaps rightly, the words 'from the beginning of the creation' (Gr. ἀπὸ δὲ ἀρχῆς κτίσεως) to mean 'at the beginning of the Creation-story' (of Genesis). The quotations are from Gen. 1^{27}, 2^{24}. The point of Our Lord's reply is that the divine intention for marriage is that it should be an indissoluble relation taking precedence even of the relation to parents.

9. *man*, i.e. the husband. No public authority dissolved marriage, whether under Jewish or under Roman law. Cf. 1 Cor. $7^{10f.}$

10. This sounds once more as if it were introducing the interpretation of Our Lord's principle that was current in the Church, as e.g. in 4^{10} and elsewhere in Mark. But the point is considered again below (see note on v. 12).

11. This lays down the rule of the absolute indissolubility of marriage, and the absolute wrongness of divorce and remarriage.

12. According to Jewish law a woman had no power to divorce her husband at all. But it was allowed by Roman law (cf. 1 Cor. 7^{13}), and even in Rabbinic law a woman, under certain circumstances, could compel her husband to divorce her. Cf. Box, *Divorce in the New Testament.*

The point here raised would be a real issue for Christians in Gentile countries. This makes it plain therefore that the rule in Mark was at any rate one interpretation, current in the Church, of a Christian's duty when living in heathen surroundings.

But does the rule, thus definitely enacted, and only (or mainly) applicable in places where Roman and not Jewish law ran, come from Our Lord Himself or only from the Church? That He actually spoke these words was obviously soon doubted. Thus the Western text reads in this place 'and if a woman leave her husband and marry another' (καὶ ἐὰν γυνὴ ἐξέλθῃ ἀπὸ τοῦ ἀνδρὸς αὐτῆς καὶ ἄλλον γαμήσῃ). In Mt. 5^{32}, 19^{9}, Lk. 16^{18} the phrase of Mk. 10^{12} appears as 'and if a man marry a woman who has been put away'. Furthermore Matthew modifies the statement of Mk. 10^{11} by inserting the exception 'except for fornication'.

On the other hand it is urged that (1) Jews in Egypt certainly allowed wives to divorce their husbands for certain reasons: (2) Even in Palestine divorce by women was not unknown. Salome, according to Josephus, *Ant.* xv. 7. 10. divorced her husband Costobar: (3) Our Lord might have had in mind the famous and recent case of Herodias, who had 'left her husband and married another'; and therefore the saying in vv. 11, 12 (whatever reading we adopt in v. 12) might be an authentic saying of Our Lord's.

This query must therefore be left undecided. But, whatever our opinion on it, this much is certain; (1) Jesus goes back to the divine intention for marriage. How far the principle of the absolute indissolubility of marriage may be reducible to a law intended to apply generally in a society where all are not Christians must be a question of debate; it is no doubt arguable, and is argued, that accommodation to human weakness is still necessary. But there is no doubt of the ideal principle which Our Lord declares in v. 9, whether He spoke vv. 11, 12, or not. (2) For Christians therefore Our Lord's declaration of the principle must be the guide of their ideas and the rule of their behaviour. (3) If Our Lord's principle seems too absolute for practical enforcement under present conditions, the same is true of many other principles of His (e.g. that of non-resistance). Our Lord is concerned to set forward the conditions of life in the Kingdom of God. But Christians are to try to live—often at great cost and even if it requires heroism—as much as they can by the principles of that Kingdom even now.

As to Matthew's exception of fornication, it seems very hard to think other than that his is a glossed version, and that the mitigation was introduced because some could not believe that Jesus would be stricter than even the strictest Jewish Rabbis, or could not believe that His rule could be so uncompromising. If Our Lord gave the rule, He gave it unconditionally; the form of it in Matthew does not read at all like His usual method of laying down principles.

Opinions will probably differ for ever as to whether the rule, as found in Mark, is too rigid to be applied, and too rigid to be even wise. No doubt there is much to be said on both sides. On the one hand, there are many 'hard cases'; on the other, the preservation of a high ideal of marriage is so vital that to some no enumeration of hard cases will seem to make a tampering with the indissolubility of marriage socially worth while. But it is interesting to note that Montefiore, who questions the wisdom of the absolute rule (though he doubts if it comes from Jesus Himself) admits that in any case (1) Jesus here puts His finger on the great weakness of Judaism, the status in which it placed women, the inequality of rights as between men and women in regard to marriage, and the facilities for divorce which Rabbinic law allowed, and (2) that Jesus' championship of womanhood is wholly admirable and beautiful; and he aptly cites in this connexion the 'exquisite' story of Jn. 8$^{1-11}$.

13. This little incident is parallel to that in 9^{36}. But it seems unnecessary to suppose that they are doublet versions of a single incident. Both may well have happened. Our Lord's love of little children inspired the Church's practice of infant Baptism. His appreciation of the beautiful qualities of childhood is unparalleled in antiquity and has exercised an enormous effect on human thought and conduct.

touch. There might be some idea, in the minds of some who 'brought' them, of a 'magical' efficacy in His touch. But is there any reason to suppose that they sought for more than the consecration of the great Teacher's blessing?

14. The disciples' attempt to save their Master from trouble is natural enough. But we love Our Lord's 'indignation', a trait which Mark alone mentions here (ἠγανάκτησε).

of such. Such in qualities? Perhaps; it certainly seems so in v. 15. But here perhaps the thought is rather of position. 'Such' in insignificance. The qualities suggested in v. 15 must be those which make children such ideal people to 'receive' a gift, such as simple trust, receptivity, dependence, no thought of merit.

16. *took them in his arms.* Cf. 9^{36} note.

17. He goes forth out of the house, and is met by one who, saluting Him with conventional effusiveness, asks how he may inherit 'eternal life', which no doubt means 'the Messianic Kingdom'.

18. It is as unwarrantable to read this phrase as involving an acknowledgement by Jesus that He is not 'good', that He is 'conscious of sin' (so Montefiore and others), as it is to read in it a covert claim to be divine (so some orthodox commentators). The phrase is a mere disclaimer of flattery. Our Lord puts it aside; goodness is of God alone, and if Jesus *is* good, to God be the praise. Our Lord's moral perfection includes human humility. Mt. 19^{17} changes the phrase here (which Lk. 18^{19} retains) to 'Why askest thou me concerning that which is good?' no doubt in order to avoid the inference which has been drawn by Montefiore.

19. The quotations are from Ex. 20$^{13-16}$, Deut. 5$^{17-20}$, though for some reason the fifth commandment is put last; 'do not defraud',

substituted for the tenth commandment because He is addressing a rich man, recalls such passages as Ex. 21^{10}, Deut. 24^{14}, Ecclus. 4^{1}.

Our Lord quotes the commandments in the negative form. He might have quoted more positive enactments from Deut. 6^{5}, Lev. 19^{18}. But the point here is not specially that of negative against positive morality. What matters in any case is 'how' duty is done, rather than the mere doing of it; and the 'how' depends on what a man 'is'. Our Lord's point is 'You know your rules of duty; you say you observe them, but have you the spirit of a passion for righteousness in this observance?' He offers him a test. To inherit eternal life is not simple. Is he equal to an action which will prove him to realize that an enthusiasm for sacrifice is needed? But even the selling of all that he had would be but another 'observance', unless the 'how' of it was right (cf. 1 Cor. 13^{3}); so he must also 'come, follow me'. The sacrifice will be a sign of sincere wholeheartedness; but it will be but a beginning of the life of discipleship which will lead to eternal life.

Notice (1) he was obviously dissatisfied with his own state. He wanted to do more. Our Lord issues a tremendous challenge to his earnestness, and a warning against self-trust. (2) Our Lord 'loved' him (Mt. 19^{16} and Lk. 18^{18} omit this touch). There is no hint that he was unduly self-righteous.

21. The test here is for the particular man. It need not be taken as a universal rule of Christian discipleship, though in individual cases it has aroused an enthusiasm of literal obedience (Antony, Francis of Assisi) which has done marvels for the Gospel. But it does imply a principle of detachment from worldly advantages, which is to be a guide to all Christians, and which may make (or must make) hard demands on any of them. That Our Lord had in particular a bias in favour of poverty, or at least a haunting dread of the dangers of wealth, is undeniable.

22. *his countenance fell.* Gr. *στυγνάσας*. Who will wonder or judge him? And do we know if this was not the beginning of a self-mistrust which may eventually have led him far?

23. Another reference to Jesus' 'look'.

24. 'for them that trust in riches' should probably be omitted. It is possible that either vv. 24 and 25 should then be transposed, or that the latter half of v. 25 should be excised. The sequence of thought would then be better.

Jewish Rabbis certainly recognized the temptation of wealth

and taught the duty of almsgiving. But they also tended to treat riches as the most obvious blessing, and even as a sign of God's approval.

25. The phrase is proverbial. There is no authority for the idea that there was a small postern gate at Jerusalem called 'the needle's eye'.

The words τρυμαλιᾶς ῥαφίδος are both rare.

Cf. Gen. 18[14]. Man is required to make his effort. But the success in the long run is God's doing.

29. *for my sake and for the gospel's sake.* Cf. 8[35].

30. Wellhausen suggests placing a colon after 'a hundredfold'. That which follows would then be perhaps a Church gloss on Our Lord's words.

in this time he will receive a new set of ties, of a spiritual nature. Cf. 3[35]. The reference to renunciations with persecutions would come home to the Church of Mark's time. The compensations 'in this time' are to be found in the new brotherhood of the Christian society.

the world to come, lit. 'the coming aeon' or 'dispensation'; and 'aeonian' life. In the coming Kingdom of God.

31. Cf. 9[35]. This may mean either that the rich and great will not necessarily be the chief, or that the earliest disciples will not therefore hold the highest places.

X. 32–45. *Third Prediction. Rank in the Kingdom.*

32. This vivid picture is peculiar to Mark. We are not told why 'they' were amazed (Turner supports the conjecture 'he was amazed' ἐθαμβεῖτο for ἐθαμβοῦντο) or afraid. But this, the first mention of Jerusalem as the goal of the journey, makes the reason obvious. The coming issue is beginning to cast its shadow before.

they that followed. Perhaps 'they as they followed' (οἱ δὲ ἀκολουθοῦντες). But there may be a distinction between the Twelve and other followers in Jesus' company.

33. The new points in this prediction are (1) the delivery to the the Gentiles (the Romans), (2) the mocking, spitting, and scourging. We may feel that here certainly it is again possible that the prediction has been made more precise after the event.

We note that each prediction is introduced as if it were made for the first time. It lies to hand to suspect that they are three versions of one prediction; and in this case, as in that of the prediction in 9^{30}, the warning is followed by a quarrel for precedence, which increases the suspicion of a 'doublet' in these two narratives. But on the other hand it is not unlikely that Our Lord recurred to His warning more than once at this time.

35. The story is very candid. Luke omits it. In Mt. 20^{20} the request is made by the mother of the two disciples. Note that they call Jesus 'Master' (=Rabbi), even when making this request to Him.

Bacon thinks this passage an expression of a claim to special veneration made by some church party on behalf of the two martyr witnesses, which claim Mark by this story means to disallow. It might be that this theory explains the preservation of the story. But that does not diminish its claim to authenticity.

37. *in thy glory*, at His Parousia.

38. The phrase of the 'cup' (which recurs in Mk. 14^{36}) has parallels in Is. 51^{22}, Lam. 4^{21}. That of the 'baptism' (*βάπτισμα βαπτισθῆναι*) is found in Lk. 12^{50}. Bacon thinks the phrasing may have been influenced by sacramental associations in the Church. Of course the words imply an expectation of calamity.

39. The death of James is recorded in Acts 12^{2}. Church tradition ascribed to John a long life and a peaceful death, but suffering in the form of 'relegation' to Patmos (Rev. 1^{9}). But Papias is said to have recorded another tradition that John was killed by the Jews. The authorities that tell us this fact about Papias are scarcely of convincing weight. They are a MS. of the ninth-century *Chronicon* of Georgius Hamartolus, and a seventh- or eighth-century MS. of an epitome of a fifth-century work by Philip of Side. Harnack and others reject the story. The only argument in its favour is that the prediction here would perhaps not have been preserved in this form if it had not been fulfilled. That may or may not be so. But the phrase here need not be pressed to mean a martyr's death and nothing else.

40. The phrase, like that in 13^{32}, implies a certain 'subordination' of the Son (in His incarnate manifestation) to the Father. To carry it farther, as some speculations did, and make it imply an eternal subordination, within the Godhead, is unwarrantable.

for whom it hath been prepared. The phrase here is quite vague, 'those who are destined for it'. In Mt. 20^{23} the phrase is made more precise.

42. The question of precedence in the Kingdom is lost in Our

Lord's proclamation as to the principles of true pre-eminence now, in the Church.

The two words for dominion mean respectively the exercise of paramount lordship (κατακυριεύουσιν) and that of authority, whether primary or subordinate (κατεξουσιάζουσιν). The variant in Lk. 22^{25} is interesting, and may be more original.

they which are accounted. Gr. οἱ δοκοῦντες. It is the same turn of phrase as in Gal. $2^{2,6,9}$. It need not imply here, any more than there, a tone of irony, as if these rulers were only so in appearance, the true ruler being God.

43. The noble conception of the greatness of service has already been enunciated in 9^{35}.

45. *a ransom.* The word is found in the N.T. only here and in the parallel passage in Mt. 20^{28}. Luke omits the saying. The idea of ransoming could be applied to a slave or captive, to land, to the firstborn, or to compensation for a crime or for a forfeited life.

for many. The preposition (ἀντί= *lit.* 'instead of') need not be pressed to convey a crude substitutionary idea. 'For the sake of' is a quite adequate rendering. 'Many' is due to Isa. $53^{11,12}$. It does not limit the scope of Our Lord's sacrifice merely to the 'elect'. We find 'all' in 1 Tim. 2^{6}.

Is this phrase here an authentic saying of Our Lord's, or is it due to the doctrinal teaching of the Church? Many scholars take the latter view, and the arguments for it are stated with great elaboration in Rashdall, *The Idea of Atonement*, pp. 49ff. We may agree with him (1) that there is some doctrinal colouring in Mark (cf. Introd. A. ii); (2) that the verse here stands somewhat solitary in Mark and indeed in the gospels (though in Mk. 14^{24} there is a statement of some vicarious purpose in the death): (3) that Luke's omission of the phrase is curious and not easily explicable. It would be quite in accordance with the doctrines of Paul and of the Church in general, as 1 Cor. 15^{3} makes plain. Luke must have omitted it, because it did not occur in his main teaching source (Q) nor in his special source, or else (less probably) because it did not occur in his edition of Mark.

But on the other hand we may maintain (1) that those scholars who say that the phrase here is 'irrelevant to its context' or is in a 'different order of ideas' from what precedes ('ransoming' instead of 'serving') seem to be quite hypercritical. 'Serving' finds its climax in 'dying to ransom'. It is the ultimate service to any one to die for his deliverance. (2) If Our Lord could foresee His death, He could also foresee that others might benefit by it. The reluctance of some scholars to admit this possibility is really surprising. For (i) the idea in itself is not far-fetched or unworthy. That he is dying for the good of others is what in one way or another many a martyr for many a cause has believed or hoped. (ii) The idea is the burden of Isa. 53, and, as applied to the Maccabaean martyrs, it is found in 2 Macc. $7^{37,38}$, and even more unequivocally in 4 Macc. 6^{29}, 17^{20-22}, in such language as 'Make my blood their purification, and take my life to ransom their lives', 'through them our country was purified, they having as it were become a ransom for the nation's sin'. (iii) It is true that Isa. 53 does not seem to have been given a Messianic application by the Jews; but what of that? Are we really to believe that Our Lord was not capable of coupling the idea of the Messiah with the idea of Atoning Suffering? The early Christians certainly did so. May it not be that this was exactly the chief respect in which Our Lord's Messianic teaching was a novelty to them?

Rashdall's *animus* (for such it almost seems to be) against the claim that the verse is authentic is excited by the fact that on this verse theories of the Atonement have been built, with which he strongly disagrees, as e.g., that Christ's death is 'the only way by which sin is forgiven', and that the 'whole conception of Our Lord's mission is to be interpreted in the light of this solitary utterance'. With such doctrines Rashdall may be right in disagreeing; at any rate we need not discuss here the doctrine of the Atonement. But the verse itself, taken as it stands in its context, is singularly simple and natural.[1]

Of course, if any one interprets Our Lord's mission by this verse alone, he is a bad theologian. Our Lord's mission was to be Himself, to love and help and teach as well as to die. His death was the crucial act of His life, and the crowning revelation of Himself. *Finis coronat opus.* But it is a defective soteriology which isolates the death from the life, as if the work of Atonement lay in the one to the exclusion of the other.

But the single phrase in itself is not to be condemned as unauthentic because of dogmatic prepossessions against the use that

[1] A notable criticism of Rashdall's theory is contained in a University sermon by Prof. C. F. Burney (*The Old Testament Conception of Atonement fulfilled by Christ.* Oxford University Press).

has sometimes been made of it. All that Our Lord says is that His giving of His life will be of ransoming efficacy for others. *How* this will be so He neither says nor hints. The explanation of the 'how' of the effect He leaves to His Church to find out. He Himself merely states *that* it is so. And we see nothing unnatural in supposing that He could hope and believe that His death would be of help to men and of service for the bringing of God's Kingdom. (Cf. Introd. C. ii.)

X. 46–XVI. 8. THE MINISTRY IN JERUSALEM

X. 46–XIII. 37. THE APPEAL TO JERUSALEM

X. 46–52. *The Approach.*

46. Jericho is about fifteen miles from Jerusalem. Jesus was now within the sphere of power of the Roman governor and the Sanhedrin. His progress through Jericho is a kind of ovation which leads up to the Messianic entry into Jerusalem. This no doubt was the reason why this story was remembered, in which a Messianic title is for the first time publicly ascribed to Jesus, and is not repudiated by Him.

Bartimaeus is the Aramaic for 'son of Timaeus' (Timaeus perhaps is short for Timotheus). Possibly the Greek is a gloss on 'Bartimaeus' or perhaps Bartimaeus became a Christian and was known in the Church under that name.

beggar Gr. προσαίτης, a late word, found also in Jn. 9^{8}.

47. Jesus' fame had spread to Judaea. The title 'son of David' here makes its first appearance in Mark. In 12^{35-37} Our Lord raises a question about the title, and it may be that Mark was himself unattracted by the 'Son of David' idea. At any rate he supplies no genealogy of Jesus. Actual Davidic descent was claimed by some Jewish families, and some of these were poor and obscure.

48. *hold his peace,* so as not to trouble the ovation by interposing his miseries.

50. The graphic details are found in Mark alone.

51. *Rabboni* a fuller form of 'Rabbi', which occurs here and in Jn. 20^{16}. Mt. 20^{33} has 'Lord' (*κύριε*), as has Lk. 18^{41}.

52. *thy faith*; his belief in Jesus' power and willingness.

hath made thee whole. Gr. σέσωκέν σε='hath saved thee'. The word 'save' is probably used in the general sense 'to make sound' though it may also suggest that Bartimaeus was, in a fuller sense, 'saved' too. But 'followed' here (ἠκολούθει) does not imply that he became a Christian. Mt. 20^{34} adds that Our Lord touched the blind eyes as well.

The symbolism of 'opening the blind eyes' may account for the placing of the story at this point, just before the challenge to Jerusalem. But the supposition of such symbolical purposes may be carried into fantasy.

XI. 1–XII. 12. *The Entry and the Challenge.*

This section hangs together. It consists of the narratives of the Entry, of the Purging of the Temple, and of Jesus' answer to the demand as to His authority. The episode of the Fig-tree is an interlude, symbolically connected with the general subject (see note *ad loc.*), while the parable of the Vineyard may be considered as the final affront to the authorities, and as the final verdict on their attitude to Our Lord. At 12^{13} the story begins a fresh phase, that of set attacks by the authorities on His teaching, and of His dealings with these attacks.

1. Bethphage is mentioned in the Talmud, but its site is unidentified. Bethany is unknown outside the gospels, but is probably the modern El-Azariyeh, 15 furlongs from Jerusalem, on the south-eastern slopes of the Mount of Olives, which lies on the road from Jerusalem to Jericho.

2. The village is unnamed; perhaps Bethphage is meant.

Wellhausen forbids us to rationalize here, and it may be that Mark intends to imply that Jesus' knowledge of where the colt was to be found was supernatural. But there is no reason why we should not believe that Our Lord had friends in the vicinity. This was not his first visit to Jerusalem.

That no man had ever yet sat on the colt is perhaps an item of reverential significance, imported by Christian narrators from the LXX version of Zech. 9^{9} which speaks of a 'new' (unbroken) 'ass'.

3. *The Lord* (ὁ κύριος). Cf. note on 5^{18}. To Mark and his readers this would doubtless signify Jesus, as 'the Lord' of Christian belief. But in Jesus' mouth it may have meant no more than 'the Master'. Notice that the meaning of the Greek here is 'the Master hath need of it and is straightway sending it back hither' (when he has done with it). The R.V. translation is influenced by Mt. 21^{3} where the future 'will send' is used.

4. *in the open street.* Gr. ἐπὶ τοῦ ἀμφόδου, a rare word, found in the Bezan Codex at Acts 19[28].

5. *certain.* Idlers standing by. Lk. 19[33] says 'the owners'.

7. This is a royal entry. Cf. 2 Kgs. 9[13], 1 Macc. 13[51]. We do not know whether Our Lord planned it deliberately, or whether it was a spontaneous action of the pilgrim-crowd (most of whom would be Galilaeans), which He allowed. It obviously created a popular atmosphere of Messianic expectation. But by using the ass instead of the horse, Our Lord was signifying that He was a meek and not a warlike Messiah, fulfilling the picture in Zech. 9[9]; He did not wish His entry to give the signal for political agitation.

8. *branches* Gr. στιβάδας 'layers of leaves'. Mt. 21[8] says 'branches from the trees'. Lk. 19[36] omits the detail. The use of palms rests only on the authority of Jn. 12[13].

9. The quotation is from Ps. 118[26]. Originally it was a welcome to any pilgrim 'Blessed in the Name of the Lord is he that cometh'. But the Psalm was connected with the hope of national restoration, and was used liturgically at the Feast of Tabernacles. Perhaps 'he that cometh' had already assumed a Messianic implication. To Mark the special significance would be undoubted. Zech. 14[4] foretells that the Messiah is to appear on the Mount of Olives.

Hosanna = 'Save now'. But Mark may have taken it as an ascription of praise. 'Hosanna in the highest' might, however, mean 'Help, Thou who art in the highest' or 'Help, let them (the angels) say in the highest places'.

11. No action results. We are surprised that neither Sanhedrin nor Romans interfered to check the uproar. But it was pilgrimage-time, and no actual disturbance seemed intended. It must, however, have been a grievous disappointment to the excited crowd that Our Lord ended such an entry with an anticlimax. He seemed ready to be acclaimed as Messiah, and yet did nothing startling. 'He looked round' (surely to prospect His ground and not as a mere sightseer), and that was all. This chilling of the popular anticipation may have been the first stage in the process which made the crowd ready to shout against Him a few days later. He had made fools of them. Mt. 21[12], Lk. 19[45] with more dramatic sense, but probably less correctly, make the cleansing of the temple follow at once on the entry.

The subsequent story is contracted by Mark within a week. To Wellhausen this seems too short; and he certainly can quote

Mk. 14^{49} 'I was daily in the temple teaching', and says with some force that two days' teaching (11^{15}–12^{38}) hardly fits such a phrase. Since this is the only period in which Mark places Jesus in Jerusalem, he may have put into his story as much as he knew of what Our Lord had done at any time there; or he may have squeezed into a week happenings which took longer. But we cannot feel certain of this. 14^{49} might refer to other occasions, as well as to the present few days. And, if we remember (1) that Our Lord had visited Jerusalem before, and (2) that His Galilaean fame had spread to Judaea and must have roused the suspicious attention of the authorities before now, we may feel that the Messianic demonstration of a day or two would be enough to determine them to finish with Him as quickly as possible. They had in a sense been ready for Him before He appeared.

12. Why should figs be looked for, if it was not the season, and why should the tree be cursed because it had none? Gore calls it a 'miracle of judgement'; and no doubt it symbolizes the rejection of unfruitful Israel. But if Our Lord did the miracle as a symbolic lesson, why is the symbolism not elucidated? We may prefer to take it as a parable (such as that in Lk. 13^{6-9}) which in the tradition became translated into a miracle. J. Weiss (borrowing from Schwartz) suggests that this change may have been helped by the presence of some conspicuous withered tree in the vicinity, to which a story had been attached, ascribing its withering to Jesus' curse.

13. Even the early figs do not ripen before May.

14. The sequel is deferred till v. 20. (Mt. 21^{18} makes the withering follow immediately.) The story of the cleansing of the Temple is dovetailed in, and its sequel in turn is deferred till v. 27. See note on 3^{21}.

15. This then is what Jesus had come to Jerusalem for. And it was a momentous action. (1) It made a claim to prophetic authority and more. It is 'the only act in Our Lord's life which explains His Crucifixion as a Messianic agitator by the Roman authority' (Bacon). And yet it was not such an act of violence as would at once force the governor to intervene. (2) It was a direct affront to the priestly authorities. The Temple was in their charge; the market was for the sale of victims for the sacrifices; it was recognized by the priests, who in fact derived a large income from the monopoly. Thus Jesus was attacking both their prestige and their pockets.

In the fourth gospel this act is placed at the beginning of Our Lord's career (Jn. 2^{14}). But this seems on every ground an improbable date. Even now, when He was famous, and the mob was at any rate to some extent His follower, He can only have carried this act through by an assertion of moral authority, which for the moment deterred the priests from calling the temple-guard and violently opposing Him.

money-changers. Gr. κολλυβιστῶν. The half-shekel tax for the Temple had to be paid in Phenician money.

16. Mark alone preserves this detail. To carry vessels through the Temple (perhaps using it as a short cut between different parts of the city) was already forbidden by the authorities (cf. Jer. 17^{27}); but the prohibition must have been a dead letter. Note that Our Lord's protest is against popular irreverence, as well as against priestly abuse.

17. The first part of the verse is from Isa. 56^{7}, the second part from Jer. 7^{11}. The fact that it was the Court of the Gentiles where it had thus become impossible to pray gives a special point to 'for all the nations'.

In the Temple stronghold 'an utterly worldly aristocracy maintained itself in diplomatic bargaining with Rome at the expense of the masses of the people. These were utterly estranged from the worship. . . . The extortion practised by the priesthood under the guise of Mosaic requirement is something wellnigh incredible. And under the unscrupulous "hissing brood of Annas" it was carried to lengths hitherto unheard-of. The requirement of priestly inspection of sacrificial victims gave opportunity for an odious monopoly. Annas himself maintained a "Bazaar of Doves", where priests controlled the sale of this offering, prescribed in the law as *that of the poor*. Even the lower orders of the priesthood were shamelessly mulcted, whilst assassination and intrigue marked the lives of a high priestly caste, whose very name of "Sadducee" became a synonym for blank irreligion (Acts 23^{8})'. (Bacon.)

18. This is the first time that we hear of the 'chief priests' combining with the Scribes against Jesus.

19. Mt. 21^{17} says 'to Bethany'. Lk. 21^{37} implies that, like many others at feast-time, when the city was overcrowded, Our Lord and His disciples bivouacked on the hill-sides. To stay in Jerusalem would obviously have been very dangerous.

22. This saying applies but poorly to the incident of the fig-tree, suggesting as it does that any thaumaturgy is possible to faith. Mt. 17[20], Lk. 17[6] place a similar saying in different contexts. It looks as if the connexion here was Mark's work.

23. A Jewish proverbial saying called a great teacher a 'remover of mountains'.

24. The compelling power of faithful prayer, the principle here so vehemently asserted, is something which devotion attests abundantly.

25. Obviously a stray saying, attached here by Mark. It occurs in Mt. 6[14]. It is perhaps an echo of the Lord's Prayer, which Mark does not give us.

The appellation 'Father in heaven' for God is not found elsewhere in Mark, though suggested in 14[36]. It is frequent in Matthew and occurs in Lk. 11[13].

Stand. The normal Jewish attitude of prayer, kneeling being for special occasions.

26. This verse is in some MSS., but is probably an insertion here from Mt. 6[15].

27. An inquiry, which the authorities had a right to make, into the justification for the act of expulsion in v. 15. Cf. the demand in 9[11].

30. Our Lord's authority was prophetic, like that of John the Baptist. But to Mark, for whom John is simply the herald of Jesus, the connexion would be even more direct. John had borne witness of Him.

31. The dialogue is of course imagined by the Evangelist.

32. Gr. *ἀλλὰ εἴπωμεν Ἐξ ἀνθρώπων; — ἐφοβοῦντο τὸν ὄχλον.*

XII. 1. This is an allegory rather than a parable. Its point is unmistakable, and it must frequently have been used in controversy between Church and Synagogue. But is it then not original to Our Lord? It is said that it cannot be, because it presupposes Christ's death; but He had already foreseen His death. It is said that He would not have claimed for Himself a position of greater importance than that of the prophets (as is claimed for Him in Hebr. 1[1f.]). But is that not exactly what He was doing? And if the Church had invented this parable, would it not have given it a turn to foreshadow the Resurrection? It seems quite credible that Our Lord thus adapted the parable of Isa. 5[2f.] in order to make a last appeal to the conscience of the Jewish leaders and to challenge them to face facts.

The suggestion has been made that the son in the parable is intended for John the Baptist, and that Christian usage changed the application to Our Lord Himself.

These are the ordinary operations of vineyard-keepers in Palestine. The 'hedge' was usually a stone fence; the 'pit' was a trough in which the grapes were pressed; the 'tower' was for the keeper to watch on, in case thieves or animals should come; it was also used as a store-place.

in parables. Only one parable is given, perhaps from a collection. But the phrase may simply mean 'parabolically'. Cf. 3^{23} and Ps. 78^{2}.

let. The lettings of a vineyard might be for the year or for life. Some were even hereditary.

4. *wounded in the head.* The Greek word ἐκεφαλίωσαν occurs nowhere else in literature, though it is a regular formation from κεφάλιον 'head'. A v.l. is ἐκεφαλαίωσαν which would be 'to deal summarily with'. A possible emendation is ἐκολάφισαν 'beat'.

5. Actual martyrdoms of prophets are not recorded in the O.T., though Jeremiah's sufferings are. But the prophets had usually been failures in their own day, and Jerusalem was not undeserving of the title 'thou that killest the prophets'.

6. *a beloved son.* Cf. 1^{11}.

7. Perhaps they thought the owner was dead. But we need not press the legal point in commenting on the story in the allegory.

9. If this is (it need not be so definite) a hint at the doom of Jerusalem, it is paralleled by 13^{2}. That Our Lord foretold the doom of the city is in every way credible; in so doing, He was in line with predictions of many O.T. prophets.

unto others, i.e. to the Christian Church, as Mark and his readers would understand it. Cf. Mt. 19^{28}.

10. *even*; because it was a well-known one. The quotation is from Ps. 118^{22-23}, where Israel is the stone, despised by the nations. To the Christians it became a favourite proof-text, Jesus Himself being the stone. Its use as such may well go back to this saying of Our Lord's.

11. This verse may be due to Christian use, unless Our Lord adds it merely to finish the quotation.

12. Cf. 11^{18}. The next verse begins the set questionings of the Jewish party-leaders. But we are not told how soon this followed

on what had preceded. Did Our Lord spend a day or two in other public teaching? Cf. 11^{11} note.

XII. 13–44. *Counter-challenges.*

13. *they.* Who? Probably the verse looks back to 11^{27}.

The Pharisees were hostile to the Roman power, though they eschewed political affairs. The 'Herodians' would be friendly to Rome; they would be adherents of Antipas, and perhaps were Galilaeans up for the Feast. Herod is said by Lk. (23^7) to have been in Jerusalem at the time. The combination of Pharisees and Herodians has already been found in 3^6.

The question, introduced with so much affected deference, was a cunning one. Was the tax to Rome allowable by the *Torah* or not? The fiercer kind of Jewish Nationalists said No. And all Jews hated the tax, because it was a tax, because it was a symptom of foreign dominion, and because, having to be paid in Roman money, it had the Emperor's head on it (the local coins struck by the Procurator did not), and this offended Jewish anti-idolatrous susceptibilities. Moreover, all the taxation for Rome was additional to the heavy Jewish taxation for the Temple and priesthood. Grant, *Economic background of the Gospels* points out that this double taxation led to an economic stress which probably helped to inflame Messianic feeling.

If Jesus answered Yes, He offended all Nationalist feeling. If He said No, He might become or be denounced as a revolutionary agitator.

14. *the way of God* = religion.

tribute (*κῆνσον*, a Latin word) was a poll-tax of apparently a *denarius* (equivalent to about 9½*d.*) per head.

15. *bring.* Not because He had never seen one, but to illustrate His answer. Roman coins would not be in use in the Temple.

17. Directly, Our Lord's answer evades the issue. He refuses to discuss questions of political theory. But His answer implies a giving-up of the idea of the theocracy as a worldly kingdom, and would disgust the fiercer Nationalists; though most of the Pharisees would agree with His pronouncement. To Mark's readers the section would be valuable as an evidence that Christianity was not disloyal to the Empire.

Caesar's authority, Jesus means, is actual and recognized. As such, it must be borne, even if tyrannical or uncongenial. The phrase has since been extended to claim (as in Rom. 13^1) a divine sanction for 'the powers that be'.

But the addition of 'unto God the things that are God's' goes deepest. The two spheres, Caesar's and God's, are different. To give to Caesar his due is not incompatible with giving to God His. Caesar requires material, God requires spiritual, tribute. Therefore even an unjust subjection need not hinder one from doing God service.

18. This is the only direct reference in Mark to the Sadducees. The name is perhaps derived from Zadok, David's priest (2 Sam. 8^{17}, 1 Kings 2^{35}), from whom they claimed descent. They consisted mostly of the high-priestly families, and their centre was

Caesar's penny. A denarius of Tiberius

therefore Jerusalem. They were rich and overbearing, and as conservative ecclesiastics, they rejected the new-fangled doctrine of the Resurrection, which had become popular in Judaea in the last 150 years, and had been espoused by the Pharisees. The explanation of their tenets is inserted for Mark's gentile readers. Cf. Acts 23^8.

It is questioned whether, after the great affront of 11^{18} (and of the parable in 12^{1-11}), an academic debate like this would have been likely to take place between the Sadducees and Our Lord. This doubt may be too subjective. But it is possible that the section is misplaced, the evangelist wishing to give illustrations of controversy with each of the sections of Jewish leaders. To his readers the section would appeal, as voicing the more spiritual Resurrection doctrine of Christianity against the more crude and materialistic doctrine current in some sections of Pharisaic Judaism.

19. The so-called 'Levirate' law is stated in Deut. 25^5 and illus-

trated in Gen. 38^{8}. It may have originated in the desire that some one should exist who had the duty of making offerings to the dead man; later it would be maintained to prevent the breaking up of a family. Wellhausen says that by now it was probably a dead letter. But the question seems to have been a stock 'poser' for the Pharisees; though that some of them could have met it is proved by a passage in the Rabbinical tract *Berachoth* 17a (quoted by Montefiore), 'In the world to come there is no eating or drinking or marrying or envy or hate; but the pious rest with crowns upon their heads, and are satisfied with the glory of God'.

24. The O.T. 'scriptures' imply the Resurrection (v. 26), and the 'power of God' is equal to producing different orders of existence (v. 25).

25. Angels are also mentioned in 13^{32}. The Sadducees did not believe in them.

26. The 'Section of the Bush' (this may be the meaning of the Greek) is found in Exod. $3^{2\,f.}$. Perhaps this was a stock answer of the Pharisees.

27. God's love and value for man is not exhausted by this life. This is in fact the only religious argument for the belief in immortality.

28. Once again we find a kinship between the teaching of the best Pharisees and that of Jesus. Mt. 22^{34} omits this feature of the story. We find an echo of it in Lk. 20^{39}; and in Lk. 10^{25} it is a 'lawyer' who gives the summary of the Decalogue.

What commandment (Gr. ποία). This may mean 'are the moral rules in the Law more important than the ceremonial?' Some of the Rabbis certainly said so, especially in the Judaism of the Dispersion. Or it may be an effort to find out whether Jesus 'summarized' the Law; many Rabbis did try to do so, but others objected to the attempt, as drawing a distinction between rules, all of which were divinely ordained. Rabbinical calculation found 365 prohibitions and 248 positive commands in the Law.

29. This, from Deut. 6^{4}, forms part of the *Shema,* the Jewish Creed for everyday use. The second half (v. 31) is from Lev. 19^{18} (in Jewish idea, however, the scope of 'neighbour' is restricted to Jews). We do not know if the combination of these two passages was first made by Jesus. But the great saying of Rabbi Hillel (60 B.C.–A.D. 20) should be quoted: 'Do not to another what thou wouldest not that he should do to thee; this is the whole law, the

rest is commentary'. The Hebrew of the Passage in Leviticus has 'heart, soul, and strength'. The LXX translates the Hebrew for heart sometimes by 'heart' and sometimes by 'mind'. Mark here gives both.

32. The sentiment recalls 1 Sam. 15^{22}, Hos. 6^{6} and the general teaching of the pre-exilic prophets. The best thought of Judaism had learnt to regard the moral as more important than the ceremonial. But the encumbrance of its sacrificial system undoubtedly hampered the growth of Jewish liberalism in this respect.

34. In 10$^{17-31}$ the 'Kingdom' is in the eschatological future. Here, some think, it is treated as if it were present already. But do the words really mean more than that the scribe is nearly qualified for the Kingdom?

It may be that Our Lord's last remark was so spoken as to awe the hearers, and so questioning ends.

35. Is this section (35–37) authentic? It has been urged that (1) the controversy has a tone of Rabbinical scholasticism, which is not usual in Our Lord's mouth; (2) the quotation was the favourite text in the Church for use in connexion with the Ascension (so in Acts 2^{34}), and may have been read back into Our Lord's mouth by later usage; (3) the controversy seems to represent Our Lord as almost 'playing with' His Messianic claim. He appears to question whether the Messiah need be literally a son of David. And yet the idea is in Isa. 11^{1}. If Jesus believed Himself to be the Messiah, did He exclude thus (and only by implication) an element which was fundamental in Jewish anticipation? And if He did mean to exclude it, He certainly did not succeed. The idea of Jesus' Davidic descent is rooted in Christian tradition. Paul allows it (Rom. 1^{3}, 2 Tim. 2^{8}), and it is formally asserted in the genealogies of Matthew and Luke.

This last point, however, proves too much. For, if this idea was thus a root-element in Christian belief, we cannot see how the Church would have been likely to concoct an incident like this, in which the idea is at least questioned. We could only suppose that it came from a section of Church opinion, which tried to spiritualize the conception of 'Son of David', as applied to Jesus, and to discard its genealogical associations; and of such a tendency of Christian thought we have no other indication.

We may prefer to think then that Jesus was conscious of Davidic descent, but that He wished by this question to suggest that He was more than a mere descendant of David, and that

His Messianic claims rested on more than physical ancestry. It is certain that Mark (as contrasted with Matthew) lays no stress on the 'Son of David' type of Christology. Cf. Note 1 to Introd.

36. *David.* Our Lord assumes the Davidic authorship of the Psalms. 'The Psalms of David' was the current Jewish name for the Psalter. But Ps. 110 is addressed to some priest-king, perhaps Simon the Maccabee, and is thought to be of Maccabaean date.

The reading of R.V. marg. which may be right, recalls Ps. 8^6.

in the Holy Spirit. Cf. Acts 2^{30}.

37. The pleasure of the common people was probably at His teaching in general. We note that Mark tells us nothing of any teaching that Jesus may at this time have given to His disciples privately. John 14–16 attempts to supply this lack.

38. *robes* Gr. *στολαῖς*. The long robe of the grandee.

40. This was true only of some scribes. There were good as well as bad in the profession. But Josephus (*Ant.* xvii. 2) speaks of the Pharisees as 'making men believe that they are favoured by God' and 'influencing women'.

The Greek is anomalous *τῶν γραμματέων . . . οἱ κατέσθοντες*.

long prayers. The 'phylacteries' of Mt. 23^5 (*lit.* 'amulets'. They were small boxes, worn by strict Jews and affixed to their doorposts, containing texts from Scripture) were called in Aramaic *Tephillim* = 'prayers'. Mark may have misunderstood the Aramaic word.

The Woes on the Scribes and Pharisees are recorded at much greater length in Mt. 23^{4-36}, Lk. 11^{39-52}, 20^{46-47}, doubtless from Q. Mark is probably quoting Q from memory. He mentions only the scribes' love of precedence, their grabbing, and their hypocrisy.

41. They are now in the Court of the Women. The 'treasury' consisted of thirteen trumpet-shaped chests to receive alms. The present incident is annexed to the preceding verses by the word 'widow' (in vv. 40 and 42), and by the wish to contrast the generosity of a poor woman with the extortion of the scribes.

The gifts at Passover-time would be numerous.

42. *mites.* Gr. *λεπτά*. *Farthing.* Gr. *κοδράντης*, a Latin word transliterated. The value of the 'mite' is explained for the benefit of Western readers. The mite was worth about $\frac{1}{3}$ of a farthing.

44. *all her living.* Gr. *ὅλον τὸν βίον* = 'her whole life'.

XIII. 1–37. *The Doom.*

This chapter is unique in the gospel. It is a continuous discourse, such as Mark has nowhere else attempted. And its character is unexampled. The discourse is a *cento* of reminiscences of current ideas and phrases in Jewish apocalyptic writings. It produces a strong impression of being a composite product.

It is very hard to believe that it is the record of an authentic discourse of Our Lord's. Of course there is no documentary proof against its genuineness. And we cannot deny that apocalyptic ideas occur elsewhere both in Mark and in Q. Thus in Mark we have such phrases as 'the Kingdom of God', the 'Son of Man', 'the world to come', the prophecy of 14^{62}, 'the nearness of the Kingdom' (9^{1}); whilst Q gives us passages like 'it shall be more tolerable for Sodom in that day', 'the men of Nineveh shall stand up in the judgement', 'they shall come . . . and sit down at meat with Abraham and Isaac and Jacob in the Kingdom of God', or the words in Mt. 19^{28}, $24^{26\text{ f.}, 37\text{ f.}}$, Lk. 22^{30}. Furthermore it is agreed that early Christian belief was agog with eschatological anticipation. The early speeches in Acts are full of the idea of the Parousia of Christ, and Paul (e.g. in 1 Thess. $5^{1\text{ f.}}$, 2 Thess. 2^{2}) gives evidence of the heated expectations of its imminent approach that were current in the Christian society. He tries to discourage too confident speculations. But that, especially in times of persecution (such as the Church had to undergo under Nero and later under Domitian) the cry 'How long?' arose with insistence in Christian circles, is unquestionable. (Cf. Rev. $6^{9\text{-}11}$.)

To a Church in such a state of mind this chapter would come with a very direct message both of comfort and of warning. Christ had foreseen all these tribulations. They were the beginning of the throes which would usher in the Parousia. The remarkable feature in the chapter, however, is that it is obviously meant to warn men against believing that the climax may come at once. True, it will come, and soon (v. 30); but the tribulation is but the beginning of the throes that prelude the Parousia (v. 8); the end is not yet (v. 7). God alone knows the date (v. 32); but the gospel must first be preached unto all the nations (v. 10). This attempt to damp eschatological enthusiasm is of course one that Paul also made; but we have no reason for denying that it was also the aim of the generality of the Church leaders, as time went on and the Parousia delayed. The enthusiasm would no doubt persist in the minds of many Christians; in the second century it changed into 'Millenarianism', and the Church teachers of that time had to combat that; it is probable that the earlier form of such views was similarly combated by others of the Apostles besides Paul.

The Church atmosphere of Mark's time was therefore such that eschatological ideas would be very rife in it. But the problem is, to what (if any) extent could such ideas genuinely claim Our Lord's authorization? To answer this question precisely is impossible. We cannot, with any respect for our authorities, deny the presence of some eschatological colouring in His teaching. But we cannot say exactly *how far* He went in using technical apocalyptic language of the symbolic pictorial type, and how far such language was put into His mouth by Christian comment. Nor, if He used such language (as to some extent He must have), can we say how far He *consciously* employed prophetic 'foreshortening' of the time in order to give immediate urgency to His exhortations, and how far His human mind was *actually circumscribed* within the form of thought of His own time and people. This latter question is part of the wider problem of the limitations of Our Lord's knowledge in His earthly life, and common sense warns us that we are quite incapable of settling the problem by any *a priori* decision.

Looking at this chapter in detail, there are a certain number of verses in it, as to which we can feel that there is nothing in them which Our Lord might not have spoken. Most will not find it hard to credit that He could foresee the doom of His nation and the persecution of His disciples. That He should speak of His triumph, and should put such a forecast under the apocalyptic form of a Parousia; that, as Gore puts it, He 'may have thrown the doom of Jerusalem on the back-ground of universal judgement'; this is in no way incredible. And, if He so spoke, we can understand the urgency of His exhortations to watchfulness and prayer. The following verses in this chapter seem therefore to be such as cannot be reasonably rejected as unauthentic: 2 (the destruction of the Temple), 11 (the promise of help in trial), 26, 28–32 (the Parousia), 33–37 (the exhortation to watchfulness). Nor is there much difficulty in believing 9, 12, and 13 (the prediction of persecution), and even 15 and 16 (the warning to quick decision), to be either authentic or based on actual sayings of Our Lord. Verse 10 (evangelism of the world) will always cause doubts to those who believe that Our Lord on earth limited the scope of His message to His own nation, and did not think of Himself as founding a world-wide religion; to us such a view seems to have little to recommend it, and we think it more likely that the evangelical programme of some of the O.T. prophets (Israel, and through Israel, the world; cf. Isa. 42^{1}, 49^{6}, 19^{23} Jonah) was one which Our Lord had consciously before Him; that v. 10 here is therefore a substantially authentic word of His.

But when, passing beyond such verses, we look at the framework in which they are set, we cannot feel comfortable in the thought that these are Our Lord's own utterances. The chapter is, in short, a map of the future, and its eschatology is crude; it marks off divine events by material signs, used not for mere symbolic picturesqueness, but as definite factors in the horoscope of mankind. This is not the sort of transmutation of eschatological ideas which we have every reason otherwise to think that Our Lord tried to effect.

Of course this is a subjective test to apply, and we may admit that we modern Westerns are not good judges of eschatological language. Allen, in fact, roundly tells us that we refuse to credit the authenticity of this language because we do not like it ourselves. But there is really more than this in our objection. Somehow or other, the gospels have painted to us a picture of Jesus, which possesses certain characteristics; for instance, independence and originality of teaching, and spiritual depth of ideas. Much of this chapter is not independent or original, and its eschatological ideas are not of the type that Our Lord gives us elsewhere.

Nor, by questioning the authenticity of parts of this chapter, do we thereby discredit the whole gospel record. After all, we have had elsewhere to note some passages where, by obvious comparison of authorities, we could see that Our Lord's sayings had been altered in phraseology, and had been coloured by later Church ideas. The present chapter is in our view only an extreme illustration of this process. And though it may be difficult in not a few cases throughout the gospel to be sure what were the *ipsissima verba* of Jesus, we have quite enough to make us sure that the picture of Him as One Who spake as never man spake, and Who was as never man yet was, is a true picture. Indeed it is not going too far to say that, in the last analysis, it is the Christian picture of Jesus which we use to test sayings ascribed to Him. He is Himself the critic of His biographers. And this is probably quite the most illuminating, and may be quite the most scientific, test that we can apply.

In Introd. F. ii the general purport of this chapter, its reference to the Neronic persecution, and the arguments as to the date of the gospel to which it gives rise, have already been considered. The theory that some Jewish, or more probably Jewish-Christian, apocalypse has been incorporated in this chapter has also there been mentioned. The only definite argument for it rests on the parenthesis in v. 14 (on which see note *ad loc.*); but the theory is not at all improbable in itself. The original apocalypse may have consisted of vv. 5–8, 14–20, 24–27. These by themselves would make up a compact little apocalypse, giving (1) the omens or 'throes', (2) the great tribulation, (3) the Parousia. Into this the evangelist has inserted predictions of persecution, and a 'doublet' warning of false-Christs, while he has prefixed a saying about the destruction of the Temple, and added an epilogue affirming the certainty of the event, dealing with the matter of its date, and ending with a warning to be watchful. This literary analysis is of course purely conjectural, and is quite incapable of verification.

1. Herod's magnificent Temple was begun in 20–19 B.C., and was not completed till A.D. 26. It was burnt during the capture of Jerusalem by Titus in A.D. 70.

2. Our Lord's foreboding of doom is parallel to that of some O.T. prophets e.g. Jer. 26^{6}, Mic. 3^{12}. The idea that Zion was inviolable and the Temple was indestructible, because there was the earthly seat of God's glory, was firmly rooted in Jewish popular belief. Our Lord's prediction would horrify any Jewish hearers. The spiritual implication of the event is brought out in Jn. 4^{21}.

Some MSS. add to this verse 'and after three days another shall rise without hands', but this is probably a gloss from 14^{58}.

3. The four disciples of 1^{16-20}, not otherwise grouped together.

on. Gr. εἰς = 'into'; a harsh use.

4. *These things.* Quite vague in reference. Strictly it should refer to the destruction of the Temple. But the verse is probably an artificial connexion between the prophecy about the Temple and that of the Parousia. In effect what follows is designed to answer Christian questionings as to the 'end', after which the Messianic age was to begin.

5–13. *The beginning of throes.*

6. *a.* The first sign is Pseudo-Christs (repeated in vv. 21, 22).

Nobody that we know of claimed to be Messiah till Barcochba who led the last great Jewish revolt in A.D. 132. But probably a Messianic element was present in the earlier agitations of men like Theudas, Judas of Galilee (Acts 5[36,37]), and the Egyptian of Acts 21[38]. Note that if this verse was of Our Lord's speaking, it ought to suggest that these 'many' would call themselves *Jesus* returned; nobody ever did this. The 'in my name' must certainly mean 'claiming to be Christ'.

7. *b.* Second sign. Wars, earthquakes, and famines. These are regular features in the Jewish apocalypses. The 'wars' would be the minor disturbances in Palestine, which preluded the rising of A.D. 66; and the Empire was very restless in the latter years of Nero's reign. Of 'famines' we have the instance referred to in Acts 11[28]. We know of 'earthquakes' at Laodicea and at Pompeii in A.D. 61–62.

8. These are 'the beginning of travail' (ἀρχὴ ὠδίνων), but 'the end is not yet'. The 'throes' may have been a technical phrase in Jewish use for the evil days to come before the new age. The word is used of birth-throes (cf. Isa. 26[17], Jer. 22[23], Hos. 13[13], Mic. 4[9]) and of death-throes (cf. Acts 2[24]).

9. *c.* Third sign. The persecution of Christians.

councils (Gr. συνέδρια = 'sanhedrins'), local assemblies of Jewish elders. 'Governors' would be Roman officials. 'Kings' would include both the Herods and the Emperor. The persecution of Nero was at its hottest in Rome, but it no doubt led to outbreaks elsewhere. And the story of Acts gives examples of the bringing of Christians before various sorts of authorities, and of their sufferings there, before Nero's persecution began. Cf. also 2 Cor. 11[24 f.].

for a testimony. The martyrdom would be a proclamation of the gospel.

10. *d.* Fourth sign. The nations must have heard the gospel before the 'end' comes. (Cf. 14[9]). This would seem to remove the end to a distant future. But the world was a small place to the ideas of the time; and the Christians expected miraculous help to further the work. How slowly, however, they realized the call of the world is shown in Acts.

It must be owned that this verse is not only hard to reconcile with v. 30, but also reads as an intrusion among the external signs otherwise enumerated. One wonders if it is not a gloss here, though possibly based on some genuine saying of Our Lord's (see note at beginning of chapter). Burkitt thinks that the true punctuation gives the sense 'for a testimony to them and to all people' (εἰς μαρτύριον αὐτοῖς καὶ εἰς πάντα τὰ ἔθνη), with which Mt. 10[18] corresponds. Mt. 24[14], however, repeats the verse in the form of the R.V. translation here.

11. *the Holy Ghost.* Undoubtedly personal. Cf. Acts 6[10], 7[55]. It is a promise of inspiration at the moment of trial, and gives the germ of what is elaborated in the fourth gospel into the doctrine of the 'Paraclete'.

12. *e.* Fifth sign. Social divisions. Cf. Mic. 7[6], Lk. 12[51]. This is again a commonplace in apocalyptic writings, and is an obvious inversion of Mal. 4[6].

13. Cf. Mt. 5[11]. The general hatred of Christians is a climax of both the third and the fifth signs. For the last clause Allen quotes as parallels 4 Ezra 6[25] 'Whosoever shall have survived all these things . . . shall be saved, and shall see my salvation and the end of the world', 7[27] 'Whosoever is delivered shall see My wonders'. We cannot be sure whether in the Marcan context it means that those who last through it all shall see the Parousia (as in v. 30) or that a reward after death is assured to the faithful. Perhaps Mark's readers would find both meanings in the phrase.

14–24. *The great tribulation.*

14. From Dan. 9[27], 11[31], 12[11]. Daniel refers to the erection of an altar to *Zeus Ouranios* in the Temple by Antiochus Epiphanes (167 B.C.); the event is recorded in 1 Macc. 1[54,59]. The Hebrew is *Shiqqutz Shomem* 'the profanation that appals'. *Shiqqutz* was used by Jewish writers instead of *Baal* = 'Lord' = *Zeus*, while *Shomen* was a play on the word *Shamayim* = 'heavenly' = *Ouranios*.

Note that 'abomination' is neuter (βδέλυγμα), while 'standing' is masculine (ἑστηκότα). The grammar is not too harsh for Mark, but it seems to indicate that the author had in view not the destruction of the Temple, but a personal Profaner. For further consideration of the reference and of the bearing of 'where it ought not' cf. Introd. F. ii. Luke, writing probably after the destruction of the Temple, changes the phrase to refer to the besieging Roman armies (21[20]).

The parenthesis may suggest that a written apocalypse is the basis of the prediction. But it may possibly be taken as an advice to the reader to note the new turn given to the Daniel prophecy.

The people are to flee not to Jerusalem (for things would be worse there), but to 'the mountains' (quite vague). In the siege of

Jerusalem the Christians, warned, it was said, by a divine monition, fled to Pella beyond the Jordan before the fall of the city. But it is quite unnecessary to see a reference to this in the present verse.

17. The weak will be specially distressed. But the verse may be an echo of the apocalyptic detail that 'pregnant women shall bring forth untimely births' (4 Ezra 6^{21}) at the Messianic tribulation.

19. From Dan. 12^{1}. Cf. Jer. 30^{7}, 1 Macc. 9^{27}, Rev. 7^{14}.

20. Because of the elect (which to Mark and his readers would mean the Christians) the time will not last long. This idea occurs in Dan. 12^{7} (where the time is cut down to $3\frac{1}{2}$ years) and is repeated in the apocalypses. Cf. 2 Thess. $2^{6,7}$.

21–22. A repetition of vv. 5, 6, but with the addition that the impostors shall work wonders. Cf. 2 Thess. 2^{9}, Rev. 13^{13}.

24–27. *The Parousia.*

24. The horror spreads. A cosmic overthrow, such as the apocalypses revelled in picturing, follows. Cf. Isa. 13^{10}, 34^{4}. But then the Parousia will take place.

26. From Dan. $7^{13,14}$. Cf. Mt. 24^{30}. The Messiah is a 'heavenly Man' as in the apocalyptic book of Enoch, where he is even called 'Son of Man'.

27. The angels are regularly represented as Messianic agents at the Parousia. Cf. Mt. 13^{41}, Jude 14 (quoting the book of Enoch).

The 'elect' to Mark would be the Christians. In Jewish eschatology they would be the Jews of Palestine and of the Dispersion. For the 'four winds' cf. Zech. 2^{6}.

from the uttermost part of the earth &c. This is a mixture of Deut. 30^{4} and 13^{7}. The phrase is paralleled in some MSS. of Enoch 57^{2} 'from the extremity of earth to the extremity of heaven'. Holtzmann suggests that it means 'from the east (the end of earth as a Jew faced eastwards with his back to the sea) to the west (the end of heaven over the sea, where the horizon ends)'.

28–37. *Exhortation to watch.*

This is to happen soon, and yet only God knows the time. It looks as if the Christians had confused what Our Lord may have said about the destruction of Jerusalem with what He may have said about the Parousia. But Our Lord may have used 'prophetic foreshortening' about the events; only He repudiates the desire to calculate dates about them, such as Jews frequently exhibited; and in every age many Christians have shown the same itching curiosity.

The 'parable' is a mere simile. For the fig-tree as presaging summer (or rather spring) cf. Song of Sol. 2^{13}. 'Summer' here probably means 'the glad time' (following the tribulation). Schwartz suggests that a popular superstition may have said that the flowering of some dead fig-tree near Jerusalem would signal Messiah's advent. This suggestion has already been adverted to in the note on 11^{12}.

29. *he*. It might be '*it*'. The Greek here has no pronoun.

30. Verses 30–32 seem to contain genuine sayings of Our Lord, but they are not consistent with one another in this context (contrast 30 and 32) and can hardly have been spoken at the same time.

31. An assurance of fulfilment. Christ will come as promised. Cf. 2 Pet. 3^{10-13}.

32. The Son is placed above the angels as in Hebr. $1^{1f.}$. The verse would be (like Acts 1^{7}) a justification for Our Lord's not having dated His Parousia. Luke omits the verse altogether. In Mt. 24^{36} many MSS. omit 'neither the Son'. We may agree with Schmiedel that such a saying could not have been invented. The explanations of Our Lord's ignorance which the Church fathers give are (1) that the Son in His human nature did not know the time, (2) that His ignorance was 'economic', i.e. that He withheld His knowledge for men's good, (3) that the verse means 'apart from the Father the Son does not know the time'.

The absolute use of 'the Son' here is not found elsewhere in Mark. It occurs in Mt. 11^{27}, Lk. 10^{22} and is frequent in John.

34. Another simile. It recurs with variations in Mt. 24^{42}, Lk. 12^{37-40}, and is paralleled by the parables of the talents in Mt. 25^{14-30}, and of the pounds in Lk. 19^{11-27}.

35. The four Roman night-watches of three hours each, beginning at 6 p.m.

37. *you*, i.e. the four. We are thus brought back to the inquiry in v. 3. For a similar recurrence to the beginning after a long section of teaching cf. the last clause in 9^{50}.

XIV. 1–XVI. 8. The Passion and Resurrection

XIV. 1–72. *The Last Night.*

The question of the date of the Last Supper is a complicated one. There is a clear conflict of chronology between John and Mark (whom Matthew and Luke follow). According to Jn. $13^{1,29}$, 18^{28}, $19^{31,42}$ we get a perfectly clear and consistent scheme. The 'day of Preparation', Nisan 14, began at 6 p.m. on the Thursday; on the afternoon of Friday (still Nisan 14) the Passover lambs were sacrificed in the Temple. The Passover meal was eaten on the night of Friday, Nisan 15 beginning at 6 p.m. on Friday, and being the Sabbath. Sunday, Nisan 16, began at 6 p.m. on Saturday. According to John, therefore, Our Lord was crucified on the day of the killing of the Passover lamb, and the Last Supper was not the Paschal meal at all.

We may add (though, standing by themselves, the references would not come to much) that with John's scheme correspond (*a*) Paul's phrase 'Christ our Passover hath also been sacrificed' (1 Cor. 5[7]), (*b*) the phrase in Lk. 22[15,16], if it is interpreted (as it is by many) to mean that Our Lord's desire to eat this Passover with His disciples was not to be fulfilled.

The Marcan chronology is quite different. According to Mk. 14[1,12] the Last Supper was the Passover Meal, and took place on the evening of the Feast, which would be Friday evening, Nisan 15, when the Sabbath had begun. The Crucifixion then would have taken place during the morning of Saturday (the Sabbath!); and we cannot call the Sunday 'the third day' after Saturday.

On the other hand Mk. 15[42] places the Crucifixion on the 'day before the Sabbath'. Further, Mk. 14[2] certainly implies that Our Lord was crucified before the feast. Finally, if the night of the Last Supper and the next morning were Passover day, how, during such a time, could Jewish men carry swords (14[47]), go to work (15[21] if this implies that Simon had been at work. Work on the day of the Passover was not forbidden, but customarily ceased at noon), buy linen (15[46]) and spices (16[1])?

Not only, therefore, does Mark place the Last Supper a day later than John does, but Mark's account is not consistent with itself.

Various efforts to harmonize the two schemes have been made; thus (1) it is suggested that Jesus expected to be arrested at any time, and anticipated the Passover meal. The Last Supper then was a sort of irregular equivalent for the Passover. (2) It is suggested that, since the Passover fell on a Friday this year, the observance of it was shifted to Thursday, because otherwise the roasting of the Passover lambs would have gone on after the Sabbath began at 6 p.m. on Friday evening. This might explain the use of the word '*must* (Gr. ἔδει) be sacrificed' in Lk. 22[7].

But these theories are not very convincing. They smack of

special pleading. The general opinion of scholars tends to believe that John has preserved the right dating and the correct tradition as to the meal. No doubt he was interested in the Christian doctrine of Christ crucified as the Christian Passover; but the actual event (Christ's Crucifixion and the time of the Passover sacrifice) may have given rise to the doctrine, rather than the doctrine to the record. John's chronology is probable and self-consistent, Mark's is neither.

In details, moreover, the Last Supper does not seem to be the Passover meal. There is no mention of the lamb. The blessing of cup and bread takes place at the end of the meal, whereas in the Passover supper it came before the meal. At the Passover meal, four cups of wine were blessed, and each of those present had his own cup; at the Last Supper we hear of only one cup, of which all partake. Finally, if the Last Supper was the Passover, Our Lord's command 'do this' would probably have been understood to mean an annual commemoration like the Passover; whereas from the start (as is evidenced by Acts 20[7] and all other testimonies) the Christians observed the Eucharistic commemoration weekly on the day of the Resurrection.

There is a great deal to be said in favour of the suggestion (which has been put forward by many scholars) that the Last Supper was not the Passover meal at all, but was a specimen of a weekly social-religious meal customary amongst many Jews in pre-Christian times and since which is called the *Kiddûsh*.[1] On Friday afternoons small groups of friends would meet in private houses for a social meal, at which a religious tone was deliberately given to the conversation. These societies were known as *Chabûr-oth*, from the word *Chabêr* 'friend, comrade'. The meal was prolonged till dusk. When the Sabbath began at 6 p.m., the president took a cup of wine, blessed it and passed it round. This ritual was called 'the sanctification of the Sabbath'. It also took place before great festivals, both the Sabbath and the festival being commemorated. So at the Passover Kiddûsh, the cup would be

[1] The account here given is taken from Oesterley, *Jewish background of the Christian liturgy*, pp. 156 f., which presents the clearest treatment that is known to me of the whole point at issue. The theory with the relevant arguments was first put forward by G. H. Box in a paper published in the *J. Th. S.* for April 1903, entitled 'The Jewish Antecedents of the Eucharist'; it was restated by the same author in a paper published in the *Jewish Guardian* for 7 December 1923, entitled 'The Jewish background of the institution of the Eucharist'.

blessed and partaken of and the institution of the Sabbath would be commemorated; then the bread would be blessed and distributed, and the deliverance from Egypt would be recalled.

The suggestion is that Our Lord and the Twelve formed such a *Chabûrah* (cf. Jn. 15[14] 'ye are my friends'); that they met for the Passover Kiddûsh (though on Thursday, not on Friday, for a reason to be given below); that Jn. 14–16 gives us what may be based on the conversation that then took place; and that the institution of the Eucharist was but the Kiddûsh ceremony, to which Our Lord now attached a new meaning for His followers. If so, then all the actions, so unsuitable to Passover-day, the carrying of arms and the rest, would have taken place on the day of Preparation, the Passover meal itself not being due till the evening of the Friday. We can also understand how the Christians came to replace the weekly Kiddûsh by the weekly Eucharist. Finally, if the Last Supper was the Kiddûsh, the cup was blessed before the bread, and this is in fact the order that we find in Lk. 22[17], 1 Cor. 10[16,21] (though in 1 Cor. 11[23-27] Paul places the blessing of the bread first. Lk. 22[20] is generally agreed not to be a part of the original text).

On this occasion the Kiddûsh was held on Thursday instead of Friday, because the Sabbath coincided with the first day of the Passover (Jn. 19[31]). By ancient Jewish use a feast superseded a Sabbath. The social meal could not be held on Friday afternoon because the Passover lambs were then being slain, nor on Friday evening, because the Passover was then being eaten. So it would have to be transferred to the Thursday afternoon; at 6 p.m. would begin the day of Preparation, and the Passover Kiddûsh would be said, which inaugurated the feast.

If this suggestion, which is so attractive as to seem wellnigh convincing, be adopted, we have then to account for the confusion in the Synoptic chronology. Firstly then, we may say that the Kiddûsh would be full of the Passover atmosphere; it was said on the day of Preparation, which in popular idea began the feast; and the Sabbath was always mentioned, whenever the Kiddûsh was said. Thus the Last Supper would have become connected in the disciples' minds with the Passover, and would easily and naturally come to be thought of as the Passover meal.

Secondly, it is possible that Roman liturgical use regarded the Easter Eucharist as the substitute for the Jewish Passover, and that Mark was (unconsciously) influenced by the Roman point of view. We know that in the next century a dispute arose between the Roman and the Eastern churches as to the proper day for observing Easter. The East claimed the authority of John and of 'immemorial use' to observe Good Friday on Nisan 14, and Easter on the third day (reckoning inclusively) after, whatever the day of the week (they were thus called 'Quartodecimans'); whilst the Roman custom was to observe Easter on the Sunday after the Paschal moon, and Good Friday on the third day before, irrespectively of the Nisan date. This controversy has a kind of preliminary in the divergence of record as to the date of the Last Supper, Mark representing the Roman, and John the Eastern tradition.

1–2. *The plot.*

1. Jewish reckoning was inclusive; 'after two days' would thus mean 'on the second day after'. The story is now at Wednesday afternoon. An informal council (a full Sanhedrin would include 'elders' as in 14^{53}) is held, and it is decided to take Jesus 'with subtilty', so as to avoid exciting a disturbance, which might arise if it were done during the feast, i.e. publicly, when crowds were assembled.

The Passover and the seven-day feast of Unleavened Bread were in origin distinct festivals. The latter began on Nisan 15, with the Passover Meal after 6 p.m. But we find the two combined in 2 Chron. 35^{17}, and Josephus speaks as if the two terms were equivalent. Thus he speaks of 'the feast of Unleavened Bread, which we call Passover' (*Ant.* xiv. 2. 1. So also *ib.* xvii. 9. 3); while in *Ant.* ii. 15. 1 he says 'We keep a feast for eight days which is called the feast of Unleavened Bread' (cf. also *B.J.* ii. 1. 3, v. 3. 1, *Ant.* xi. 4. 8, ix. 13. 3), the 'eight days' including the Passover.

2. Mark's report of their deliberation may be hearsay, but is more probably deduced *a posteriori* from the way in which they acted.

3–9. *At Bethany.*

3. Simon the leper (if he was present, he must by now have recovered) is otherwise unknown to us; he may have been well known to the Palestinian church. Jn. 12^{2} says this incident took place in the house of Martha and gives the woman's name as Mary. Simon may have been some relative of Martha's. The coincidence that Martha's brother was called Lazarus, and that the Lazarus of the parable of Luke 16 may have been a leper, is curious.

Jn. $12^{1,12}$ places this anointing before the entry into Jerusalem. Luke omits it here, and places it at $7^{36f.}$. It may be that Mark has interposed it here to suit the context. Certainly v. 10 would follow excellently on v. 2. We have already noted (on 11^{19}) that Luke does not represent Our Lord as lodging at Bethany but as bivouacking in the open.

spikenard. Gr. νάρδου πιστικῆς. The second word is unknown. If connected with πίστις 'faith', it must mean 'genuine'. Is it perhaps a form of 'πιεστικῆς'; from πιέζω 'to squeeze', so meaning 'concentrated'? The Vulgate has *nardi spicati.* σπίκατον was a kind of ointment.

Mark alone mentions the breaking of the flask.

4. *Some.* Mt. 26^{8} says 'the disciples', as some MSS. of Mark also have here. Jn. 12^{4} says 'Judas'.

5. On the value of the *denarius* see note on 6^{37}. The word for 'murmured' is that used in 1^{43}. It is a strong word.

6. *A good work.* Gr. καλὸν ἔργον. The generosity had been lavish (though 'she has done what she could' need not mean that she had spent her all); but special occasions justify special actions. Her devotion had prompted the homage, and Our Lord reads into the act more than she could have intended. He was in no danger of disesteeming the works of charity to the poor.

8. The Greek is strange, προέλαβεν μυρίσαι. Anointing a dead body before burial was not unknown among the Jews.

We may suppose that the woman meant her homage to be an acknowledgement of Jesus' anticipated kingship, and that Our Lord's reply means 'not a throne, but a sepulchre is my lot'. That He spoke so openly, not only of His death, but also of His burial, and that nobody seems astonished, is strange. But perhaps His words have been made more definite in retrospect.

The woman's action may have been intended to provoke Him to an act of Messianic revolutionism. At any rate His enemies could easily misrepresent it. Perhaps Our Lord realized this contingency. His treatment of the act, however, gave the deathblow to any hope of an earthly kingdom. Thus it may have provided the last impulse to Judas' disloyalty.

9. Here too the wording may have been recast *ex post facto*. It is strange that the woman's name is not given here. The word 'gospel' must mean the gospel about Jesus, the Christian Gospel, though preached, not written.

10–11. *The betrayal.*

No doubt the contrast between the woman's homage and the treachery of Judas is intentional.

10. We are given no reason for Judas' action. Jn. 12^{6} suggests that he was avaricious, but that is scarcely enough to explain his treason. Probably he had been disappointed by Our Lord's refusal to figure as the popular Messiah; perhaps he wanted to force Him to a position where He must declare Himself in public. Jn. 18^{2} tells us that what he betrayed was the place where Jesus could be caught without publicity. Did he also betray His claim to be Messiah, and so put the fatal question of 14^{61} in the high-priest's mouth?

one of the twelve. Gr. ὁ εἷς, perhaps 'he that has been mentioned as one of the Twelve', or it may be to distinguish him from another Judas. The repetition of the words, when Judas is mentioned again in 14^{43}, is evidence of the Church's horror at this deed of one of Our Lord's chosen disciples. Mark does not record his remorse.

11. *money.* Mt. 26^{15} mentions the sum. Cf. Zech. 11^{12}.

12–16. *Preparation for the Supper.*

12. This is incorrect, unless Nisan 14, the day on which the Passover was sacrificed, is included in the feast of Unleavened Bread (cf. note on v. 1 above). It also squares badly with v. 1, for it seems to be the next day after. It is suggested by Allen that the original reading here might have been πρὸ τῆς ἡμέρας; he points out that Marcan usage would rather say τῇ μιᾷ (as in 16^{2}) than τῇ πρώτῃ (as in the unauthentic 16^{9}) for 'the first day' of the feast. But the corruption, if it be one, is reproduced in Mt. 26^{17}.

13. The story is parallel to that of the preparations for the entry in 11^{2}, and perhaps Mark regarded Our Lord's knowledge as miraculous. But it is not necessary to deny that it may be explained by previous arrangement. Perhaps He already suspected Judas' treachery, and wished even His disciples not to know too soon where they were going to be. It is said that a *man* bearing a water-pot would be unusual in the East. Church tradition may be correct in believing that the house of the Supper was the house of Mark's own mother, which subsequently was the Church's head-quarters (Acts $12^{12f.}$).

14. *guestchamber.* Gr. κατάλυμα. Cf. Lk. 2^{7}.

15. *upper room.* Gr. ἀνάγαιον, ἀνώγεων in classical Greek.

17–25. *The Last Supper.*

If, as has been suggested above, this was not the Passover, but the Kiddûsh, we wonder why Our Lord went to Jerusalem at all. The Passover had to be eaten in Jerusalem, the Kiddûsh need not; and Jerusalem was dangerous to Him. This we cannot explain except by guesses, which are free. But (*a*) the gospel tradition is unanimous in placing the meal in Jerusalem, and (*b*) the Kiddûsh explanation is the only one which properly fits the circumstances.

Mark's account of the Supper is very brief, and deals only with the evidence that Jesus knew of Judas' betrayal, and with the institution of the Eucharist.

17. *evening.* Gr. ὀψίας. This need not mean more than late afternoon. The Passover meal was late at night. The Kiddûsh began in the afternoon.

18. *sat*; better 'reclined' (Gr. ἀνακειμένων). The recumbent posture had become usual, even at the Passover.

The reference to Ps. 41^9 is obvious. Our Lord makes an indirect appeal to Judas. That the traitor was directly and publicly indicated is contrary to all reasonable probability, and we must read the story in Mt. 26^{25} in the light of this conviction. Jn. 13^{26} is at once qualified by Jn. $13^{28f.}$. In Mark's story all that is said is that one of them will be a traitor.

19. *is it I?* Gr. μήτι ἐγώ 'Surely it is not I'. John (*l.c.*) fills the scene out.

20. If this was the Passover, the dish would be that of unleavened cakes and bitter herbs.

one of the twelve. Why not 'one of us' or 'one of you'? No doubt the motive referred to on v. 10 above explains the use of the phrase here.

21. ὑπάγει='is given up'. 'Even as it is written of him' may be a reference (as in 14^{49}) to Isa. 53. We have already seen reason for thinking it probable that Our Lord applied that prophecy to Himself.

22. Our Lord had often presided at the Kiddûsh before. But this was a special occasion. What may we take it to have meant at the moment?

(1) To the disciples the primary idea would be of brotherhood. To a Semite, table-fellowship is in itself a kind of sacrament. Our Lord was using this Kiddûsh to lay special emphasis on the

bond which united them to Him and to one another. The words of 1 Cor. 10^{17} express this idea in the Christian Eucharist.

But (2) the circumstances were special. Jesus was, as by now they must have realized, in imminent danger. His acts and words (and no doubt also His manner) gave to the occasion the special solemnity of a farewell, and of a farewell before death.

And (3) He was voluntarily risking this death; He had been telling them (v. 21) that He was risking it in obedience to God's will and in accordance with God's counsel. They were thus being invited to a communion not only with a departing friend, but with one who was departing to a martyrdom for God's cause.

And (4) His invitation was given in mysterious words which must mean something special. 'Take, this is my body, this is my blood'—the words expressed a very peculiar intimacy of union; the disciples were to become one with Him in the closest of all ways, by assimilation in some sort of His Self. But the words also gave emphasis to an idea, with which the mere Passover associations of the meal must already have charged the air, the idea of sacrifice. Here was One Who was offering His life 'a ransom for many'. And He was asking them to re-knit themselves to Him with a very special intimacy, at the moment when His martyrdom for God was approaching. It is not going into fancy to think that, with the idea of communion, the idea of sacrifice must also have been throbbing in their minds during this solemn scene. That they understood things very clearly at present may be doubted. But however ill-defined their impression, however puzzled and perplexed their minds, such in some way may have been their impressions as they partook of the bread and the cup thus blessed by their Leader.

(5) To Our Lord Himself the words and acts no doubt meant something more and more definite; how much more we dare not speculate too subtly; but this at least may be said with reverence: (*a*) perhaps He meant the words to be a call to His disciples to join with Him in His act of self-offering. Was it at least a pathetic request for their loyal comradeship right through to the end, and was their desertion of Him in the garden the proof that they had not understood or were not equal to His request? (*b*) To Himself it was certainly an act of self-dedication. He is willing to surrender Himself 'for many'. His blood is to be 'the blood of the covenant', the seal of a new agreement between God and God's people, analogous to the Mosaic covenant. (*c*) And we cannot say

that in His mind the scope of His self-offering was now limited to His own people. If He thought of His death as the death of God's Messiah or God's Servant (cf. Isa. 53), then it was the Absolute Martyrdom. Its benefit was absolute and not particular. All other martyrdoms for God were fore- or after-shadowings of His. On behalf of the 'gentiles' as well as of the Jews, it was to be a travail leading to triumph (cf. Isa. 52^{15}, 53^{11}).

(6) Did He ordain the repetition of the rite? The command 'do this in remembrance of Me' is found only in 1 Cor. 11$^{23-25}$ and in Lk. 22^{19}, which is supposed to have been influenced by Pauline ideas. Neither in Mark nor in Mt. 26$^{26-29}$ nor in Lk. 22$^{14-18}$ do the words occur.

As to this, we may say (*a*) that neither Mark nor his readers can have had any doubt that the rite was intended to be repeated. From the first, so far as we have any testimony, the weekly Eucharist was the special rite of the Lord's Day. Whether Jesus in word enacted this or not, the Church did continue the observance. That the Christian sacramental system was the creation of Paul is a theory for which there is no real evidence and in which there is no solid probability. The Church was 'communicating' before Paul ever became a Christian.

(*b*) Nor is it wholly true to say that Christian sacramental doctrine is the invention of Paul's genius. He himself tells us that he 'received' (1 Cor. 15^{3}) the doctrine that Christ died for our sins; and in that, which must have been the Church's belief from the start, lies the germ of all sacramental doctrine. No doubt, in interpreting the sacraments, Paul uses language of 'mystery', and no doubt he goes deeper into the *modus operandi* of sacramental grace than those who were apostles before him. But Paul was not speculating *in vacuo*. The Church had its Eucharist before Paul was converted, and in that Eucharist it was conscious of a spiritual experience, before Paul came to help the Church to understand that experience.

(7) The 'mystery', in fact, lay in the Person of Jesus Christ, and in the fact of His abiding Life in the society of His followers. Paul helped the Church to realize the greatness of the mystery, he did not give to the Church a mystery which was not already there. Jesus was the Fact, Paul was but the great interpreter of that Fact. Jesus was the Foundation, Paul was but the master-builder on that Foundation.

(8) Speaking critically, we may admit that there is room for

doubt as to the *exact* words with which Our Lord instituted the Eucharist. But we are not entitled to question that the whole atmosphere of the scene in the Upper Room was charged with the ideas of Communion and Sacrifice. After the Resurrection, Our Lord's followers, finding that what He had imparted in the Upper Room He was still able (and even more fully) to impart to any two or three gathered together in His Name, continued to meet weekly for their 'Breaking of the Bread', for their 'Supper of the Lord'. More and more they learnt, by the teaching of Paul, of others, and of fuller experience, to understand what this rite could be to them; but the experience was theirs from the beginning; and the power of the ordinance in the Church's life shows that the basis of their belief about it was an authentically divine reality. Christian sacramental belief is the interpretation of a genuine experience, and not the outcome of a theoretic speculation, whether of Paul or of any one else.

23. Mark places the blessing of the bread before that of the cup. Contrast Lk. $22^{17f.}$. Clearly tradition was uncertain about the order. If the meal was the Kiddûsh, the cup came first.

24. *covenant,* the Hebrew *Berith* = 'bond' or 'agreement'. The reference is back to the Mosaic covenant. Cf. Ex. 24^{8}; also Jer. 31^{31}, Zech. 9^{11} for applications of the idea.

25. The wine is to be not 'new-made' (νέον) but a new kind of wine (καινόν). For the idea cf. Isa. 25^{6}. In the 'Kingdom' to come at Messiah's Parousia, there will be a new sort of cup-sharing. We are not told if Jesus Himself ate and drank with His disciples at this point or not. His words suggest that He did. The gist of the verse is that if death is certain, so is reunion.

26–31. *On the Mount of Olives.*

26. The Passover meal ended with the second part of the *Hallel*, Pss. 115–118, the first part, Pss. 113–114, being sung earlier in the meal. A Kiddûsh might well end with a hymn also.

They 'went out', because they were not sleeping in Jerusalem.

27. The verse recalls Zech. 13^{7} but agrees neither with the Hebrew nor with the LXX text of that verse. Perhaps its form comes from its use as a Christian proof-text. The suggestion here is that Our Lord doubted the endurance of His disciples in the trial that He anticipated.

28. Cf. Mk. 16^{7}. This verse is difficult in its context, and may

be a later insertion. Obviously Mark is leading up to a Resurrection appearance in Galilee, though his (authentic) Gospel ends at 16^{8} before that is related. Mt. 28^{16} gives such an appearance. Luke locates the Resurrection appearances in Jerusalem. Both traditions existed; and, for those who believe that Our Lord did rise from the dead, both may be true.

30. Did Our Lord mean literally two crowings of a cock, or did He speak in general terms of 'cockcrow'? Or is the phrase here a reference to the Roman signal called *gallicinium* ('cock-crowing') which would be given to the guard on the castle of Antonia?

The story of Peter's denial, thus foretold by Our Lord, would be distressing reading to the Roman Christians. It undoubtedly must rest on Peter's own record. By the time Mark wrote, Peter had finally redeemed himself by a glorious martyrdom.

32–42. *The Agony.*

32. Gethsemane means 'oil-press'. It may have been an olive plantation. Jn. 18^{1} describes it as a garden beyond the river Kidron.

33. The special Three, present also at the Transfiguration, to the story of which this story bears some striking resemblances, e.g. 9^{6} compared to 14^{40} and to Lk. 9^{32}. In both cases the disciples witnessed a mystery which they failed to understand. To Christian readers the story here would be an object-lesson of the spirit in which to face martyrdom.

The word 'to be greatly amazed' (ἐκθαμβεῖσθαι) occurs in 9^{15}, $16^{5,6}$; 'to be sore troubled' (ἀδημονεῖν) is found in Phil. 2^{26}. The horror of anticipation is heavy on Our Lord's soul, and, true man, He shrinks from that which lies before Him, though He is prepared to go through with it, if God wills that He should. For a comment on this scene cf. Heb. 5^{7-10}.

34. *even unto death.* Cf. Ps. $42^{5,6}$, (LXX) 88^{3}, Jonah 4^{9}, Ecclus. 51^{6}.
watch. 'Keep awake' (γρηγορεῖτε). 'Watch with Me', or 'watch for danger'.

35. If the disciples could not hear, they could at least infer. They saw His agony, and then they saw His calmness.

36. For the idea of the 'cup' cf. 10^{38}. The words 'Abba, Father' are found in Rom. 8^{15}, and may have become a Church formula. 'Abba', of course, means 'Father'. Our Lord may, however, have used both words; He probably, like most Jews, was to some extent bilingual.

This verse was used by Church fathers to prove the existence of a real human will in Jesus.

37. *Simon,* used for the first time since 3^{16}.

38. The verbs change from the singular of v. 37 to the plural. The sentence echoes the Lord's Prayer, and is addressed to Christians generally.

41. Ironical? Or is it a question 'are you still sleeping'? But 'now' is in the Greek 'henceforth' (τὸ λοιπόν).

it is enough. The Gr. ἀπέχει is very rare in an impersonal use. De Zwaan, finding it used in papyri as a receipt-term, suggests that it means 'he (Judas) has received his full pay'; but this would be very abrupt.

sinners. Not only gentiles here, but all His enemies.

42. There can be no idea of flight. Let them go and meet their enemies bravely.

43–52. *The Arrest.*

43. The Sanhedrin had power in certain cases to order arrest and inquiry. The 'multitude' would be the temple-police or a hastily armed rabble. But Jn. $18^{3,12}$ seems to suggest that a band of soldiers had been obtained from Pilate, perhaps on the plea that Jesus was dangerous.

44. *token.* Gr. *σύσσημον,* a late word. A kiss was the customary greeting for a Rabbi. Of course, Jesus was known, but Judas wanted to make sure that the right man was not missed in the darkness.

45. *ἐλθὼν προσελθών.* The scene is extraordinarily vivid. He came, and then came up, and 'fervently kissed' Him (*κατεφίλησεν*). Mark records no address to the traitor.

47. Mark says 'a bystander'. Mt. 26^{51} makes it one of Jesus' company, Luke leaves it vague (22^{50} 'a certain one of them'), Jn. 18^{10} names Peter, and gives the servant's name as Malchus. Luke also mentions the healing of the ear. Two of the disciples had swords, according to Lk. 22^{38}.

48. Jesus was being treated like a bandit.

49. *daily.* We have already noted that this scarcely seems to square with merely two days' teaching in the Temple during the Paschal Week. See note on 11^{11}.

but this is done that. Gr. *ἀλλ' ἵνα* is very elliptical. On the reference to the scriptures cf. note on v. 21.

50. The Apocryphal gospel of Peter says that they fled to Galilee. But this is certainly not Mark's idea, as is proved by 14^{54}, 16^{7}.

51. This curious little incident, which leads to nothing, and seems quite pointless, is recorded in Mark alone. It is not surprising that it has been thought to be a personal reminiscence of Mark's own. If the Supper took place at his mother's house, and if Judas first led the band there, he may have hurried on to give the alarm, arriving, however, too late. He had on him only a linen upper garment; under that either nothing or only undergarments (γυμνός could mean either).

53–65. *Before the Sanhedrin.*

53. Are we to suppose (1) that the Sanhedrin met at midnight to hold a trial? How were the witnesses procured at that hour? They then separate only to hold another meeting in the morning (15[1]). (2) Is it also credible that these Jewish aristocrats indulged in the horseplay of v. 65? Luke's story seems here to be more likely than Mark's (in his whole Passion story Luke is much more independent of Mark than he is usually, when he is going over the same ground). According to him (Lk. 22[66]) the Sanhedrin does not meet till morning, and (Lk. 22[63]) the insults are the work of the temple-police.

53. The high-priest was Caiaphas A.D. 18–36. Jn. 18[13] places a preliminary examination before Annas between the arrest and the examination by Caiaphas.

54. It was bold of Peter to follow, after the scene in the garden. Cf. Jn. 18[16]. 'The light' in Greek is τὸ φῶς, vulgarly used for 'fire'.

55. It seems that (*a*) a trial for life could not by Jewish law be held at night, and it needed a special court; (*b*) the Sanhedrin had no right to try capital cases at all (Jn. 18[31]); (*c*) the high-priest's palace was not the proper place for an assembly of the Sanhedrin. But the fact is that this is not, speaking correctly, a 'trial' at all. It is a preliminary examination, to see if a case can be made out to present to the Roman governor for a verdict of death. This explains the seeming inconsequence of the proceedings. At first it looked as if nothing but a charge of blasphemy would be made out, and that would probably not move Pilate to give the desired sentence. This, perhaps, explains Mark's idea that even the witnesses of v. 57 were not satisfactory. Then the high-priest challenges Jesus as to His Messianic claim, and elicits the reply of v. 61. This was enough to warrant the priests in presenting Him to Pilate as a dangerous Messianic agitator. (The charge in Lk. 23[2], if actually made, was a flagrant untruth.)

Of course, to the Sanhedrin, to foretell the destruction of the Temple would be flat blasphemy. So, probably, also to claim to be Messiah, though it does not come under the strict definition of Lev. 24^{10-23}. But it was not enough for the priests to be convinced that Jesus was in Jewish ears a blasphemer. They had to prove to Pilate that He was dangerous.

Mark was no lawyer, and no disciples were present at the inquiry. They could only depend on hearsay to know what had happened. But in any case Christian writers were keen to show that Christianity was not disloyal to the Empire. Mark would want to make it clear that Jesus was not a *political* offender. Hence his presentation of the case, which probably gives the popular Christian view, a view which in fact was true, if not technically correct, is that the Jews were responsible for the Crucifixion, and that Jesus was condemned for the blasphemy of His Messianic claim and His outraging of Jewish ideas, and not for any offence against Roman law and order.

58. That Jesus had actually said something like this is quite likely. Perhaps He spoke about a new sanctuary of a spiritual order. The witnesses may have made an ingenious combination of genuine sayings. Cf. Mk. 15^{29}, Jn. 2^{19}, Acts 6^{14}.

59. Mt. 26^{60} does not say this about the last two witnesses. A suggested explanation of Mark's view has been given above (note on v. 55). The requirement of exact agreement of two witnesses is laid down in Numb. 35^{30}, Deut. 17^{6}, 19^{15}.

61. For the silence of Jesus cf. Isa. 53^{7}. 'The Blessed' is a Jewish reverential equivalent for God, as is 'the Power' in v. 62. The Messiah in Jewish minds would, of course, be a 'son of God', cf. Ps. 2^{7}, $89^{26,27}$; but, of course, not in the metaphysical sense implied in Christian theology. No thought of the Messiah as a 'Person' in the Godhead is found anywhere in Jewish literature.

62. The answer combines Dan. 7^{13} and Ps. 110^{1}. The Messianic claim is now made openly and directly.

63. The rending of clothes was a sign of grief or horror.

64. They could not condemn Him to death (cf. note on v. 55), but they could adjudge Him to be worthy of presentment to Pilate as a capital offender.

65. For the insults cf. Isa. 50^{6}. Lk. 22^{63}, far more probably, makes them the work of the temple-guard, and not of the

grandees themselves. The covering of the face, and the word 'Prophesy' is explained in Mt. 26^{68}, Lk. 22^{64}, as being a combined sneer; 'Prophesy who smote Thee'. In Mark the two items are separated, and 'Prophesy' might mean 'we will teach you to be a prophet'. Is the 'covering of the face' the sign of condemnation, as with Haman (Esther 7^{8})? The phrase at the end is strange: ῥαπίσμασιν ἔλαβον should mean 'took charge of Him with blows'; some MSS. have ἔβαλον 'aimed blows at Him'. The mention of 'officers' (better, 'servants' ὑπηρέται) looks like a gloss, perhaps inserted under the influence of the Lucan account to explain that the servants were the actors in the scene. Mark's 'some' above certainly looks as if it referred to the Sanhedrin.

66–72. *Peter's denials.*

68. Many MSS. omit 'and the cock crew'. The Greek word for porch or fore-court is προαύλιον.

69. *the maid.* Mark seems to mean the same maid. Mt. 26^{71} makes it a different one. 'Thou art a Galilaean' would no doubt be in reference to his dialect, as Mt. 26^{73} says.

71. *curse,* Gr. ἀναθεματίζειν, 'to invoke a curse on oneself if one is lying'. 'To swear' is the simple ὀμνύναι 'to assert with an oath'.

72. *When he thought thereon.* Gr. ἐπιβαλών. Its meaning in this context is very uncertain. Possible renderings are 'realizing', 'throwing himself outside', 'covering his head', 'answering' (to himself), or simply 'he set to and wept'. None of these is really convincing. The Greek word properly means 'to throw upon'.

The story of Peter's denial is wonderfully vivid, and can only be based on Peter's own witness. It is a human document of a singularly affecting character.

XV. 1–41. *The Crucifixion.*

1–15. *Before Pilate.*

1. *morning*; somewhere about 6 a.m. Mark places the Crucifixion at 9 a.m. (v. 25); the darkness begins at noon (v. 33) and Jesus dies at 3 p.m. (v. 34, 37). There seems something artificial about these three-hour divisions; but the times need only be taken as approximate. Jn. 19^{14} seems to show divergence from the Marcan arrangement of time.

The meeting here mentioned would be a second one. On the improbability of this see note on 14^{53}. Lk. 22^{66} makes this morning meeting the one at which Jesus is questioned. The phrase translated 'held a consultation' is of uncertain reading in the Greek, *συμβούλιον ποιήσαντες* or *ἑτοιμάσαντες*; the former would mean 'made a plan' as in 3^6; the latter might mean 'got ready their arrangement' or 'got a council ready'.

There was reason for hurry, both because of the feast, and lest a rescue might be attempted.

Since the deposition of Archelaus in A.D. 6, Judaea had been directly ruled by a Roman *procurator*, under the *legatus* of Syria. Pilate was the fifth of these, and was governor A.D. 26–36. He resided at Caesarea, but was in Jerusalem for the feast (Mark takes it for granted that his readers know about this); it is uncertain whether he occupied Herod's Palace in the west quarter of the City, or the Castle of Antonia at the north corner of the Temple area. Pilate's character is described in a letter of Agrippa I quoted by Philo (*de leg.* 38), as obstinate and merciless, and he is there accused of most crimes that an official can commit; 'receiving of bribes, violence, robbery, ill-treatment, oppression, illegal executions, savage cruelty without end'. (Cf. also Lk. 13^1). But it is probable that the Jews exaggerated in their denunciations of him. The gospel records give a more favourable impression, at least by comparison with the Jewish priesthood; but the Christians probably tended to treat his character mildly, in order to establish the point that the Jews were responsible for Jesus' death, and that the Roman governor really believed Him to be innocent.

2. Pilate cannot say 'the Messiah' but gives the idea a non-Jewish turn. It is hyper-critical to say that Mark makes Pilate ask this question before he has heard the charges. Jn. 18^{28} must be right in making this scene take place outside the palace, so that the Jews should not be defiled by entering it.

Thou sayest; scarcely so much a 'qualified admission' as a refusal to answer at all. What was the use of answering? Pilate meant one thing, Jesus another, by the phrase. Jn. 18^{36} makes this clear.

3. *many things.* (Gr. πολλά) Probably rather 'accused Him much'.

6. The gospels are our only authority for this custom, which may simply have been a practice of Pilate alone; but it is not at all improbable. Livy V. 13 is quoted for a parallel, and a papyrus of the first century A.D. relates that a certain Phibion

was released by a Roman prefect in deference to a popular demand.[1]

7. The Greek (ὁ λεγόμενος Βαραββᾶς) means 'the so-called Barabbas'. Was Barabbas a nickname? It is a strange name 'son of the father'. An early text of Mt. $27^{16,17}$ gives the name as 'Jesus Barabbas' (Jesus = Joshua was a common Jewish name), and Origen (*in Matt.* 121) approved the suppression of the first name as unsuitable to a sinner, but obviously considered it part of the correct text. Many scholars accept the reading. The point that Barabbas, a real agitator, was released, while the innocent Jesus was crucified as an agitator, is obvious.[2]

8. *went up*. Gr. ἀναβάς. It looks as if there were some confusion between two mobs, one accompanying the priests, an anti-Jesus mob, and another, a pro-Barabbas mob, coming to ask for the release of Barabbas.[3] If so, and if Barabbas' name was Jesus,

[1] In an article by Langdon in *Expository Times*, April 1918, Babylonian custom is cited to show that, in the ancient Babylonian-Assyrian calendar, the king was required, on certain days of the month Marchesvan, to recite a penitential psalm and to free a prisoner.

[2] An article by Couchoud and Stahl (*Hibbert Journal*, Oct. 1926), makes great play with the singularity of the name. The authors suggest (apparently quite seriously) that the story of the release of Barabbas is connected with a conflict within the Church between (1) the idea of Jesus as 'Son of the Father' (which is Johannine and anti-Jewish) and (2) the idea of Jesus as Messiah of Israel (which is the idea of the Synoptists and is Judaistic). The incident was inserted as a piece of symbolic polemic against the former ideas; in effect it says 'Your Jesus the Son of the Father was released; it was Our Jesus the Messiah of Israel who was crucified'. Such criticism does not help the scientific study of the gospels. However, it is at least a novelty to find Mark placed on the side of the Judaistic ideas.

This theory is only an extreme example of that style of 'symbolist' criticism, of which Loisy is the great protagonist, and with which Bacon is badly bitten (though neither Loisy nor Bacon indulges in such fancy guessing as this illustrates); it seems incapable of believing that any of the evangelists can have written with the simple purpose of trying to tell the story as best they could; it is always agog to discover some symbolic purpose in the several incidents of the gospel story, and to suggest that the incident has been invented or trimmed up to suit that purpose. In its search for symbolic purposes no distance is too far to fetch material; and the result is that the gospel-story evaporates into the thin air of symbolic fantasy. One wonders what such critics think really did happen to set Christianity going.

[3] This had occurred to me independently; I then found that Rawlinson makes the same suggestion and has worked it out as in the rest of the above note.

Pilate may have mistaken the pro-Barabbas demonstration as one in favour of Jesus of Nazareth, and so asked the question of v. 9. The priests then took up Barabbas' cause, as a way of escaping the danger of their victim's release.

10. This sounds exactly like the sort of idea which would occur to a shrewd man of the world. Pilate knew that Jesus was not a political agitator; he also knew that the priests' concern for loyalty to the Empire was a pretence. To him the situation was an outburst of jealousy towards a rival religious teacher. The annoying thing was that an uproar might ensue, if he did not yield; and of all things Pilate was most anxious to keep the peace. He would try to save the accused, but he would not risk a riot for the sake of strict justice to an obscure Jew.

11. *stirred up* (ἀνέσεισαν found also in Lk. 23⁵). The priests perhaps played on the mob's enthusiasm for an agitator who had given Rome trouble, and perhaps (if Barabbas was a Jerusalemite) on their preference for a Judaean to a Galilean. Cf. also the suggestion on v. 8 above.

13. Mere fickleness, or the mob's lust for violence?

14. Nothing is said of the insult to Caesar (Lk. 23², Jn. 19¹²). But the continual repetition of the phrase 'King of the Jews' is intended to make it clear that Jesus had been falsely represented to Pilate as being a Messianic agitator.

15. *content* Gr. τὸ ἱκανὸν ποιῆσαι = *Lat. satisfacere.* The word for 'scourged' (φραγελλώσας) is also a latinism. It was usual to scourge criminals before their execution. The scourge (*flagellum*) was a whip of leather thongs, loaded at intervals with pieces of bone or metal. The criminal was sometimes lashed to a column for the scourging.

16–20. *The mocking.*

16. *court,* better 'palace' (αὐλῆς). 'Praetorium' would mean the official head-quarters. The 'band' or 'cohort' (σπεῖραν) might be 600 strong; but of course the phrase 'the whole band' here is not to be taken exactly; it only means 'all who were on duty'. These soldiers would not be Jews, as Jews were exempt from military service.

17. There is nothing improbable in this incident. Lk. 23¹¹, however, says the mocking was done by Herod's men. The 'irony' of their mock homage is obvious to Mark.

The purple would be a soldier's red cloak, to represent the imperial purple, while the crown of thorns would be for the royal diadem, or for the laurel wreath of the general; and the reed would be the sceptre (Mt. 27^{29}). But Mark's account is imperfect; the reed appears only as a weapon in the soldiers' hands. The 'worship' would be to the mock King, and not to a mock god.

21–41. *The Crucifixion.*

21. *compel, lit.* 'impress'. The Greek word ἀγγαρεύουσιν is of Persian origin, the ἄγγαροι being the Persian couriers. Criminals had to carry the transverse beam (the *patibulum*) of their cross to the place of execution, where the upright would be already in place. Perhaps Our Lord fell under the weight.

from the country. Gr. ἀπ' ἀγροῦ. The corresponding Hebrew would mean 'from field work'; but this is not necessarily the sense here. Simon of Cyrene [1] (there were many Jews in Cyrene), and his two sons were probably well-known persons in the Roman church. A 'Rufus' is mentioned in Rom. 16^{13}, who may be one of Simon's sons.

22. Golgotha is not called a hill, but a place. Hebr. 13^{12} shows that it was 'outside the gate'. The place was so named because of its shape (Lk. 23^{33}). 'Calvary' is the Latin equivalent. A legend connected it with the burial-place of Adam's skull. The traditional site is now included in the Church of the Holy Sepulchre.

23. Charitable women of Jerusalem provided wine mingled with frankincense for use on such occasions as this, to deaden the pain. 'Myrrh' is therefore probably a mistake. Wine and myrrh was an ordinary drink. Jesus refuses the draught; He will have no alleviation.

24. This was a regular custom. Of course it fulfils Ps. 22^{18}, but Mark does not refer to the prophecy.

25. A case of Semitic parataxis.

The hands were nailed to the cross-piece, and a wooden ledge was provided for the body. It is doubtful if the feet were usually nailed. Lk. 24$^{39-40}$ suggests that it was so in this case; that may

[1] Even this simple incident cannot pass our symbolists. A heretic called Basilides (in the Second Century A.D.) propounded the view that Simon suffered in place of Jesus; the mention of Simon's name in the gospels, says Salomon Reinach, is put in in order to contradict that view. If the evangelists had to hunt for all the whimsies that occurred to heresiarchs or other theorists and to insert contradictions of them in their story, they must have been kept busy; and they must have been men of singular genius to produce a story with any interest at all in it, let alone such a story as the evangel, if this sort of research was their pre-occupation. It is a great deal more simple, and infinitely more scientific, to believe that Simon of Cyrene is mentioned because the incident connected with his name actually happened. See note on 15^{7}.

be due to Ps. 22[16], Jn. 20[20,25] seems to imply that there were nail-marks only in the hands.

26. This was the *titulus*, which was affixed to the cross, stating the criminal's offence. Swete gives other instances: *Impie locutus*, *Hic est Attalus Christianus*. According to Jn. 19[20] Our Lord's *titulus* was written in Hebrew (Aramaic) and Greek and Latin, and Jn. 19[21,22] suggests, as is very possible, that Pilate meant it as a covert sneer at Jewish Messianic ideas. The text of the inscription varies in the various gospels.

27. Robbers, perhaps followers of Barabbas, whose execution was due.

28. Some MSS. reproduce here the phrase from Lk. 22[37], which is a quotation from Isa. 53[12].

29. An obvious echo of Ps. 22[7,8]. The charge is that of Mk. 14[58]. No doubt this was the popular view of Jesus' crime.

31. It may be unlikely, as many commentators point out, that the priests and other grandees had stayed on the spot; they had to go away for the Passover sacrifice. But we cannot be sure that their vindictiveness did not chain them to the spot; and anyhow it was the sort of thing that they might be saying, even if Mark has only imagined the words for them. To call this detail obviously unhistorical is not scientific criticism. In particular Montefiore's critical judgement seems to have gone wandering, when he reached this chapter.

32. 'Believe' is used absolutely.

33. The darkness was clearly miraculous to Mark, but he only says that it covered the whole *land*, not the whole earth; and even that need only be a loose phrase for an extraordinary gloom. This could not be an eclipse, as Luke says (23[45]), since the Passover season was that of full moon. The words may look back to Amos 8[9], and the detail may be a piece of symbolism. The idea of such a phenomenon at the time of great calamities was common.

34. The quotation is from Ps. 22[1]. Some critics regard it as the Christian interpretation of an inarticulate cry; on the other hand Schmiedel considers that a cry seeming to express Jesus' despair at the shipwreck of His hopes could not have been invented.

Ps. 22 is a psalm of dereliction turning to triumph, and we cannot be sure that Our Lord does not only 'precent' the first verse, whilst the whole psalm is in His mind. The utterance is the supreme mystery of His Passion, and can require volumes for its study. But if we can imagine the blank feeling of hopelessness that comes on a good man's mind, as he walks through a series of mean streets, or experiences the sordid depths of human wickedness—if we can suppose him rebelling against the feeling and crying desperately to the God Who seems not to be there—if we can go farther and believe that God loves such rebellion, for only a good man could commit it, we may have some faint idea of what Our Lord may have been feeling, when this terrible cry burst from Him. He was in the heart of the very slum of human sin, and He cries to the God Who seems not to be there, because He knows that God is there.

The cry in Mark is in the Aramaic form. In Mt. 27[46] *Eli, Eli* is the Hebrew form. In the D Text of both Matthew and Mark, the whole is in Hebrew *Eli, Eli, lama azabhthani*. The Aramaic *Eloi* could not be misunderstood for a cry to Elijah; the Hebrew *Eli* might. Probably therefore Our Lord used the Hebrew form.

36. The account is confused. The 'one' who ran was probably a soldier; would a Jewish bystander have been allowed to give the criminal drink? Some of these soldiers were recruited from Samaria, and so may have known of Elijah, for a kind of Judaism existed at Samaria. If the soldier said the words attributed to him, 'let be' (ἄφετε) must mean 'allow me'. Mt. 27[49] gives the remark to 'the rest', which seems more likely. Some MSS. in fact have 'they said' here. The drink was probably the soldiers' *posca* or sour wine.

Elijah was he who was to prepare for the Messiah's coming; and a Jewish legend spoke of him as a helper in times of distress.

37. Our Lord's loud cry appears in all the records. He died not slowly as was usual, but quickly and in full physical vigour.

38. There were two veils in the Temple, one covering the entrance to the Holy Place, and one that to the Holy of Holies. The latter is probably meant. The incident may be symbolic, like the miraculous darkness. It is mystically treated in Hebr. 10[19 f.]. It would symbolize either the sorrow of God's house, or the opening of access to God, or the imminent destruction of the Temple and the passing of Judaism.

39. *centurion* (κεντυρίων, a latinism). Tradition gives his name as Longinus. Mt. 27[54] says that he was also influenced by the natural phenomena. Mark seems to refer his awe only to the vigour of the last cry, or to the whole demeanour of Our Lord. The centurion's word may have been taken by Mark as a Christian utterance, or as an unconscious confession of a truth of which the centurion is ignorant. But if the centurion was a heathen, 'a son

of God' (there is no article) might only mean in his mouth a demi-god. Lk. 23^{47} has 'a righteous man'.

Verses 40 and 41 prepare for what follows. We have not previously heard in Mark of these women, who ministered to Our Lord in Galilee (Lk. 8^{1-3} has some of them). The Virgin Mother is not mentioned. Bacon says they are introduced (like Simon of Cyrene) as sponsors of the tradition, but is that in the least likely as the explanation of this mention? The facts of the Crucifixion were known publicly, and the Church needed no special sponsors for the story.

Mary Magdalene (of Magdala) is mentioned in Lk. 8^{2}, but need not be the woman of Lk. 7^{37}. James 'the less' (Gk. 'the little one', either in years or in importance) may or may not be the son of Alphaeus of Mk. 3^{18}. In 15^{47} Mary is called 'Mary of Joses' and in 16^{1} 'Mary of James', which would normally imply that she was their daughter, which is impossible. But we are told that the description of women by their children is common among modern Arabs. Of Joses we know nothing. Salome is called the mother of the sons of Zebedee in Mt. 27^{56}.

XV. 42–XVI. 8. *The Burial and the Empty Tomb.*

42. *even.* Gr. ὀψίας. Cf. 14^{17}n.

'The Preparation' had become practically a regular term for Friday; Mark explains it (προσάββατον) for his gentile readers. This verse is the first clear intimation that Jesus was crucified on a Friday. Jn. 19^{31} says that this sabbath was 'a high day'; on the Friday night the Passover would be eaten, and the feast of Unleavened Bread began. Cf. note at beg. of c. 14.

43. Arimathaea = *Ramathaim.* One Ramathaim is mentioned in 1 Sam. 1^{1}, another in 1 Macc. 11^{34}. Joseph was of good position (εὐσχήμων. Mt. 27^{57} says he was 'rich'), and a 'councillor' (βουλευτής); this may mean that he was one of the Sanhedrin (Lk. 23^{51} plainly so understands it and says that Joseph had not consented to the council's action), but it may equally mean only that he was one of the 'elders' of his town, a sort of 'alderman' (Lat. *decurio*). He was 'looking for the Kingdom of God'; Mark may understand by this that he was a disciple of Our Lord's, as Mt. 27^{57} and Jn. 19^{38} say. But the phrase by itself need mean no more than is meant in the case of Simeon (Lk. 2^{25}, cf. also Lk. 2^{38}). Many Jews were looking for the Kingdom in a really spiritual sense; their Messianic anticipation was not that of the vulgar sort. Joseph's

boldness consisted in his braving not only of Pilate's displeasure, but of the feelings of the Jewish aristocrats.

The need for haste lay in the law of Deut. 21^{22-23}. We gather the impression that this was a hurried burial, and that the women (16^{1}) came to carry out the usual rites more fully and reverently than had been possible in the late afternoon of Friday. Jn. $19^{39f.}$ gives an opposite impression, and does not mention that women brought any spices.

44. *already.* A crucified man might linger for days and eventually die of starvation and torture as much as of anything else. Obviously the centurion had not yet reported to Pilate, if indeed he was under any necessity to do so; we do not know how long a time elapsed between Our Lord's death and Joseph's action; perhaps an hour or so; but Joseph had still time to buy linen before the Sabbath began.

45. The Roman custom was to let the bodies rot where they hung, but perhaps in Palestine they acted otherwise in deference to Jewish religious ideas. If so, probably the criminals would be buried in a common grave. But it seems that permission was at least sometimes granted to relatives or friends to bury the bodies. The fact that a comparative stranger buries Jesus emphasizes the desertion of His disciples.

corpse. Gr. *πτῶμα,* as in 6^{29}. 'He granted the corpse' (ἐδωρήσατο may hint that Pilate asked for no bribe) may reproduce the actual Latin phrase *donavit cadaver.*

46. Mt. 27^{60} adds that this was a new tomb of his own, as yet unused. Jn. 19^{39} says that Nicodemus also helped in the burial. The tomb would be rock-hewn, like most of those round Jerusalem, and the stone would be not only to save the body from animals, but also to save men from touching the dead body, which was a Levitical defilement.

XVI. 1. The Sabbath ended at 6 p.m. on Saturday. Did the women come then, as soon as they had bought the spices (they might, however, have bought the spices before the Sabbath began, though this is perhaps less likely, as the time was so limited)? Verse 2 says that they came at sunrise, i.e. very early on Sunday morning, unless Allen is right in suggesting that this phrase is due to misunderstanding of an Aramaism for 'when the new day was beginning'. Mt. 28^{1} speaks uncertainly; his words might mean Saturday evening or Sunday morning. Lk. 24^{1} is definite that it was dawn. Jn. 20^{1} says it was yet dark.

It is obvious that the women would have come as soon as they could after the Sabbath was over; but their way might be difficult to find, if it was quite dark. Mark, writing for Roman readers, probably has dawn in mind, especially as the Church's Easter celebrations began at dawn.

4. *for it was exceeding great.* The 'for' would be more logical if the clause was part of the women's question; unless the meaning is that, because the stone was so big, they could see that it had been removed, even when they were some way off.

5. This is certainly meant for an angel, as in Acts 1^{10}. The belief in angelic manifestations was universal in the Church and was common amongst Jews.

6. 'Jesus the Nazarene' sounds strange in this context.

7. Cf. 14^{28}. Clearly this gospel was leading up to an appearance in Galilee to Peter (specially mentioned because of his denial) and the disciples.

8. Their fear was the result of awe. According to the account, they disobey the angel's order. Perhaps the story was going on, or went on, to explain what happened; perhaps the women distrusted their own experience; or perhaps the tradition of the empty tomb only spread later in the Church, the earliest tradition being that of Appearances. Paul (1 Cor. $15^{1f.}$) says nothing of the empty tomb more definitely than his statement that Christ 'hath been raised on the third day' (ib. v. 4); he mentions no Appearance to women.

Mark's story breaks off very abruptly, even more so in the Greek (ἐφοβοῦντο γάρ) than appears in the English translation. On the problem of the conclusion of the gospel see a later note. The last sentence may have originally contained an object for 'feared', such as 'the Jews' or 'the people'. But that is only a guess.

A commentary is not the place for a discussion of the pros and cons of the Resurrection doctrine. But it may be said (1) that of all ways of dealing with the gospel story of the Resurrection, the rationalizing way is the most unsatisfactory. K. Lake's theory for instance—that the neighbourhood was full of rock-tombs, that the women in their perturbation went to the wrong tomb, that a young man told them that they were mistaken and pointed to the right tomb, and that they, in fear lest their sympathy for Jesus should be discovered, ran away and told nobody about the incident; that then, after the stories of the Appearances began to be known, the women began to connect their experience with these stories, and turned the young man into an angel who had told them that Jesus was risen (it was only necessary to add the clause 'he is risen' to the original communication, and so v. 6. is produced), and that so the story of the empty tomb arose—this theory is extraordinarily ingenious; and there is an end of it.[1] Its ingenuity is its own destruction. It will never convince any one; did it even convince its author?

(2) The evidence for the continued life of Jesus after death and for His appearances to His disciples undoubtedly contains some mutually conflicting details. Did Jesus appear in Galilee or in Jerusalem or in both? But, however the details vary, the evidence for the fact that the disciples believed themselves to have seen Jesus alive after His death is unanimous, and is irrefragable unless—a desperate hypothesis—we believe the disciples to be singularly successful liars or grossly self-deceived.

(3) The story of the Church's life through the ages increases the volume of testimony. The Church is built on the belief in the living Christ, and the story of the Church makes it hard to credit that this belief is an illusion.

(4) But, only those to whom Jesus is such as Christianity believes Him to be can feel really sure that the story of the Risen Christ is true. It is true because it is congruous with Himself; such as He could not be 'holden of death'. And one to whom the Christian experience of meeting the risen Christ has at all become his cannot doubt that His disciples met Him; nor can he question that He conquered death as He had conquered sin, in unique fashion. We do not say that He is God because He rose from the dead, but we say that we are sure He rose from the dead, because He is God.

XVI. 9–20. EPILOGUE

It is universally agreed that these verses were not part of the original conclusion of the gospel. The evidence for this inference is overwhelming: (1) the narrative takes a fresh start in v. 9, as if what preceded had not been there, and Mary Magdalene is mentioned as if for the first time. The verses read like an epitome, and not like a piece of living gospel record; and the incidents cited seem to presuppose the stories of the other gospels (especially Luke) and even, in one case, a presumably later tradition. The style and phraseology are very different from Mark's; this differ-

[1] Lake, *Historical Evidence for the Resurrection of Jesus Christ.*

ence is perceptible even in the English version; in the Greek it is unmistakable. (2) The verses do not occur in the two great MSS. Aleph and B, nor in the Latin MS. *k*, nor in the Sinaitic Syriac version, nor in three of the oldest MSS. of the Armenian version. In four Greek uncials they are preceded by the shorter ending (see below), and are but an alternative to it. Eusebius and Jerome note their absence from the best Greek MSS. of their time. In an Armenian MS. of A.D. 986 the verses occur, with a rubric 'of the presbyter Ariston'; this 'Ariston' may be meant for Aristion, an elder mentioned by Papias; the rubric is a scribe's conjecture and is quite valueless, but it further attests the existence of doubt as to the Marcan authenticity of these verses.

These verses were known to Tatian (A.D. 140), are perhaps quoted by Justin (A.D. 160) and v. 19 is quoted as from 'Mark' by Irenaeus (A.D. 180). Thus they were probably written near the beginning of the 2nd century; and scholars think it more likely that they proceed from Rome than from Asia. The Asiatic tradition (that of the fourth gospel) is far less drawn upon in the verses than the Lucan.

The verses are fitted so badly to 16^8 that they were probably written at first not as a continuation of the gospel, but for catechetical use, and were then attached to the gospel, because it ended so abruptly, or because the shorter ending was considered unsatisfactory.

The shorter ending runs on from v. 8: 'And all that had been commanded they briefly reported to Peter and those who were with him. And after this Jesus Himself appeared to them, and from the East and as far as to the West sent forth through them the sacred and incorruptible proclamation of eternal salvation.' This occurs in four Greek uncials before the longer ending, and in other MSS. and versions, either in the text or in the margin. It was obviously written in order to give the gospel a proper conclusion, and is obviously not Marcan.

The reason for the very abrupt ending of the Marcan narrative at 16^8 can only be a matter of conjecture. (1) Wellhausen and Meyer believe the gospel to have ended there, and to be complete as the author designed it. But that is really incredible. Mark is no stylist; but could even he end his work with v. 8? And is it not plain that he is leading up to the story of an Appearance to Peter? If the gospel never went farther than 16^8, we must conclude that, either owing to persecution or to some other unknown cause, the author never completed it. (So Rawlinson.)

(2) But may the gospel have been mutilated? What, if so, it originally added we cannot tell; a Resurrection Appearance to Peter certainly; possibly even it carried the story on through the period covered by Acts i–xii, until the point when the gospel first reached Rome by the preaching of Peter or of some one else.

Some critics think the conclusion was deliberately suppressed, in the interests of the tradition that the Resurrection Appearances took place in Jerusalem and not in Galilee. But that is not very likely; for the Galilee tradition lived on in the Church, and is found in Mt. 28, as well as in Jn. 21.

There remains the theory of accidental mutilation; that the gospel came to be preserved in only one copy, from which the last page or two had been torn off. This is the usual hypothesis; but it is not free from difficulty. It is true that Mark's gospel suffered neglect, by comparison especially with Matthew, after the second century began. But Luke shows no sign of knowing of such a Galilaean Appearance to Peter as Mark seems to be leading up to; nor does the vague story of Mt. 28^{16-20} seem to be based upon such a record as, we must suppose, Mark would have given. Thus it seems that neither Matthew nor Luke had a 'Mark' which went beyond 16^{8}. This drives the date of the mutilation back into the first century; and it is less probable that, at so early a date, the gospel could exist only in one copy and that a torn one. The suggestion that Jn. 21 gives the substance of the original conclusion of Mark has been made.[1] To discuss it properly, it would be necessary to go somewhat fully into the character of that chapter, which is an appendix written by the disciple of 'John' (whoever John may have been), probably after the author's death. Rawlinson (pp. 269, 270) rejects the suggestion, though his reasons for doing so do not appear conclusive. But, if this suggestion is not accepted, we must confess that we have no probable indication anywhere of what the original ending of Mark contained; and we may be driven back to believe that the gospel never was completed by its author.

9. Lk. 24^{1-11}, 8^{2}; perhaps Jn. 20^{11}.

12. Lk. 24^{13-32}. Verse 13 contradicts Lk. 24^{34}, and may be influenced by Lk. 24^{41}.

in another form (ἐν ἑτέρᾳ μορφῇ) is due to the non-recognition of Jesus by the two disciples; the writer seems to have thought it was due to some metamorphosis (like that of the Transfiguration); but this is a misunderstanding of Luke who guards against such an idea in vv. 16, 31.

[1] By Streeter. *Four Gospels*, pp. 352 ff.

14. Lk. 24^{36-43}, Acts 1^{1-8}, Mt. 28^{19}. But this epitome is notabl in two ways; (1) it lays a very strong emphasis on the unreadines of the disciples to believe in the Resurrection; this seems addresse to sceptical Christians in general, rather than to the Eleven i particular; (2) in v. 16 we have (no doubt on the basis of passage like Acts 16^{31}, Jn. $3^{5,18}$) a very strong declaration of the ecclesiastical point of view which became crystallized in the formula *extr ecclesiam nulla salus.*

Between vv. 14 and 15, we find a passage inserted in a fifth centur Greek MS., discovered in Egypt in 1906, now known as W. Thi passage (the 'Freer Logion', so-called from the name of the origina owner of the MS.) was: 'And they replied saying, This age of lawlessness and unbelief is under Satan, who by means of evil spirits doe not permit the true power of God to be apprehended; wherefor reveal thy righteousness now. They were speaking to Christ, an Christ said to them in reply: The limit of the years of the authorit of Satan has been fulfilled, but other terrible things draw near. An on behalf of sinners I was delivered over unto death, that they migh turn unto the truth and sin no more, in order that they may inheri the spiritual and immortal glory of righteousness, which is heaven' Jerome quotes the opening words of this Logion in a Latin versio (from which in fact the meaning of the Greek text, which is partiall corrupt at that point, has to be supplied) and says that it is found i certain copies and especially in Greek codices (*adv. Pelag.* ii. 15). I is a mere gloss, perhaps of the early second century, when the Churc had known persecution and was dreading more, but the expectatio of an early Parousia was still alive, and needed still to be curbed.

15. How curt is this epitome is shown by the fact that the com mission to evangelize follows without any transition upon the rebuk for unbelief.

17. The 'signs' are mostly paralleled from N.T. records; exorcism and healings *passim*, new tongues from Acts 2, 1 Cor. 12, 14, the tak ing up of serpents from Acts 28^{3-5}, Lk. 10^{19}. The drinking of poiso has no N.T. parallel, but Eusebius (*H.E.* iii. 39. 9) states that Papia recorded of Justus Barsabbas that he drank poison and by the grac of the Lord suffered no harm. The tradition that John the Apostl did the same (he is constantly represented in art with a poison-cup i his hand) appears to be of much later date.

19. Acts 1^{9-11}, 2^{33}.

INDEX TO NOTES

(The references are to Chapter and Verse in the Commentary.)

Abomination, 13^{14}
Adoptionism, p. 140
Agapé, 6^{41}
Apostles, 3^{14} 6^{7}
Apostolic poverty, 6^{9}
Aramaisms, $1^{21\ 23}$ $2^{4\ 19}$ $3^{17\ 18\ 28\ 29}$ 5^{41} 6^{9} $7^{11\ 34}$ 8^{24} 12^{40} 15^{34}
Aretas, 6^{17}
Arimathaea, 15^{43}
Asceticism, 9^{43}
Assassins, 3^{19}

Baptism, 1^{9}, p. 136
  Infants, 9^{42} 10^{13}
Barabbas, 15^{7}
Bath qol, p. 140
Beelzebub, 3^{22}
Bethany, 11^{1} 14^{3}
Bethphage, 11^{1}
Bethsaida, 8^{22}

Caesarea Philippi, 8^{27}
Caiaphas, 14^{53}
Cananaean, 3^{18}
Capernaum, 1^{21}
Christ, 1^{1} 8^{29} 9^{41}
Corban, 7^{10}
Crossbearing, p. 200

Dalmanutha, 8^{10}
'David', 12^{36}
Decapolis, 5^{20} 7^{32}
Demons, 4^{39} $5^{2\ 7\ 9\ 10}$ 9^{22}
Denarius, 6^{37}
Dereliction, cry of, 15^{34}
Divorce, $10^{4\ 9\ 12}$
Docetism, p. 140
Doublets, 4^{26} 6^{51} 8^{1} $10^{13\ 33}$ p. 238

Easter, 16^{1}
Eucharist, 6^{41} 8^{17} 14^{22} p. 245
Exorcism in Christ's Name, 9^{39}

Faith, 2^{5}
Fasting, 2^{18}
Fig-tree, 13^{28}

Galilee, 1^{9}
Gallicinium, 14^{30}
Gehenna, $9^{43\ 48}$
Gerasa, $5^{1\ 7}$
Gethsemane, 14^{32}
Golgotha, 15^{22}
Gospel, $1^{1\ 14}$ 8^{35}

Hardening of Jews, 3^{5} 4^{12} p. 166
Herod Antipas, $6^{14\ 17\ 18\ 20}$
Herodians, 3^{6} 12^{13}
Herodias, $6^{14\ 17\ 18\ 22}$ 10^{12}
Herod, Philip, 6^{17}
Herod's Temple, 13^{1}
Holy Spirit, $1^{8\ 10}$ 3^{29} 13^{11}

Iscariot, 3^{19}

Jairus, 5^{22}
James, 10^{39}
Jesus
  and His kin, $3^{31\ 35}$ 6^{3}
  avoids Herod, 1^{14} $3^{6\ 7}$ $6^{13\ 56}$ 7^{31} 8^{22} 9^{30} 10^{1} p. x 179
  challenges the authorities, p. 197
  humility of, 10^{18}
  ideas of, on children, 10^{13}
  —on demoniacal possession, 3^{23} p. 146
  —on disease and sin, p. 153
  —on eschatology, p. 236
  —on His Death, 8^{32} 10^{45} 12^{1} $14^{8\ 21\ 22}$ p. 200
  —on His Messianic position, 2^{10} $8^{29\ 32\ 38}$ 10^{46} $11^{7\ 11\ 15}$ 12^{35} 14^{62} p. 141, 145, 154, 198
  —on scope of His Mission, 7^{27} p. 236
  limitations of knowledge, 13^{32}, p. 236
  preaching of, $1^{15\ 16\ 45}$ 2^{17} $9^{37\ 39}$ p. 141, 144
  teaching of, about Caesar and God, $12^{13\ 17}$
  —about detachment, 10^{21}
  —about duty 10^{19}
  —about immortality, 12^{27}

Index to Notes

Jesus (*cont.*)
—about marriage, 10[5 6 11 12]
—about Mosaic Law and tradition, 7[8 15] 10[5] 12[29]
—about prayer, 11[24]
—about ritualism, 7[2 15]
Temptation of, 1[12]
Trial of, before Caiaphas, 14[55]
John the Apostle, 9[38] 10[39]
John the Baptist, 1[1 5 6 8] 2[18] 6[17] p. 135
Judaism and women, 10[12]
Judas, 14[10]

Kiddûsh, 14[17] p. 244
Kingdom of God, 1[14 15 17] 4[11 26 31] 9[48] 10[12 17 30] p. 137, 141, 145

Last Supper, 14[22] p. 242
Latinisms, 5[9] 6[27] 7[5] 12[42] 15[15 39]
Law of Moses, 7[9 10] 12[28 32]
Levi, 2[14] 3[19]
Levirate Law, 12[19]
Lord, The, 5[18] 7[28] 11[3]

Machaerus, 6[17]
Mark. *See* Aramaisms, Latinisms
Christology in, 1[1 2] p. 140
chronology in, 3[31] 6[56] 9[1] 15[1], p. 157, 160, 243
conclusion of, p. 267
Galilaean Ministry in, p. 195
geography in, 4[1] 5[1] 6[32 33 53] 7[24 31] 8[10 22] 10[1] p. 178
interest in exorcisms, p. 146
theory of demonic recognition, 1[24] 3[11]
use of Q, 1[2 12] 3[23 28] 4[21] 6[7] 8[12 34] 9[50] 12[40] p. 136, 139, 196
Matthew. *See* Levi
Messiah, 13[26] 14[61]
Midrash, 9[7] p. 140
Millenarianism, p. 236
Miracles, 4[41] 5[39] 6[41 51] 11[12]
Mustard-seed, 4[31]
Mystery of gospel, 4[11] p. 166

Nazareth, 1[9]
Nero's persecution, 13[9]

Parable, 3[23] 4[12 13 26 31 33] 7[17] 12[1] 13[28] p. 166
Parousia, 9[1] 10[37] 13[24 27 28 32] 14[25] p. 235
Passover, 14[1 18] p. 243
Peter's confession, 8[29]
Pharisees, 2[16] 3[6] 12[13 26 28 40]
Phylacteries, 12[40]
Physicians, 5[25]
Pilate, 15[1 2 6 10]
Preparation, 15[42] p. 243
Priests, 11[17 18]. *See* Sadducees
Pseudo-Christs, 13[6]
Publicans, 2[14]

Quartodecimans, p. 246

Ransom, 10[45]
Resurrection story, 16[8] p. 266
Ritualism, Jewish, 7[2 3]
Roman provincial government, p. 197
taxation, 12[13]

Sadducees, 12[18] p. 197. *See* Priests
Saliva, 7[33]
Salome, 6[17 22]
Sanhedrin, 8[31] 14[1 43 55]
Scribes, 1[22] 2[16] 11[18] 12[40]
Shewbread, 2[26]
Simon of Cyrene, 15[21]
Simon the leper, 14[3]
Son of David, 10[47] 12[35]
Son of Man, 2[10] p. 154
Subordinationism, 10[40]
Suffering Servant, 9[11] 10[45] p. 145
Symbolism in gospel story, 8[1] 10[52] 15[33 38] p. 259, 261
Synagogue, 1[21 22] 5[22]

Temple-market, 11[15]
Testimonies, 1[2] 14[27]
Transfiguration, 9[2]
Treasury, 12[41]
Twelve, the, 3[13 19] 4[40] 6[13] 8[17]

Unction, 6[13]

Virgin Birth, 6[3]

Zealots, 3[18]

PRINTED IN GREAT BRITAIN AT THE UNIVERSITY PRESS, OXFORD
BY VIVIAN RIDLER, PRINTER TO THE UNIVERSITY